Letts
EDUCATIONAL

ADVANCED SUBSIDIARY

Revise AS
Psychology

Author

Cara Flanagan

Contents

Specification lists   4

AS/A2 Level Psychology courses   8

Different types of questions in AS examinations   11

Exam technique   13

What grade do you want?   15

Four steps to successful revision   16

Chapter 1   The study of psychology

1.1 Key approaches and the development of psychology   17

Sample question and student answer   26

Practice examination questions   27

Chapter 2   Cognitive psychology

2.1 The cognitive approach   28

2.2 Short-term and long-term memory   30

2.3 Forgetting   38

2.4 Critical issue: Eyewitness testimony   43

Sample question and student answer   48

Practice examination questions   49

Chapter 3   Developmental psychology

3.1 The developmental approach   50

3.2 Cognitive development   53

3.3 Attachments in development: The development and
variety of attachments   60

3.4 Attachments in development: Deprivation, separation and
privation   69

3.5 Critical issue: Day care   75

Sample question and student answer   78

Practice examination questions   79

Chapter 4   Physiological psychology

4.1 The physiological approach   80

4.2 Genetic explanations of behaviour   85

4.3 Bodily rhythms   89

4.4 Stress: Stress as a bodily response   *93*

4.5 Stress: Sources of stress   *97*

4.6 Critical issue: Stress management   *101*

     Sample question and student answer   *104*

     Practice examination questions   *105*

Chapter 5   Individual differences

5.1 The individual differences approach   *106*

5.2 Studying gender   *108*

5.3 Abnormality: Defining psychological abnormality   *111*

5.4 Abnormality: Biological and psychological models
of abnormality   *114*

5.5 Critical issue: Eating disorders   *120*

     Sample question and student answer   *127*

     Practice examination questions   *128*

Chapter 6   Social psychology

6.1 The social approach   *129*

6.2 Attitudes and prejudice   *131*

6.3 Social influence: Conformity and minority influence   *141*

6.4 Social influence: Obedience to authority   *148*

6.5 Critical issue: Ethical issues in psychological research   *154*

     Sample question and student answer   *158*

     Practice examination questions   *159*

Chapter 7   Research

7.1 Quantitative and qualitative research methods   *160*

7.2 Research design and implementation   *165*

7.3 Data analysis   *172*

     Sample questions and student answers   *174*

     Practice examination questions   *175*

     Index   *176*

Specification lists

AQA A Psychology

MODULE	SPECIFICATION TOPIC	CHAPTER REFERENCE	STUDIED IN CLASS	REVISED	PRACTICE QUESTIONS
Unit 1	**Cognitive psychology: Human memory**	2.1			
	Short-term and long-term memory	2.2			
	Forgetting	2.3			
	Critical issue: eyewitness testimony	2.4			
	Developmental psychology: Attachments in development	3.1			
	The development and variety of attachments	3.3			
	Deprivation and privation	3.4			
	Critical issue: day care	3.5			
Unit 2	**Physiological psychology: Stress**	4.1, 4.2			
	Stress as a bodily response	4.4			
	Sources of stress	4.5			
	Critical issue: stress management	4.6			
	Individual differences: Abnormality	5.1			
	Defining psychological abnormality	5.3			
	Biological and psychological models of abnormality	1.1, 5.4			
	Critical issue: eating disorders – anorexia nervosa and bulimia nervosa	5.5			
Unit 3	**Social psychology: Social influence**	6.1			
	Conformity and minority influence	6.3			
	Obedience to authority	6.4			
	Critical issue: Ethical issues in psychological research	6.5			
	Research methods				
	Quantitative and qualitative research methods	7.1			
	Research design and implementation	7.2			
	Data analysis	7.3			

Examination analysis

The specification comprises six compulsory modules (3 examination units).

Unit 1	Two structured questions on cognitive psychology, candidates must choose one. Two structured questions on developmental psychology, candidates must choose one.	1 hr test 33.33%
Unit 2	Two structured questions on physiological psychology, candidates must choose one. Two structured questions on individual differences psychology, candidates must choose one.	1 hr test 33.33%
Unit 3	Two structured questions on social psychology, candidates must choose one. One compulsory structured question on research methods.	1 hr test 33.33%

AQA B Psychology

MODULE	SPECIFICATION TOPIC	CHAPTER REFERENCE	STUDIED IN CLASS	REVISED	PRACTICE QUESTIONS
Unit 1 PSO1	**Introducing psychology**	10.1			
	Key approaches and the study of psychology	1.1, 2.1, 5.4			
	The biological approach	4.1, 4.2			
	Methods of research	7.1, 7.2			
	Representing data and descriptive statistics	7.3			
	Ethics	6.5			
	Studying gender	5.2			
	Explaining gender	–			
Unit 2 PSO2	**Social and cognitive psychology**	2.1, 6.1			
	Attitudes	6.2			
	Social influence	6.3, 6.4			
	Social cognition	–			
	Social psychology of sport	–			
	Perception and attention	–			
	Remembering and forgetting	2.2, 2.3			
	Language and thinking	–			
	Cognition and law	2.4			
Unit 3	**Practical work**	–			

('–' means not covered in this book as they are optional modules)

Examination analysis

The specification comprises three units. There is considerable choice in units 1 and 2 of the examination.

Unit 1	Candidates must answer three structured questions: • one on either key approaches or the biological approach • one on either explaining gender or studying gender • one compulsory question on research methods.	1 hr 30 min test	35%
Unit 2	Candidates must answer three structured questions: Eight questions set, one from each of the eight sections in social and cognitive psychology (see list above). • a minimum of one on social psychology • a minimum of one on cognitive psychology • plus one from either cognitive or social psychology.	1 hr 30 min test	35%
Unit 3	Practical investigation: one 1500 word report, externally assessed.		30%

Edexcel Psychology

MODULE	SPECIFICATION TOPIC	CHAPTER REFERENCE	STUDIED IN CLASS	REVISED	PRACTICE QUESTIONS
	Cognitive, social and development processes				
	The cognitive approach (key assumptions, methods)	2.1			
	Memory and forgetting	2.2, 2.3			
	Key application (eyewitness testimony)	2.4			
Unit 1	The social approach (key assumptions, methods)	6.1			
	Obedience	6.4			
	Prejudice	6.2			
	The cognitive-developmental approach (key assumptions, methods)	3.1			
	Cognitive development	3.2			
	Key application: education	3.2			
	Individual differences, physiology and behaviour				
	The learning approach (key assumptions, methods)	1.1			
	Classical and operant conditioning	1.1			
	Key application: behaviour modification	5.4			
Unit 2	The psychodynamic approach (key assumptions, methods)	1.1			
	Freud's theory	1.1			
	Key application: mental health	5.4			
	The physiological approach (key assumptions, methods)	4.1, 4.2			
	States of awareness	4.3			
	Data gathering exercise				
Unit 3	Ethics	6.5			
	Methods used in psychological research	7.1, 7.2, 7.3			

Examination analysis

The specification consists of three compulsory units.

Unit 1	A set of compulsory structured questions.	*1 hr 30 min test*	*33.33%*
Unit 2	A set of compulsory structured questions.	*1 hr 30 min test*	*33.33%*
Unit 3	Practical investigation: one 1500 word report, no inferential statistics, externally assessed.		*33.33%*

OCR Psychology

MODULE	SPECIFICATION TOPIC	CHAPTER REFERENCE	STUDIED IN CLASS	REVISED	PRACTICE QUESTIONS
Units 1&2	**Cognitive core studies**				
	Loftus and Palmer (eyewitness)	2.4			
	Deregowski (perception)	–			
	Baron-Cohen et al. (autism)	–			
	Gardner and Gardner (Washoe)	–			
	Social core studies				
	Milgram (obedience)	6.4			
	Haney, Banks and Zimbardo (prison simulation)	6.3			
	Piliavin et al. (subway samaritan)	6.1			
	Tajfel (ethnocentricism)	6.2			
	Developmental core studies				
	Samuel and Bryant (conservation)	3.2			
	Bandura et al. (imitating aggression)	1.1			
	Hodges and Tizard (attachment)	3.4			
	Freud (Little Hans)	1.1			
	Physiological core studies				
	Schachter and Singer (emotion)	–			
	Dement and Kleitman (dreaming)	4.3			
	Sperry (split brains)	4.1			
	Raine et al. (murderers)	–			
	Individual differences				
	Gould (IQ testing)	4.2			
	Hraba and Grant (doll choice)	–			
	Rosenhan (sane in insane places)	5.3			
	Thigpen and Cleckley (multiple personality)	–			

Examination analysis

The specification comprises twenty key studies, examined in units 1 and 2, plus a unit on practical work.

Unit 1 Core Studies 1 (questions on the core studies)
20 compulsory short answer questions — 1 hr — 33.3%

Unit 2 Core Studies 2 (essay questions related to core studies)
Part A: choice of 1 from 2 structured essays (50%)
Part B: choice of 1 from 3 structured essays (50%) — 1 hr — 33.3%

Unit 3 Practical work examination. Candidates should complete a practical folder containing notes about four specified practical activities. The examination will ask questions about these four practical activities, as well as questions on general issues of methodology. — 1 hr — 33.3%

AS/A2 Level Psychology courses

AS and A2

All Psychology A Level courses being studied from September 2000 are in two parts, with three separate units or modules in each part. Most students will start by studying the AS (Advanced Subsidiary) course. Some will then go on to study the second part of the A Level course, called the A2. It is also possible to study the full A Level course, both AS and A2, in any order.

How will you be tested?

Assessment units

For AS Psychology, you will be tested by three assessment units. For the full A Level in Psychology, you will take a further three units. AS Psychology forms 50% of the assessment weighting for the full A Level.

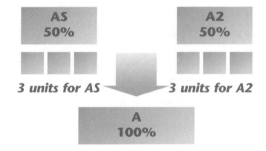

Each unit can normally be taken in either January or June. Alternatively, you can study the whole course before taking any of the unit tests. There is a lot of flexibility about when exams can be taken and the diagram below shows just some of the ways that the assessment units may be taken for AS and A Level Psychology.

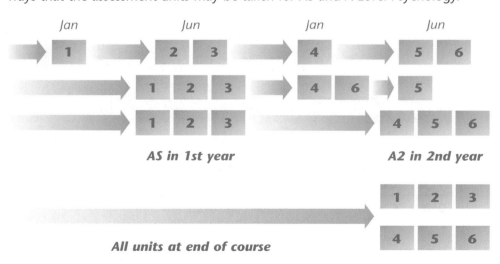

If you are disappointed with a module result, you can resit each module once. You will need to be very careful about when you take up a resit opportunity because you will have only one chance to improve your mark. The higher mark counts.

A2 and Synoptic assessment

For those students who, having studied AS, decide to go on to study A2, there are three further units to be studied. Similar assessment arrangements apply except some units, those that draw together various elements of the course in a 'synoptic' assessment, have to be assessed at the end. The question style is intended to be a progression from AS.

Coursework

Coursework will form part of your A Level Psychology course. In some specifications this does not come until the A2 part of the course.

Key skills

It is important that you develop your key skills throughout the AS and A2 courses that you take, as these are skills that you need whatever you do beyond AS and A Levels. To gain the key skills qualification, which is equivalent to an AS Level, you will need to demonstrate that you have attained Level 3 in Communication, Application of number and Information technology. Part of the assessment can be done as normal class activity and part is by formal test. It is a worthwhile qualification, as it demonstrates your ability to put your ideas across to other people, collect data and use up-to-date technology in your work.

What skills will I need?

Following an examination course means that much of your learning is guided by how it will ultimately be assessed. Examination boards set out their assessment objectives: these are skills and abilities you should have acquired by studying the course. In the new A Level examinations there are three skill clusters, which in brief are: describe (AO1), evaluate (AO2), and conduct (AO3). There is also an assessment of the Quality of Written Communication (QoWC).

These objectives are shown below.

Knowledge and understanding (AO1)

• Knowledge and understanding of Psychological theories, terminology, concepts, studies and methods in the core areas of cognitive, social, developmental, individual differences and Physiological Psychology.
• Communicate knowledge and understanding of Psychology in a clear and effective manner.

Analyse and evaluate (AO2)

• Analyse and evaluate psychological theories, concepts, studies and methods in the core areas of cognitive, social, developmental, individual differences and Physiological Psychology.
• Communicate knowledge and understanding of Psychology in a clear and effective manner.

In general, the AS assessment contains more AO1 assessment than AO2.

Design, conduct and report (AO3)

- Design, conduct and report psychological investigation(s), choosing from a range of methods, and taking into account the issues of reliability, validity and ethics.
- Collect and draw conclusions from data.

Quality of Written Communication (QoWC)

The Quality of Written Communication is assessed in all AS and A2 assessment units where candidates are required to produce extended written material. Candidates will be assessed according to their ability to:

- select and use a form and style of writing appropriate to a complex subject matter
- organise relevant information clearly and coherently, using specialist vocabulary when appropriate
- ensure text is legible, and spelling, grammar and punctuation are accurate, so that meaning is clear.

Key Term Throughout the book AQA Key Terms are highlighted with this symbol.

Different types of questions in AS examinations

Short-answer questions

A short-answer question may test recall or it may test understanding by requiring you to recall information from your studies. This style of question is used in OCR units 1 and 2. For example:

> Milgram's study of obedience is often criticised for being unethical, though Milgram himself made a robust defence of it. Give **two** examples of how the ethics of this study can be defended.
>
> *(Specimen paper for Unit 1)*

Structured questions

Structured questions are in several parts. The parts are usually about a common context and they often become progressively more difficult and more demanding as you work your way through the question. They may start with simple recall, then require more elaborate description of a study or a theory. The most difficult part of a structured question is usually at the end, where the candidate is asked to analyse the evidence related to a specific issue.

When answering structured questions, do not feel that you have to complete one question before starting the next. The further you are into a question, the more difficult the marks are to obtain. If you run out of ideas, go on to the next question. Five minutes spent on the beginning of that question are likely to be much more fruitful than the same time spent wracking your brains trying to think of an explanation for an unfamiliar phenomenon.

Here is an example of a structured question that becomes progressively more demanding.

(a) Explain what is meant by the terms 'obedience' and 'conformity'. [3+3 marks]

(b) Describe **one** research study that has explored conformity.   [6 marks]

(c) Milgram's and Zimbardo's studies provoked public outcry because of the ethical issues raised.

 Outline some ethical issues raised in social influence research and consider to what extent such ethical issues can be justified.   [18 marks]

The AQA specification A examination uses the following mark scheme to assess parts (a) and (b) of this question, and the AOI component of part (c):

Skill cluster A01

Band 3: 5-6 marks
The description is **accurate** and **detailed**.

Band 2: 3-4 marks
The description is **limited**. It is **generally accurate** but **less detailed**.

Band 1: 1-2 marks
The description is **basic, lacking detail** and may be **muddled**.

 0 marks
The description of a research study of conformity is **inappropriate** or the description is **incorrect**. Where an answer is marked out of 3, then the marks are changed accordingly.

Extended answers

In AS Level Psychology, questions requiring more extended answers will usually form part of structured questions *(AQA A)* or be the last question on the question paper *(Edexcel and OCR)*. They will be characterised by having more than 6 marks. These questions are also used to assess your abilities to communicate ideas and put together a logical argument. For example:

To what extent can forgetting be explained in terms of repression? *(AQA A)*

Discuss **two** contributions of either Freud or Rogers to the development of Psychology. *(AQA B)*

Discuss the effects of shift work on circadian rhythms. *(Edexcel)*

What impact have the findings about human behaviour and experience had on everyday life, good or bad? *(OCR)*

The 'correct' answers to extended questions are less well-defined than those requiring short answers. Examiners may have a list of points for which credit is awarded up to the maximum for the question, or they may first of all judge the 'quality' of your response as poor, satisfactory or good before allocating it a mark within a range that corresponds to that 'quality'.

The AQA specification A uses the following mark scheme for extended answer questions:

Skill cluster AO2

12–11 marks
There is an **informed commentary** and **reasonably thorough analysis** of the relevant psychological studies/methods. Material has been used in an **effective** manner.

10–9 marks
There is a **reasonable commentary** and **slightly limited analysis** of relevant psychological studies/methods. Material has been used in an **effective** manner.

8–7 marks
There is a **reasonable commentary** of relevant psychological studies/method and a **slightly limited analysis** of the relevant psychological studies/methods. Material has been used in a **reasonably effective** manner.

6–5 marks
There is a **basic commentary** but a **limited analysis** of the relevant psychological studies/methods. Material has been used in a **reasonably effective** manner.

4–3 marks
There is **superficial commentary** and **rudimentary analysis** of the relevant psychological studies/methods. There is **minimal interpretation** of the material used.

2–1 marks
Commentary is **just discernible** (for example, through appropriate selection of material). Analysis is **weak** and **muddled**. The answer may be **mainly irrelevant** to the problem it addresses.

0 marks
Commentary is **wholly irrelevant** to the problem it addresses.

Exam technique

Links from GCSE

AS Level Psychology is a step up from GCSE. You can take a GCSE in Psychology but this would mean covering very much the same information. The advantage of this is that the work will be quite easy because it is familiar, and you can focus on tackling slightly more difficult assignments and focus on those areas that are new.

Most students doing AS Level Psychology will be new to the subject but there are still links to your earlier GCSEs. Physiological Psychology is concerned with the same subject matter as Biology, and some of the things you have studied in Mathematics will come in useful here (such as drawing graphs and calculating statistics).

The most important thing to realise is that the level of this AS exam is designed to be just the right sort of step up for you, after studying GCSE. You will be required to learn about more complex ideas and, in the examination, to answer more extended questions than during your GCSE studies.

What are examiners looking for?

Psychology examiners are looking for evidence of your knowledge, but often there are no 'right' answers. There are a range of correct answers and any of these will receive credit. The examiners mark your answers *positively*. They do not subtract marks when material is missing. Instead they award marks for any material that is relevant. You must aim to demonstrate your knowledge and understanding.

Whatever type of question you are answering, it is important to respond in the correct way to the **command words** at the beginning of the question:

Recall

To identify and reinforce knowledge gained at Key Stage 4 through the study of the National Curriculum science programme, also through the study of other units in this specification.

Understand

To explain the underlying principles and apply the knowledge to novel situations (AO2).

Appreciate

To show awareness of the significance, without detailed knowledge of the underlying principles.

Discuss

To give a balanced, reasoned objective account of a particular topic.

Distinguish

To recognise comparable differences in a given context, e.g. different types of neurones within the nervous system.

Outline

To briefly describe without explanation, identifying main points.

Describe

To give details without explanation.

Evaluate

To comment on, giving advantages and disadvantages, or give a judgement.

Apply

To explain how a concept is significant when considering everyday issues or novel situations.

Some dos and don'ts

Dos

Do read all the questions first.

If you have to choose between questions make sure you choose the right question for you. Don't end up discovering that you could do parts (a) and (b) but haven't a clue about part (c).

Do answer the question.

This sounds obvious but, under examination conditions, students feel very anxious and write about anything they can think of. Sometimes they don't even read the whole question. They just look at the first few words and start writing.

Do use the mark allocation to guide you in how much you should write.

Two marks is likely to mean two valid points. If you write lots and lots for a question with very few marks you won't get extra credit and you will leave less time for the other questions.

Do write legibly and try to use technical terms and correct spelling.

There are marks in the examination for your quality of written communication, and this includes the use of technical terms. It also helps to use names and dates if you know them.

Don'ts

Don't regurgitate your prepared answer because you got a good mark for it in class. If it doesn't answer the question set, it will receive no credit.

Don't ignore features of a question.

If the question says 'describe one study of work stress', explain how the study you select demonstrates work stress. Explain any ambiguities to the examiner.

Don't leave out obvious material.

It is very easy to think 'the examiner knows this' and presume that you don't have to write down the obvious things. However, the examiner cannot be sure that you know it unless you demonstrate it.

Don't waste time.

An examination has a finite length, so don't spend time 'waffling' because you think the examiner might find something relevant in what you say. Spend time thinking and select what you say very carefully.

What grade do you want?

For a Grade A

- You must be able to cope with the evaluation as well as the description (skills AO1 and AO2).
- To do this type of work you need to practise by writing lots of answers to extended-type questions. In the AQA A questions the evaluation part of the question is always the last part.
- Increase your understanding by trying to discuss your studies with other people. For example, you might try to explain psychological research into conformity to your mother. What does it all mean?

For a Grade C

- You must have thoroughly learned the material. You will need to get virtually full marks on all the AO1 questions (description).
- Memory is improved by organising the material. Write your own notes using your own method of organisation.
- Practise examination questions and try to find out where you lost marks, and why.

For a Grade E

- Aim to get high marks on the most straightforward questions.
- Memorise the definitions of all key terms.
- Don't overlook any question. Try to write something.
- If your examination has a coursework component, make sure you get as high a mark as possible on this.
- Select one area that you especially enjoy and do the most work on this.

What marks do you need?

As a rough guide, you will need to score as follows:

average	65%	56%	50%	42%	35%
grade	A	B	C	D	E

Four steps to successful revision

Step 1: Understand

- Study the topic to be learned slowly. Make sure you understand the logic or important concepts.
- Mark up the text if necessary – underline, highlight and make notes.
- Re-read each paragraph slowly.

GO TO STEP 2

Step 2: Summarise

- Now make your own revision note summary:
  What is the main idea, theme or concept to be learned?
  What are the main points? How does the logic develop?
  Ask questions: Why? How? What next?
- Use bullet points, mind maps, patterned notes.
- Link ideas with mnemonics, mind maps, crazy stories.
- Note the title and date of the revision notes
  (e.g. Psychology: Attitudes and prejudice, 3rd March).
- Organise your notes carefully and keep them in a file.

This is now in short-term memory. You will forget 80% of it if you do not go to Step 3. GO TO STEP 3, but first take a 10 minute break.

Step 3: Memorise

- Take 25 minute learning 'bites' with 5 minute breaks.
- After each 5 minute break test yourself:
  Cover the original revision note summary
  Write down the main points
  Speak out loud (record on tape)
  Tell someone else
  Repeat many times.

The material is well on its way to long-term memory. You will forget 40% if you do not do step 4. GO TO STEP 4

Step 4: Track / Review

- Create a Revision Diary (one A4 page per day).
- Make a revision plan for the topic, e.g. 1 day later, 1 week later, 1 month later.
- Record your revision in your Revision Diary, e.g.
  Psychology: Attitudes and prejudice, 3rd March 25 minutes
  Psychology: Attitudes and prejudice, 5th March 15 minutes
  Psychology: Attitudes and prejudice, 3rd April 15 minutes
  ... and then at monthly intervals.

Chapter 1

The study of psychology

The following topics are covered in this chapter:

- *Key approaches and the development of psychology*

1.1 Key approaches and the development of psychology

After studying this topic you should be able to:

- *define psychology and identify its main characteristics*
- *outline what is involved in the scientific process*
- *explain the three main approaches in psychology: psychodynamic, behaviourist, and humanistic*
- *discuss the assumptions, methods, advantages and limitations of each approach*

LEARNING SUMMARY

What is psychology?

AQA A	general
AQA B	U1
EDEXCEL	general
OCR	U1, U2

Psychology is the scientific study of behaviour and experience. It differs from common sense in so far as it seeks to collect objective and verifiable facts about behaviour and construct empirically based theories.

The scientific process involves:

- making observations, and producing 'facts' (data about the world)
- constructing a theory to account for a set of related facts
- generating expectations (hypotheses) from the theory
- collecting data to test expectations
- adjusting the theory in response to the data collected.

Data can be collected in two ways:

- **empirically**, through direct experience or observation
- **rationally**, by constructing reasoned arguments.

> Sometimes 'approaches' are called 'perspectives'. Both describe a characteristic way of looking at the world. Every psychological theory grows out of a perspective or 'world-view'.

The psychodynamic approach

AQA A	U2
AQA B	U1
EDEXCEL	U2
OCR	U1, U2

'Psychodynamic' refers to any approach which emphasises the processes of change and development (i.e. dynamics). Freud's psychoanalytic theory is the best-known psychodynamic theory. The term psychoanalysis describes both a theory of personality and the therapy derived from it. Key assumptions of the psychodynamic approach are as follows:

- Human development is a **dynamic process** (i.e. it is driven or motivated by certain forces).
- Importance of **early experience**. Infants are born with innate biological drives, e.g. for oral satisfaction.
- **Ego defence.** If innate drives are thwarted or not satisfied, anxiety is produced. The ego defends itself against anxiety using ego-defence mechanisms (e.g. repression, denial, projection). Ego defenses can explain abnormal and/or unconscious behaviour.
- **The unconscious.** Many aspects of personality dynamics are unconscious, and their expression is indirect, for example through dreams and in 'Freudian slips'.

> Freud (1920) gave the following example of the Freudian slip: a British MP was speaking of his colleague from Hull but said 'the honourable member from Hell', thus revealing his private thoughts about the other MP.

17

The structure of the personality

- The **id** (or 'it'). This is the primitive, instinctive part that demands immediate satisfaction. Motivated by the **pleasure principle** ('it' gets what 'it' wants).
- The **ego** (or 'I') develops in the first two years of life as a result of the child's experience. Motivated by the **reality principle**, the child learns to accommodate to the demands of the environment and modifies the demands of the id.
- The **superego** (or 'above-I') develops at about the age of five. It is equivalent to the conscience.

Psychosexual stages of development

> The three strands of Freud's theory of development are: driving forces (e.g. the pleasure principle), personality structure (e.g. the id), and the organ-focus (e.g. oral).

The child seeks gratification through different body organs during development. If conflicts arising from these developmental stages are not resolved satisfactorily they can lead to 'fixations' later in adult life.

- **Oral stage** (0–18 months). Oral fixation from too much or too little gratification of the id, may result in, for example, thumb-sucking.
- **Anal stage** (18–36 months). Anal fixation could be due to either strict toilet training, or pleasure taken in playing with faeces.
- **Phallic stage** (3–6 years). A fixation on genitals leads to the Oedipus Complex (desire for mother, jealousy and guilt towards father, resolved by identification with father; this is described further in Freud's case study of Little Hans – see p.20). Girls, on the other hand, realise they have no penis and blame their mother. 'Penis envy' is resolved by a desire to have babies. This conflict resolution is weaker for girls and therefore, according to Freud, girls don't develop as strong a sense of moral justice as boys. Jung proposed an 'Electra complex' – a young girl feels desire for her father and rejects her mother.
- **Latency stage** (7 until puberty): the in-between years. Little psychosocial development takes place but children develop socially by interacting with other children, e.g. at school (although boys and girls do not interact much).
- **Genital stage** (puberty). The development of independence is now possible if earlier conflicts have been resolved.

Therapy (see Chapter 5, p.116–117).

> Freud did not mean the term 'sexual' in the way many people interpret it. 'Sexual' roughly means 'physical' or 'sensual'.

Positive points include the following:

- Freud's important contribution was to **recognise childhood** as a critical period of development, and to identify sexual (physical) and unconscious influences.
- The theory has been enormously **influential** within psychology, and beyond.
- It is an **idiographic** approach, meaning that it focuses more on the individual than on general laws of behaviour (the nomothetic approach). Psychoanalytic theory provides a rich picture of individual personality dynamics.

Criticisms of the theory are that:

- It lacks rigorous **empirical support**, especially regarding normal development. The 'evidence' comes largely from case studies of middle-class, European women, many of whom were neurotic. The data was retrospectively collected and given subjective interpretation (thus introducing potential **investigator bias** – see p.171).
- It reduces human activity to a basic set of structures, which are **reifications** (abstract concepts which are presented as if they are real things).
- It is **deterministic** (it implies that people have little if any choice or free will), suggesting that infant behaviour is determined by innate forces and adult behaviour is determined by childhood experiences.
- The original theory lays too much emphasis on **innate biological forces**.

Methods used in the psychodynamic approach

Case studies

Psychoanalytic studies focused on one person (see Freud's case study of Little Hans on p.20), though a case study could also be of one family, one school or a particular event. Case studies offer insight into unusual behaviour and provide rich details grounded in real life. They are an idiographic approach to data collection.

In a case study an individual may be interviewed to discover details of their present and past, or psychometric tests may be used to assess personality, intelligence and other abilities.

The drawbacks of case studies are that:
- they are **time-consuming** and unreliable (retrospective data, interviewer bias)
- they **can't be replicated** and it may not be reasonable to generalise the findings to all human behaviour
- there may be **ethical objections** in terms of invasion of privacy.

As already indicated, there are advantages to case studies, such as rich data.

Clinical interviews

The interview method is described on p.162–163. Clinical interviews, as used by doctors and therapists, start with a predetermined set of questions. As the clinical interview (like an unstructured interview) progresses, the questions are adapted in line with some of the responses given. This means that unexpected answers and individual differences can be accommodated. The method maximises the amount of information gained and may lead to new discoveries.

The drawback of interviews is that:
- the interviewer needs to be highly experienced because their questions may affect the kinds of answers given (**interviewer bias**).

The advantages of interviews are described on p.162–163.

Analysis of symbols in dreams

Freud proposed that the **latent content** of dreams may be represented in symbols (the **manifest content** being the dream as reported by the dreamer). Some symbols are personal, related to an individual's experiences, whereas others are universal. For instance, Freud suggested that guns or swords were representations of the penis, whereas vessels such as ships and jars represented the female genital organs. In order to interpret personal symbols, the therapist has to become familiar with an individual's life history.

A criticism of dream interpretation is that it lacks **falsifiability** (i.e. cannot be proven wrong). If the patient rejects the therapist's interpretation, this may be seen as resistance. If the patient accepts the interpretation, this confirms its accuracy.

Neo-Freudians

Other theorists, such as Erikson and Jung, produced psychodynamic theories which placed less emphasis on biological forces and more on the influences of social and cultural factors. Erikson's work with adolescents and Sioux Indians led him to believe that many aspects of behaviour were culturally rather than biologically based.

Progress check

1 Name one assumption of the psychodynamic approach.
2 Name one method used by the psychodynamic approach.

2 E.g. case studies; analysis of symbols.
1 E.g. the importance of early experience; the influence of the unconscious.

OCR core study: Little Hans

Freud (1909) Analysis of a phobia

Aims To document the case history of a boy who had developed an extreme phobia of white horses.

Procedures & Findings This was a case history of a 5-year-old boy whose father was a supporter of Freud. The case history was recorded by the father and discussed with Freud, who only met the boy twice. The chief findings of the case history (chronologically) were:

- *His 'widdler'.* Hans was fascinated by his 'widdler' (his penis). He observed that animals had big ones and probably so did both his parents because they were grown up.
- *His mother.* Hans spent a lot of time alone with his mother over the summer holiday and realised he liked having her to himself. He wished his father would stay away. He also felt hostile towards his new baby sister who further separated Hans from his mother. He expressed this indirectly in his fear of baths because he thought his mother would drop him (in fact, he *wished* his mother would drop his little sister – a desire which he projected elsewhere because of the anxiety it aroused).
- *Horses and anxiety.* There were two strands to Hans' anxiety: (1) Hans once heard a man saying to a child 'Don't put your finger to the white horse or it'll bite you'. (2) Hans asked his mother if she would like to put her finger on his widdler. His mother told him this would not be proper. Therefore Hans learned that touching a white horse or a widdler was undesirable. Hans' desire (libido) for his mother created a sense of anxiety and fear that she might leave him if he persisted in asking her to touch his widdler. Unconsciously this anxiety was projected elsewhere: he became afraid of being bitten by a white horse.
- *More anxiety* was created by the fact that Hans' mother told Hans that, if he played with his widdler, it would be cut off. Hans' father told Hans that women have no widdler. Hans reasoned that his mother's must have been cut off – and she might do the same to him.
- *Dream about giraffes.* Hans dreamt that there were two giraffes – one crumpled and one big. He took away the crumpled one and this made the big one cry out. This might represent Hans' wish to take away his mother (crumpled one) causing his father to cry out (big giraffe – possible symbol of penis). Hans sat on the crumpled one (trying to claim his mother for himself).
- *Symbolism.* Freud suggested to Hans that the black around horses' mouths and the blinkers in front of their eyes were like his father's moustaches and glasses. Hans might envy these symbols of adulthood because they might give him the right to have a woman's love.
- *Further horse anxieties.* Hans told his father that he was afraid of horses falling down, and if they were laden (e.g. with furniture) this might lead them to fall down. Hans also remembered seeing a horse fall down and thinking it was dead. Since he secretly wished his father would fall down dead this made Hans feel more anxious.
- *The 'lumf' obsession.* Hans now became preoccupied with bowel movements ('lumf'). Freud suggested that laden vehicles represented pregnancy and when they overturn it symbolises giving birth. Thus the falling horse was both his dying father and his mother giving birth.
- *The plumber.* Hans was in the bath and the plumber stuck a big borer into his stomach. Freud called this a 'fantasy of procreation'. The bath is the mother's womb (and Hans is in it). The borer is his father's penis, which created him.
- *The resolution.* Hans became less afraid of horses because he had worked through his fantasies and understood their real meaning – they were no longer

unconscious and he could deal with them. He developed two final fantasies which showed that his feelings about his father were resolved: (1) 'The plumber came and first he took away my behind with a pair of pincers, and then he gave me another, and then the same with my widdler', (2) Hans told his father that he was now the daddy and not the mummy of his imaginary children, thus showing that he had moved from wishing his father dead to identifying with him.

Conclusions This provides support for Freud's theory of psychosexual development, and evidence for Freud's explanation of the origins of disordered behaviour.

OCR Revision question
a) In the study by Freud, Little Hans is referred to as 'a little Oedipus'. Briefly describe the Oedipus complex. [2]

b) Outline **one** piece of evidence from the study that is used to support the claim that Hans is a 'little Oedipus'. [2] (January 2001, Core Studies 1, question 4)

The behaviourist approach

AQA A	U2
AQA B	U1
EDEXCEL	U2
OCR	U1, U2

Introspectionism was a highly formalised investigative technique. Individuals were trained to produce evidence about their thoughts and mental states.

This approach has its roots in nineteenth-century empirical philosophy (e.g. that of Locke) which believed that we should only study what can be directly observed (**positivism**). Watson (1913) coined the term 'behaviourism', suggesting that Pavlov's **classical conditioning** theory could be used to explain all behaviour, and that this approach was preferable to Wundt's **introspectionism**.

Thorndike (1913) expanded learning theory to include 'instrumental learning', later adapted by Skinner (1938) into **operant conditioning**. Skinner's views represent 'radical behaviourism' – the position that there are private, less accessible activities (mental events or the contents of the 'black box') but these are not needed in the explanation of behaviour.

Key assumptions of the behaviourist approach are as follows:

- Humans and non-human animals are only **quantitatively different**, i.e. they differ in terms of having more or less of something rather than differing qualitatively.
- There is no need to look at what goes on inside the 'black box' – it is sufficient to be concerned with external and **observable behaviour** only.
- All behaviour can be explained in terms of **conditioning** theory: stimulus and response (S–R) links which build up to produce more complex behaviours.
- All behaviour is determined by **environmental influences**, i.e. learning. We are born as a blank slate.

Key concepts of behaviourist (learning) theory

Classical conditioning

Learning to associate a stimulus with a response.

Before	NS (neutral stimulus, bell)	→ no response
	UCS (unconditioned stimulus, food)	→ UCR (unconditioned response, salivation)
During conditioning		NS and UCS are paired by occurring together
After	CS (conditioned stimulus, bell)	→ CR (conditioned response, salivation)

Operant conditioning

Learning due to the consequences of a behaviour (response).

			→ Reinforcement (reward) strengthens response learning
Situation (<u>A</u>ntecedents)	→ <u>B</u>ehaviour	→ <u>C</u>onsequence [ABC]	
		→ Punishment weakens response, no learning takes place	

The probability of a behaviour being repeated depends on strengthening or weakening S–R links:

> All reinforcement (positive or negative) *increases* the likelihood of a response.

- **Positive reinforcement** increases the probability of a response recurring because the response is pleasurable – for example, receiving a smile when you give someone a kiss.
- **Negative reinforcement** – escape from an unpleasant stimulus. This is also pleasurable and increases the probability of the same response in the future. For example, finding that a smile stops your mother shouting at you.
- **Positive punishment** (punishment by application), receiving something unpleasant, decreases probability of a future behaviour. For example, being told off for smiling at an inappropriate moment.
- **Negative punishment** (punishment by removal), removing something desirable, also decreases probability of future behaviour. For example, not being allowed your dessert because you didn't finish the main course.

Features of conditioning

> Skinner's approach concentrated on the effects of emitted behaviour rather than Pavlov's focus on the elicited behaviours themselves. ('To emit' means to spontaneously produce, whereas 'to elicit' means to draw forth.)

- **Generalisation**. Animal responds in the same way to stimuli which are similar.
- **Extinction**. The new response disappears because it is no longer paired with the original stimulus or is not reinforced.
- **Shaping**. Animal gradually learns a target behaviour by being reinforced for behaviours which are closer and closer to the target.
- **Reinforcement schedules**. Partial reinforcement schedules are more effective and more resistant to extinction. This may be because, under continuous reinforcement, the organism 'expects' it on every trial and therefore 'notices' its absence more quickly. Partial reinforcement includes fixed or variable ratios, and fixed or variable intervals. An example of a fixed ratio would be a reward once in every ten trials; an example of a fixed interval would be a reward every 10 minutes.

Evaluation of the behaviourist approach

Positive points include the following:

- Classic learning theory has had a major influence on all areas of Psychology – **methodological behaviourism** is the view that all approaches use some behaviourist concepts to explain behaviour.
- Behaviourism has given rise to many **practical applications**.
- It is an empirical perspective which lends itself to **scientific research**. Broadbent (1961) argued that it is the best method for rational advance in psychology.

Criticisms of the theory are that it:

> Reductionism refers to the process of reducing complex matters to a set of simple rules or components. Behaviourism is a very reductionist approach.

- **is a mechanistic** (machine-like) perspective which ignores consciousness, subjective experience, and emotions
- **excludes the role of cognitive factors** and cannot explain, for example, insight learning and cognitive maps
- denies the role of **innate factors**
- **is deterministic**: behaviour is determined by the environment
- **is reductionist**: reduces complex behaviour to stimulus–response links
- is largely based on work with **non-human animals**. Behaviourists argue that the theory of evolution shows that human and non-human animals are quantitatively not qualitatively different and therefore such research is meaningless

- can lead to the use of behaviourist principles to control others (as in some prisons and psychiatric institutions) and this could be considered unethical.

Methods used in the behaviourist approach

Laboratory experiments

These are described later in Chapter 7, on p. 160–161.

Non-human-animal learning experiments

Skinner (1938) placed a pigeon in a 'Skinner box' and if it pecked a lever, a door would open and food (the reinforcer) was delivered. The pigeon first pecks randomly around the box as part of its natural exploratory behaviour. Accidentally it pecks the lever a few times and receives food. Each experience strengthens the S–R link. Reinforcement is positive (when the lever is pecked) and also any unrewarded behaviour is 'stamped out' (when pecking elsewhere no food appears). Behaviour has thus been brought under stimulus control. If the pigeon learns to peck at a button whenever it is lit to get food, it is **learning** to discriminate between different states of illumination of the button (a discriminative stimulus).

The drawback of this approach is that it may not be appropriate to make generalisations from the study of non-human animals to human behaviour because much of human behaviour is influenced by higher-level thinking.

Social learning theory

Neo-behaviourist approaches are those which are based on behaviourist principles but use un-observable processes (mental events) in their explanations – for example, social learning theory which was developed by Dollard and Miller (1950). The key concepts for social learning theory are:

- As well as direct reinforcement and punishment, behaviour is learned through **indirect (vicarious)** reinforcement and punishment, i.e. by seeing others reinforced or punished. Much more can be learned indirectly.
- Individuals imitate the behaviour of others either because they see it **rewarded** and/or because they **identify** with significant others (e.g. people of the same gender, or TV idols, or parents). In order to imitate behaviour, one must store an internal representation of that behaviour.

Bandura *et al.* (1961) demonstrated how aggressiveness can be learned through modelling (see the OCR core study on p.24).

The advantage of this approach is that is goes beyond traditional learning theory in the inclusion of un-observable and cognitive and social factors. Its weakness is that it doesn't include the effects of emotional factors.

Progress check

1 Name one assumption of the behaviourist approach.
2 What is the difference between positive and negative reinforcement?
3 What is 'shaping'?

3 Receiving rewards for behaviours that are closer and closer to the target behaviour.
2 Positive reinforcement involves a reward whereas in negative reinforcement pleasure is derived by escaping from an aversive stimulus.
1 E.g. that everything is learned.

OCR core study: Imitating aggression

Bandura *et al.* (1961) Transmission of aggression through imitation of aggressive models

Aims Is aggression learned through imitation? Do observers imitate specific acts or do they just become more aggressive? Would children be more likely to imitate a same-sex model?

Procedures This was a laboratory experiment. The participants were children from a university nursery school, 36 boys and 36 girls aged approximately 3 to 5 years. Two adult 'models', a male and a female.

Phase 1: Exposure to aggression. Each child was taken on their own to a room where there were lots of toys including, in one corner, a 5-foot inflatable 'Bobo' doll and a mallet. The experimenter invited the 'model' to join them and then left the room for about 10 minutes. Participants had been allocated to one of three conditions on the basis of a pre-test for aggressiveness so that each group contained equally aggressive children:

> The pre-test (before the experiment) was done to ensure that there were a similar number of aggressive children in each condition, otherwise aggressiveness could have been a confounding variable.

- *Non-aggressive condition*: The model played with the toys in a quiet manner.
- *Aggressive condition*: The model spent some of the time being aggressive to Bobo, including some specific acts, e.g. repeatedly punching it on the nose.
- *Control*: The report does not say what treatment these children received.

Phase 2: Tests for imitation. In order to find out whether the children imitated the aggressive model it was necessary to 'mildly' provoke the children to behave aggressively – the children were taken to a room of attractive toys and then told they couldn't play with these. They were then taken to another room which contained some aggressive toys (e.g. a mallet, and a dart gun), some non-aggressive toys (e.g. dolls and farm animals) and a Bobo doll. The children were observed through a one-way mirror while they played. A record was made of any physical or verbal aggression and whether it was imitative of the model's behaviour.

> This study has been used as support in general for social learning theory yet the data is based on the imitative behaviour of children. Adults might not behave in the same way since they are less impressionable.

Findings *Imitation*: Children in the aggressive condition imitated specific behaviours. Children in the non-aggressive condition displayed very few of these behaviours (70% had zero scores).

Non-imitative aggression: The aggressive group displayed much more non-imitative aggression than the non-aggressive group, ie. they were generally more aggressive.

Non-aggressive behaviour: Children in the non-aggressive condition spent more time playing non-aggressively with dolls.

Gender: Boys imitated more physical aggression than girls but not verbal aggression. There was some evidence of a 'same-sex effect' between model and children.

Conclusions This provides evidence that learning can take place in the absence of either classical or operant conditioning. The children imitated the model's behaviour in the *absence* of any rewards. Bandura *et al.* suggest that Freud's concept of identification may be useful in explaining how learning took place but more investigation is needed to understand the modelling process.

OCR Revision question
a) From the study by Bandura, Ross and Ross, outline **one** difference that was found between the aggressive behaviour of boys and that of girls. [2]
b) Outline **one** possible reason for the gender differences that were found. [2]
(January 2002, Core Studies 1, question 2)

The humanistic approach

Maslow called humanistic psychology the 'third force in psychology', in its rejection of determinism and reductionism. Humanistic approaches are a reflection of modern-day society in the same way that both psychoanalysis and behaviourism are a reflection of their times.

Key assumptions of the humanistic approach are as follows:

- Each individual is *unique*. What matters is each person's subjective view rather than some objective reality. Reality is defined by the individual's perspective.
- Human nature is positive and inherently good. Each person strives for growth and **actualisation**.
- Individuals are capable of **self-determination** (free will).

Rogers was the founder of client-centred therapy, or counselling. He believed that maladjustment stemmed from receiving conditional love as a child. This results in a conflict between the self and the ideal self, and means the individual is likely to try to be someone else in order to receive the love they want.

Evaluation of the humanistic approach

Positive points include the following:

- This **subjective approach** has encouraged psychologists to accept the view that there is more to behaviour than objectively discoverable facts.
- It has had **widespread application** in counselling and client- or person-centred therapy (Rogers, 1951).

Criticisms of the theory are that:

- it is largely a vague, unscientific and **untestable** approach.

Methods used in the humanistic approach

Humanistic psychologists believe that psychological theories should be humanly rather than statistically significant, claiming that objective data can tell us little about subjective experience. New research methods are needed to properly investigate human behaviour, such as **new paradigm research** (Reason and Rowan, 1981) and **ethogenics** (Harré and Secord, 1972). Ethogenics involves a careful analysis of sequences of events, without quantifying them, to understand how successive episodes interlock.

Progress check

1 Name one assumption of the humanistic approach in psychology.
2 What is one advantage of the humanistic approach in psychology?

2 E.g. emphasises the importance of individual experience.

1 E.g. each person strives for self-actualisation.

25

Sample question and student answer

AQA B style question

from AQA B specimen paper Unit 1 Introducing psychology, question 1

(a) Identify and describe **one** characteristic of the scientific method. [3]

(b) Discuss **one** limitation of the scientific study of human behaviour. [4]

(c) Identify and describe **one** assumption of the behaviourist approach in psychology. [3]

(d) Discuss **two** contributions of either Freud or Rogers to the development of psychology. [10]

The candidate has correctly identified a characteristic of the scientific method (1 mark) and made an attempt to describe this characteristic. Some understanding is apparent but the description is not entirely clear (1 mark). (Total of 2 marks for this part.)

(a) One characteristic of the scientific method is that it is objective. This means that observations are made from an objective point of view rather than one individual's view.

The question requires a discussion rather than simply a description, as in part (a). 'Discuss' entails both description and evaluation. The candidate has offered both: a description of one limitation and then a consideration of why this is a limitation and a means of overcoming it. Additional credit might have been gained by elaborating on this final point. (3 marks)

(b) One problem with the scientific approach is that human behaviour does not lend itself to objective study. If you stand outside an individual and make objective observations of their behaviour you don't take their subjective experience into account. This latter approach is taken by humanistic psychologists.

The candidate has identified two assumptions and not given a description of either. Only one can be credited. (1 mark)

(c) One assumption of the behaviourist approach is that all that matters is observable behaviour. Another assumption is that all behaviour can be explained in terms of learning.

(d) I will write about two contributions from Freud. His first contribution to psychology was to write a theory of development. He described how biological forces interact with experience to produce adult personality. In the first stage of development the primitive force, the id, makes demands and wants immediate gratification. If these biological demands are not met then the individual has repressed desires and these will surface in later life, being expressed in different ways. For example, a repressed desire during the oral stage of development might later be expressed as a parsimonious personality.

The other elements of the personality are the ego and super-ego. The ego is governed by the reality principle. The super-ego develops out of identification with the same-sex parent. The other stages of development after the oral stage are the anal, phallic, latency and genital stages.

Freud's theory has been very influential in psychology and many other areas such as literature. His approach of studying individuals in detail produced a lot of rich data concerning those individuals. On the other hand, these individuals were a very biased sample (female, middle-class, neurotic) and therefore his theory of personality may not actually account for all people all over the world. Another criticism of Freud's theory is that it is deterministic, suggesting that adult personality is the result of innate biological forces rather than being the result of an individual's decision to behave in a particular way.

The candidate has identified two contributions from Freud and offered a good description for both, though the second one is slightly limited. Unfortunately evaluation is only offered for the first contribution which means that the overall mark would be 7. The candidate would have done better to spend less time on the descriptive material and include some evaluation of the second contribution. (7 marks)

Freud's second contribution was a therapy to treat mentally ill patients. The main features of this therapy are free association, where the therapist says something and then the patient talks freely about whatever comes into their head, and dream analysis, where the patient recounts their dreams and the therapist turns the manifest content into the latent content and tells the patient what they were really thinking. These methods give the therapist a chance to have insights into the patient's unconscious thoughts which can then be dealt with. Only that way can the patient resolve those things which are causing their neurotic behaviour.

TOTAL: 13 out of 20 marks

Practice examination questions

(a) Ivan Pavlov studied how dogs learned to salivate to the sound of a bell using the procedure shown in the table. Complete the table by writing the appropriate terms in the boxes. [3]

When answering the question, ensure that you write *enough*. The detail required is indicated by the number of marks allocated to each question. The kind of answer required is also indicated by the injunctions that are used (e.g. 'describe', 'discuss', 'evaluate').

Before learning	Food	→	Salivation
	Unconditioned stimulus		*Unconditioned response*
During learning	Food + bell	→	Salivation
After learning	Bell	→	Salivation
			Conditioned response

(b) Describe **one** advantage and **one** disadvantage of classical conditioning as an explanation of learned behaviour in humans. [4]

(c) Describe **one** other way in which humans can learn behaviour. [3]

Edexcel specimen paper Unit Test 2 question 1

Chapter 2

Cognitive psychology

The following topics are covered in this chapter:

- *The cognitive approach*
- *Short-term and long-term memory*

- *Forgetting*
- *Critical issue: Eyewitness testimony*

2.1 The cognitive approach

After studying this topic you should be able to:

- *define the term 'cognitive'*
- *describe key assumptions of the cognitive approach and evaluate its advantages and limitations*
- *discuss some of the methods used by the cognitive approach*

LEARNING SUMMARY

Key assumptions of the cognitive approach

AQA A	U1
AQA B	U1, U2
EDEXCEL	U1
OCR	U1, U2

The word 'cognitive' comes from the Latin word *cognitio* meaning 'to apprehend, understand or know'. Cognition is the activity of internal mental processing. Early psychologists such as Wundt investigated mental activity using introspection. Behaviourists such as Watson and Skinner rejected this approach, regarding mental concepts as 'explanatory fictions', i.e. mental concepts don't actually exist and only *appear* to explain behaviour. For the first half of the 20th century, cognitive psychology lay dormant and it was only revived due to the advent of the computer age.

Cognitive psychologists are primarily interested in thinking and related mental processes such as memory, perception, attention, forgetting, learning, thinking, and language. You will come across the word again when you look at *cognitive* development (Chapter 3) and social *cognition* (Chapter 6).

The key assumptions of the cognitive approach are:

An *assumption* is something which is taken as being true without any proof. It is the basis of an approach or belief.

- Behaviour can largely be explained in terms of how the **mind** operates.
- The mind works in a manner which is **similar to a computer**: inputting, storing and retrieving data.
- Cognitive psychologists see psychology as a **pure science**.

Evaluation of the cognitive approach

Weaknesses of this approach

The cognitive approach has been criticised as overly mechanistic and lacking in social, motivational and emotional factors. It is mechanistic because cognitive explanations are based on the behaviour of machines. Inevitably, this de-emphasises the importance of emotion.

Strengths of this approach

The approach has numerous useful applications, including: advice about the validity of eyewitness testimony (see p.43–47).

Methods used in the cognitive approach

Laboratory experiments

Most cognitive research takes place in laboratories. The main advantages of this method are that cause and effect can be determined and that there is good control of variables. The main weakness is that such research doesn't always apply to the real world (low ecological validity). For example, memory research focuses on one kind of memory – explicit memory.

Explicit memory is based on conscious recollection, as distinct from implicit memory which occurs without any conscious direction to remember something. The key study on p.31 illustrates this.

Field experiments

Field experiments involve the use of more natural situations. For example, Abernethy (1940) showed that students performed better if they were tested in the same room where they were taught and tested by the same person. The context (same room, same lecturer) must have acted as a cue to recall. Field experiments have greater ecological validity but less control than laboratory experiments.

Natural experiments

Natural experiments are also used in cognitive research. For example, Myers and Brewin (1994) found that individuals who were classed as 'repressors' were less able to recall negative childhood memories as compared with other personality types, thus taking advantage of naturally occurring difference between people. We can not truly claim that cause and effect have been demonstrated because the experimenter has not manipulated the independent variable nor were participants randomly allocated to conditions.

Case studies of brain-damaged patients

If a person incurs damage to part of his or her brain, we may be able to associate this with changes in behaviour. This allows us to determine what parts of the brain might be related to particular behaviours, as in the case study of HM (Milner, 1959). The man referred to as HM suffered from epilepsy of such severity that it couldn't be controlled by drugs. As a final measure, surgeons removed the hippocampus from both sides of his brain. HM's personality and intellect remained intact but his memory was affected. He had no memory for events subsequent to the operation. His memory for events prior to the operation was reasonable, though not as good as before. He could still talk and recall all the skills he previously knew (semantic and procedural memory) but his memory did not incorporate new experiences. In short, his LTM was intact but he appeared to have no ability to update it, i.e. use his STM. This case study suggests that the hippocampus may be a specific location for STM. Without STM, HM couldn't transfer data to LTM, but he could still use his long-term memory. However, there are criticisms. HM's epilepsy may have caused general brain damage and this could explain his abnormal behaviour. We also don't know whether his subsequent behaviour was caused by the trauma of the operation, rather than the loss of part of the brain. Finally, it is not reasonable to generalise from a sample of one person. However, other studies have supported the importance of the hippocampus. For example, Baddeley (1990) described similar symptoms in a man, Clive Wearing, whose hippocampus was damaged by infection.

The hippocampus is a small structure found in both hemispheres of the forebrain.

Imaging techniques

A more recent method of studying brain activity is the use of brain scans. There are a variety of these: CAT, MRI and PET scans which produce images of the brain in action. For example, Squire *et al.* (1992) used PET scans to show that blood flow in the right hippocampus was much higher when the participants were performing one kind of memory task (cued recall) than another memory task (word-stem completion).

2.2 Short-term and long-term memory

After studying this topic you should be able to:

- *define the term 'memory' and outline the main methods used to investigate it*
- *identify the stages in, and structure of, memory*
- *distinguish between short-term memory and long-term memory*
- *explain the main models of memory and assess their strengths and limitations*

Research into the nature and structure of memory

AQA A	U1
AQA B	U2
EDEXCEL	U1

There are close links between learning and memory. So, in what ways are they different from each other? Something which is learned is lodged in memory. The two terms are almost synonymous, though learning theorists (behaviourists) do not acknowledge internal mental states (therefore the concept of memory has no place in learning theory).

Definitions

Key Term **Memory** is the process by which we encode, store and retrieve information. It includes sensory memory, short-term memory and long-term memory. These concepts are defined on page 31.

A **memory trace** is the physical representation of the information in the brain.

Memory research usually involves asking a participant to learn a set of material and then to recall it, in order to assess how much they have memorised or learned. The typical methods and means used to test memory and recall are:

- **Nonsense syllables** – a participant is given information devoid of meaning, such as trigrams (e.g. BDT) or CVCs (consonant-vowel-consonant, e.g. HIG).
- **Paired associate learning** – participants are given a pair of stimuli, such as a syllable and a digit. Recall is tested by presenting the participant with a member of the pair and recording if its partner can be remembered.
- **Interference task** – participants are given a task to perform between exposure to stimulus and recall of information. (It is used to prevent rehearsal.)
- **Free recall** – information is directly retrieved from memory at will. Participants are allowed to recall items in any order they please.
- **Recognition** – identifying familiar information. Participants are shown a list of items to remember, and then later shown another longer list that contains the original items. Their task is to recognise the original items. It is a better test of memory than recall because participants recall all the items that are not available, not just those that are currently accessible.

Progress check

1 Why are interference tasks necessary?
2 Is a person likely to recall more when given a free recall task or a recognition task?

2 Recognition task.

1 To prevent rehearsal.

The nature and stages of memory

The stages involved in the operation of memory are:

1 **Input (registering/encoding information).** Sensory data is translated into a memory trace.
2 **Storage.** This may be temporary or permanent.
3 **Output.** Memories are useless unless they can be retrieved through recall, recognition, reconstruction, reproduction (rote learning), and/or confabulation.

The structure of memory

Memory can be divided into the following parts:

Sensory memory (SM)

The sensory form of a stimulus remains unaltered in the mind for a brief time. This could be an auditory or visual trace. It is rapidly lost through spontaneous decay (i.e. the trace disappears).

Short-term memory (STM)

Key Term Short-term memory refers to a temporary storage place for information where it receives minimal processing. It is relatively limited in capacity (about seven items) and decays rapidly unless maintained through rehearsal. It may be held in a visual or auditory form (code), though it is mainly the latter.

Long-term memory (LTM)

Key Term Long-term memory refers to relatively permanent storage, which has unlimited capacity and uses a semantic code. Different kinds of long-term memory have been identified:

- **Procedural memory:** knowing how. Our knowledge of how to do things, skills such as riding a bicycle.
- **Declarative memory:** knowing that. Memory for specific information or facts. This is either semantic or episodic.
  - **Semantic memory:** storage for language, other cognitive concepts and general knowledge. This is well organised, usually isn't forgotten, and doesn't disappear in cases of amnesia. Theories of loss of availability can't account for the behaviour of semantic memory.
  - **Episodic memory:** memory for personal events and people, the episodes of your life. It is this kind of memory that is tested in experimental work. It is unstructured and more rapidly lost, particularly as new information arrives and interferes.

An empirical study is a study (such as an experiment or interview) where data has been collected through direct observation or experience.

Distinguishing between short-term and long-term memory

The evidence for separate stores comes from empirical studies of:

Duration

Key Term Duration refers to how long a memory is stored. Short-term memories last a short time, between 15 and 30 seconds if not rehearsed. Long-term memories may last forever. See key studies on duration in STM (page 32) and LTM (page 33).

Capacity

Key Term Capacity refers to how much can be held in a memory store. STM has a very small capacity, estimated by Miller (see page 33) to 7±2 chunks of information. LTM is potentially unlimited. Merkle (1988) estimated (using the number of synapses) that LTM may have a capacity of between one thousand and one million gigabytes.

Encoding

Key Term Encoding describes the form or code used to store data in memory. This may be based on the sound of the information (an acoustic code), the way the information appears visually (a visual code) or may be in terms of meaning (a semantic code). STM tends to be stored acoustically whereas LTM is more semantic. (See the key study on encoding on page 34.)

Serial position effect: primacy and recency effects

Glanzer and Cunitz (1966) asked participants to recall word lists; if this was done immediately there was a primacy and a recency effect (early and later words were better recalled) due to STM and LTM effects. If there was delay of 10 seconds or more there was only a primacy effect – STM alone was affected. Primacy is due to the fact that the first items are more likely to have entered LTM. Recency occurs because the last items in the list are still in STM.

Brain damage

Amnesia affects LTM. In anterograde amnesia, permanent memories remain intact but sufferers cannot remember any new information for more than the normal STM span. This is probably because transfer from STM to LTM is lost. Examples include the case study of HM (described on page 29) and Korsakoff's syndrome, which is due to severe alcohol poisoning.

> What are some of the weaknesses with evidence from brain-damaged individuals?

Brain injury can affect STM. The patient KF (Shallice and Warrington, 1970) performed poorly on many short-term memory tasks (e.g. digit span) after a motorbike accident. However his long-term memory was normal.

Forgetting

Explanations for forgetting are different for STM and LTM. See pages 38–42.

AQA (A) Key study: Duration of STM

Peterson and Peterson (1959) Recall of trigrams without rehearsal

Aims To test the hypothesis that information held in STM disappears within about 20 seconds if rehearsal is prevented. If participants are allowed to rehearse (repeat) information, this maintains information indefinitely. An accurate 'reading' of STM requires no rehearsal.

Procedures This was a laboratory experiment. Participants were given trigrams to remember – three letters that did not form a meaningful unit, such as TVG. After each trigram they were given a three-digit number and were asked to count backwards in 3s and 4s until told to stop. This task was done to prevent rehearsal. On each trial they were stopped after different times: 3, 6, 9, 12, 15 or 18 seconds. This is called the 'Brown-Peterson technique'.

Findings If participants had to wait 3 seconds before recalling the trigram they could recall the trigram correctly 80% of the time; if they had to wait 6 seconds, 50% were recalled; and after 18 seconds, recall was reduced to 2%.

Conclusions This suggests that STM is limited to a maximum of 18 seconds when rehearsal is prevented. This supports the idea that STM and LTM are distinctly different kinds of memory as STM has a very limited duration.

Criticisms A particular kind of memory was tested in this experiment, as in many memory experiments (called 'episodic memory', see page 31). Other kinds of memory may behave somewhat differently. This means that this study lacks ecological validity (cannot be easily applied to other settings).

The fact that participants were counting numbers during the retention interval means that the numbers may have *displaced* the information in STM. This means that poor recall may not be due to decay but could be explained in terms of displacement (see explanations of forgetting in STM on page 38) – which means that the experiment does not reflect the duration of STM after all.

Bahrick *et al.* (1975) Recalling names and faces

Aims To investigate recall over a long period of time (very long-term memories, VLTM). In particular, to look at the sort of memories where an individual is highly motivated to remember details rather than the typically artificial circumstances of many memory experiments. In this case, participants' recall of classmates' details was tested decades after leaving school.

Procedures Nearly 400 participants were tested in this natural experiment, some of them had recently left school whereas others had left over 40 years ago. They were given many tasks including being asked to list all the names of the pupils in their graduating class and being asked to select familiar photographs from a set of high-school photographs (not all familiar) and to name them.

Findings Participants who were tested within 15 years of graduation were about 90% accurate in identifying faces and names. After 48 years, this declined to about 80% for names and 70% for faces.

Conclusions Despite the fact that recall was not perfect, these findings still show that participants are able to remember information over long periods of time, certainly more than is claimed for short-term memory! The study supports the existence of VLTM in a real-life setting.

Criticisms A positive feature of this study was that it investigated memory in a real-life context (high ecological validity). This gives us information about how memory functions in the real-world rather than in limited laboratory experiments in which participants have little motivation to recall information.

At the same time, such real-world investigations often lack suitable control of extraneous variables. For example, it is possible that participants actually saw their ex-classmates frequently and this might explain their high recall. In addition, as it is a natural experiment, we cannot truly claim a cause-and-effect relationship.

Miller (1956) The magic number seven

Aims Miller noted that there are many things that come in sevens (seven days of the week, seven notes on the musical scale) and wondered whether this 'Magic number 7' might be related to an individual's span of immediate memory – that is, the amount that can be held in STM at any time. This study aimed to review other research to see what support there was for this hypothesis.

Procedures The method used was a review of previous research, all laboratory experiments. Such studies presented participants with ranges of stimuli, such as dots or words. The experimenter would show participants displays with varying numbers of dots to find out how many could be identified. Or, the experimenter would give participants words to remember; the words varied in the number of letters (or bits of information) in the word or the number of syllables (chunks) in the word.

Findings Participants could reliably report up to 5 or 6 dots in a display but then accuracy deteriorated. Another finding was that participants could remember as many 5-letter words as they could 10-letter words. Participants were able to remember about 7 words no matter how many bits of information were in the word. It was the number of chunks in the word that appeared to affect recall.

Conclusions These findings led Miller to conclude that the span of absolute judgement (counting dots) is about 5 or 6 items, and that the span of immediate memory is about 7±2 chunks. This supports the view that STM is very limited and that its limit is between 5 and 9 items. However, an 'item' may consist of small chunks. The ability to chunk data is a way to increase the capacity of STM.

Criticisms Subsequent research has found that the size of the chunk does actually matter. For example, Simon (1974) found that he could remember fewer 8-word phrases than he could one-syllable words.

The concept of chunking has many useful applications. It is used in designing phone numbers and postcodes. This is a positive criticism of such research.

AQA (A) Key study: Encoding in STM and LTM

Baddeley (1966) The influence of acoustic and semantic similarity

Aims Previous research (Conrad, 1964) found that participants made mistakes when trying to recall words that sounded the same (acoustic similarity) when recall was immediate (i.e. testing STM). Baddeley sought to investigate this further: to see whether acoustic similarity affected long-term recall and to see what effect semantic encoding (i.e. when words are placed in memory on the basis of meaning) had on STM and LTM.

Procedures This was a laboratory experiment, using an independent groups design. One experiment tested STM (recall was tested immediately), and in another experiment LTM was assessed (recall was after 20 minutes). In each experiment there were 4 groups of participants: group 1 were given acoustically similar word lists (e.g. man, cab, can, cad, mad), group 2's words were acoustically dissimilar (e.g. pit, few, cow), group 3's words were semantically similar (e.g. great, large, broad, tall) and group 4's words were semantically dissimilar (e.g. good, huge, hot, safe).

Findings In the experiment testing STM it was found that group 1 (acoustic similarity) did worst. Participants recalled about 55% of the words. In the experiment testing LTM it was found that group 3 (semantic similarity) again recalled about 55% of the words. In both experiments, recall of the other three groups was about 75%.

Conclusions These findings suggest that in STM information tends to be acoustically coded (and that is why acoustically similar words were muddled up) and in LTM information tends to be semantically coded (and that is why words with similar meaning tended to be muddled up).

Criticisms This study again tests a particular kind of memory (episodic memory). Other kinds of memory may behave somewhat differently. This means that this study lacks ecological validity (cannot be easily applied to other settings).

Other research has found that STM doesn't always use an acoustic code. This depends on whether verbal rehearsal is prevented and/or whether recall is tested in an acoustic manner. For example, Brandimote *et al.* (1992) found that participants used visual encoding in STM if they were given pictures to remember (a visual task) and verbal rehearsal was prevented (they had to say 'la la la') and they were asked to recall the items by drawing them (visual recall task).

Models of memory

AQA A   U1
AQA B   U2
EDEXCEL U1

A model or theory of memory aims to describe the structure of explain how information is transferred from STM to LTM.

The multi-store model

Key Term The **multi-store model** is a representation of memory based on having more than one different kind of store for remembered information. Atkinson and Shriffrin (1968) proposed this model based on evidence related to the separate stores of memory (see pages 31–34). Information enters SM, and is initially stored in STM. If it is not rehearsed, it is lost. Continued rehearsal leads to LTM storage.

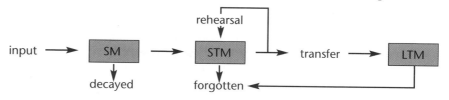

The multi-store model of memory

Evaluation

The strengths of this model are as follows:

- There is general agreement that there is an STM/LTM distinction, and this is well supported by the empirical evidence.
- The multi-store model is the basis of many later models, even if they were subsequently divided into further STM and LTM stores.

The limitations of this model are as follows.

- Rehearsal doesn't adequately explain LTM. It may *appear* that rehearsal creates a long-term memory but this may be an artefact of memory experiments where participants are asked to remember things. In most situations we do not actively try to store something in our memory.
- Alternative explanations can account for the empirical findings, e.g. the levels of processing model (see p.36) can explain differences in material recalled.
- The model is over-simplified; in practice there are no clear distinctions between stores of memory.
- It presents a passive view of memory and cannot account for active processes such as reconstruction.

The working memory model

Key Term The **working memory model** was proposed by Baddeley and Hitch (1974) as a way to represent short-term memory in terms of further sub-divisions. The use of the term 'working memory' reflects the idea that this is the area of memory that is active when you are working on information. Working memory consists of the following components:

1 The **central executive**. This component of working memory is modality-free (i.e. not visual or auditory). It is roughly the same as 'attention' (the concentration of mental effort on sensory or mental events). The central executive allocates resources to other components. Empirical support comes from studies (e.g. McLeod 1977) which show that task similarity impairs performance, e.g. playing the piano and singing a song (both are auditory). This must be due to competition within the one component.

2 **Phonological loop** deals with verbal material and consists of:
- An articulatory process. Baddeley and Lewis (1981) found that articulatory suppression did not affect decisions involving acoustic (phonological)

Articulatory suppression refers to a task which stops you articulating, i.e. speaking. The **articulatory process** is the process of speaking.

differences and therefore there must be a separate store for this.

- A **phonological store**. Baddeley (1975) gave participants a sequence of words to recall. Normally they could perform the task better with short rather than long words (called the word-length effect), but when an articulatory suppression task (counting backwards) was included there was no difference, demonstrating that the word-length effect depends on having access to an articulatory process.

3 A **visuo-spatial sketchpad** (or scratchpad) is used to hold visual memories, such as faces. Baddeley *et al.* (1975) gave participants the task of visualising a matrix of digits which was presented auditorially. If this was combined with tracking a moving light, the ability to visualise was impaired.

Evaluation

The strengths of this model are as follows:

- The model is supported by empirical evidence, especially Hitch and Baddeley (1976) who showed that dual task performance is reduced when both tasks involve the same component (e.g. the central executive is involved in a verbal reasoning task, and saying random digits, but is not involved when saying 'the, the, the'). This is hard to explain within the multi-store approach.
- It can explain how we can do two tasks at one time if they involve different stores and why we have trouble with some tasks that involve the same store.
- It concerns active processing and therefore is relevant to a wider set of activities such as verbal reasoning and comprehension.
- It describes rehearsal (the articulatory process) as only one component, which seems preferable to the central importance given in the multi-store model.
- Its division of STM into further components more accurately reflects evidence from brain-damaged patients. For example, Shallice and Warrington (1970) studied KF, who was injured in a motorcycle accident. His LTM was not affected, but his STM was much reduced in capacity. In addition, his short-term forgetting of auditory stimuli was much greater than his forgetting of visual stimuli. He could remember meaningful sounds but not words.

The weakness of this model is that the description of the central executive is somewhat vague and it may not be one thing but in fact a number of different stores/processes.

The levels of processing model

Key Term The **levels of processing model** (approach) is the view put forward by Craik and Lockhart (1972) that memories become enduring not through rehearsal but because information is processed in a meaningful way. Rehearsal is a kind of processing but it is not very deep. Craik and Lockhart believed that it is the *depth* of processing that determines whether information is stored over a long period.

The main problem with this theory is defining what constitutes 'depth'. Craik and Lockhart defined it in terms of a continuum: an example of shallow processing would be to say whether a word was written in capital letters, whereas an example of deep processing would be to say if the word would fit in a given sentence (this involves semantic processing or a consideration of meaning). A study by Craik and Tulving (1975) illustrates this point. They showed participants a list of words, each followed by a question with a yes/no answer. The questions belonged to one of three levels of analysis:

1. **Shallow** or structural, for example 'Is the word in capital letters?'
2. **Phonemic**, for example, 'Does the word rhyme with able?'
3. **Semantic** or sentence, for example, 'Would the word fit in the sentence "They met a ---- in the street?"'

Those words which had been given semantic-type questions were remembered most. The phonemic coding was next best. This shows that semantic processing creates an automatic memory, supporting the levels-of-processing theory.

There are a number of ways that complex processing can take place.

- **Elaboration.** Craik and Tulving (1975) also tested the effects of elaboration. Participants were shown a word and a sentence containing a blank, and asked whether the word fitted into the incomplete sentence. Elaboration was manipulated by varying the complexity of the sentence between the simple (e.g. 'She cooked the ....') and the complex (e.g. 'The great bird swooped down and carried off the struggling ....'). Participants recalled twice as many words for the complex sentences. The improved performance was not due to increased time spent on the task because some phonemic questions in the original study required as much time. Depth of processing involves elaboration.

- **Organisation.** Mandler (1967) asked participants to repeatedly sort a pack of cards into categories of their choosing, using anything from 2 to 7 categories and according to any system they wished. They were asked to repeat the sorting until they had achieved two identical sorts. At the end they were given an unexpected free-recall test. Mandler found that recall was poorest for those who had decided to use only 2 categories, and best for those who used 7 categories. Those participants who used several categories in sorting were imposing more organisation on the list and thus remembered more.

- **Distinctiveness.** Eysenck and Eysenck (1980) manipulated distinctiveness by using words containing silent letters or irregular pronunciation, such as 'comb'. Some participants were asked to say these words as they were spelled (e.g. pronouncing the 'b' in 'comb'). This was the shallow (non-semantic), distinctive condition. There was also a non-semantic, non-distinctive condition where the nouns were pronounced normally; as well as a semantic, non-distinctive condition and a semantic, distinctive condition, where the nouns were processed in terms of their meaning. On an unexpected test of recognition memory, words in the non-semantic, distinctive condition were much better remembered than those in the non-semantic, non-distinctive condition and almost as well as the two semantic conditions. This demonstrates that distinctiveness was as importance as depth.

> You can use this evidence to enhance your revision – the more you organise your notes, the better you will remember it! Other ideas are to elaborate it and make it **distinctive**!

Evaluation

The strength of this approach is that there is considerable empirical evidence to support the role of depth of processing, as outlined above.

The weaknesses are as follows:

- It is possible that the better recall of meaningful material is due to the way the participants' memories were tested. Morris *et al.* (1977) found that if participants were given a rhyming recognition test they remembered the words which had received shallow processing better than the more deeply processed ones.
- This model *describes* rather than explains. The concept of 'depth' is hard to define and it is circular (something which requires deeper processing is better remembered, and something that is better remembered was more deeply processed).
- The model ignores the evidence that supports the distinction between STM and LTM.

Progress check

1 How does the multi-store model suggest that data is transferred from STM to LTM?
2 How does the levels of processing (LOP) theory suggest that data enters permanent memory?

2 Complexity or depth of processing.

1 Verbal rehearsal.

2.3 Forgetting

After studying this topic you should be able to:

- describe and evaluate explanations of (and research into) forgetting in short-term memory
- describe and evaluate explanations of (and research into) forgetting in long-term memory
- explain and assess research on the effects of emotion on memory

LEARNING SUMMARY

Explanations of forgetting in short-term memory

AQA A ▶ U1
AQA B ▶ U2
EDEXCEL ▶ U1

What do you think would happen if you didn't forget most of the information that enters your mind?

Key Term Forgetting is the inability to recall or recognise information that was once stored in memory and has now disappeared (not available), or can't be 'brought to mind' (not accessible). Since STM has limited capacity and duration, the explanations for forgetting in STM are likely to be due to lack of availability (it has disappeared) rather than accessibility (being unable to 'find' it).

Trace decay

The physical trace simply disappears because it is not rehearsed or processed sufficiently. As we saw in the previous section, Peterson and Peterson provided evidence that data in STM disappears (see p.32).

Evaluation

The disappearance of a memory trace may be due to interference rather than spontaneous decay, i.e. if nothing else entered STM it wouldn't disappear.

Displacement

Information stored in STM is displaced by new information entering STM because STM has a limited capacity. This might explain Peterson and Peterson's findings (page 32) where the second set of information (participants had to count backwards in threes) displaced the initial material and caused information to disappear, i.e. be forgotten.

The serial probe technique has been used to investigate displacement. Waugh and Norman (1965) asked participants to listen to a sequence of numbers, after which the participants were given a probe (one of the numbers in the list) and asked to recall the number that came next. If the probe was near the end of the list, recall was good; if the probe was early in the list, recall was poor. This demonstrates that early numbers were displaced by later ones.

Evaluation

Waugh and Norman (1965) repeated the experiment, this time reading digits out at different speeds: at a rate of 1 per second (faster) or 4 per second (slower). If the numbers were presented faster, recall improved – which must be because the numbers had less time to decay rather than because they had been displaced; displacement would have led to the same recall no matter what the timing. This suggests that short-term forgetting is due to decay *and* displacement. Shallice (1967) found that displacement is more important. In the serial-probe task, forgetting was less if the numbers were presented faster, but there was a stronger effect when the position of the probe was moved.

Progress check

1   Why is STM explained by lack of availability rather than lack of accessibility?
2   Name two explanations for forgetting in STM.

2 Trace decay, displacement.
1 Because it is a limited capacity store and any information would be accessible.

Explanations of forgetting in long-term memory

Forgetting in LTM can be explained as lack of availability or accessibility.

Failures of availability in LTM

Encoding failure

This means that the memory is not available because you never remembered it! You may think you've forgotten something, whereas in fact you had never stored it.

Evaluation

Ebbinghaus (1885) demonstrated **re-learning savings** – that you may think you have forgotten something, but the next time you try to learn it you will be better at it. This suggests that some memory trace is there but it is possibly fragmentary.

Trace decay

This means that the physical form of memory disappears with time.

Evaluation

This is unlikely to apply to LTM. Some kinds of memory clearly do not decay, e.g. you never forget how to ride a bicycle even if you haven't done it for a long time (procedural memory). Other kinds of memory may not decay but they become inaccessible.

Interference

One set of information competes with another, causing it to be 'overwritten' or physically lost. There are two forms of interference:

- **retroactive (RI)** – a second set of information 'pushes out' earlier material
- **proactive (PI)** – previous learning interferes with current learning/recall.

This can be demonstrated by a **paired-associate** task. Participants are asked to learn two similar lists (see margin). In each list the same nonsense syllable is paired with different words (word B or C). An example of an A–B pair would be 'BEM and lawn,' and an A–C pair would be 'BEM and aisle'. If participants learn List 1 (A–B), *then* List 2 (A–C), and are asked to recall List 1 their performance will be affected by RI. If they learn List 2 followed by List 1, and are tested on List 1 again, their performance will be affected this time by PI.

Findings include:

- **Similarity causes greater interference.** McGeoch and McDonald (1931) found that if the interference task was a list of synonyms to the original list, recall was poor (12%), nonsense syllables interfered less (26% recall), and numbers even less (37% recall). Only interference can explain such findings.
- **RI is stronger than PI.**

Evaluation

Interference has limited application. It is relevant to occasions when two sets of data are very similar. This is rare in everyday life but it does occur.

Tulving and Psotka (1971) showed that the effects of interference disappear when cued-recall rather than free recall is used. Participants had to learn lists of 24 words, each organised into 6 categories. There were two tests of recall: 1. **Noncued recall:** after seeing each of their lists three times, they were asked to recall the words. They then were given another list to learn and recall. In total participants were given either 1, 2, 3, 4, or 5 lists to learn; 2. **Cued recall:** after learning all the lists they were given an interference task for 10 minutes, and then told the category names for each list they had learned, and asked to recall the words again. In the noncued recall, the more lists the participants were given the fewer words they recalled. In

---

The concept of *re-learning savings* means that even though you don't think you have learned anything when you read a textbook, it hasn't all been to waste. Why is that?

There are many different kinds of memory – such as remembering how to ride a bicycle and remembering what you learned in psychology class today. If there are different kinds of memory, then there are likely to be different kinds of forgetting.

List 1

A	B
BEM	lawn
TAQ	barge
MUZ	host
PEZ	tube
LUF	weed
ROH	mate

List 2

A	C
BEM	aisle
TAQ	cave
MUZ	bass
PEZ	vine
LUF	dame
ROH	file

One common everyday example of interference is if you are given a new locker at school – for a while you still go to the old locker (PI). If you are later given your old locker back you may go to the 2nd one for a while (RI).

the cued recall performance remained the same (about 70% recalled for each list) no matter how many words the participant learned. This demonstrates the effects of both retroactive and proactive interference, and that, given suitable cues, the participants' memories recovered from the effects of interference. This suggests that forgetting is due to a lack of good-enough cues at the time of recall.

Progress check

1 Why is trace decay an unlikely explanation for forgetting in LTM?
2 How did Tulving and Psotka demonstrate that interference doesn't affect what is actually stored in memory?

2 When they used a cued–recall task, participants were able to recall much more.

1 E.g. some memories do last forever.

People always perform better on a recognition task than on free recall. This can be explained by cue-dependent forgetting, which is the same as cue-dependent remembering because forgetting and remembering are two sides of the same coin – if you can't remember something then you have forgotten it. A recognition task provides cues for better recall.

Police reconstructions of crimes are based on context-dependent recall. When a person revisits the scene of the crime their memory is jogged. A more common example is the smell of something, e.g. the smell of the sea may jog your memory for a particular incident at the seaside.

Freud initially used hypnosis with his patients, in order to access repressed memories, but ultimately concluded that it was too unreliable.

Failures of accessibility in LTM

Cue-dependent forgetting

Tulving (1962) presented participants with a list of words followed by three recall trials. The words recalled each time differed, though the response rate remained a fairly steady 50%. This suggests that information is there but not always retrieved. Presumably, on each recall trial the participants were using different retrieval cues. Tulving and Pearlstone (1966) found that performance was three times better when participants were given appropriate retrieval cues.

- **Encoding specificity principle:** The closer the retrieval cue is to the information stored in memory, the greater the likelihood that the cue will be successful in retrieving the memory. Thomson and Tulving (1970) demonstrated this by showing that cues which are strongly associated (e.g. white paired with black) lead to better recall than weak associations (e.g. train paired with black).
- **Context-dependent recall:** Cues do not have to be a significant word, they may also be the context or state in which something was learned. In Abernethy's study (1940) on p.29, the participants may have looked around the room and certain things acted as cues which jogged their memory.
- **State dependent recall:** Goodwin *et al.* (1969) reported that drinkers who hid money when drunk, couldn't remember where it was when they were sober. However, they could recall where it was when drunk again.

Repressed memories

Key Term **Repression** is a form of forgetting. Freud (see Chapter 1) argued that painful or disturbing memories are put beyond conscious recall as a means of protecting one's ego from anxiety. The kinds of memory that are 'forgotten' or repressed range from the serious, such as childhood incidents of sexual abuse or extreme unhappiness, to more commonplace situations like 'forgetting' to clean your room.

Empirical support

Levinger and Clark (1993) gave participants word lists, including some emotionally charged words (such as 'fear'). Subsequent recall was poorer for the emotional words. However, when Parkin *et al.* (1982) repeated this experiment with delayed recall, they found improvement, which suggests that arousal had led to initial repression. Finally, there are case histories of event-specific amnesia such as Bower's (1981) report that Sirhan Sirhan, the man who assassinated Robert Kennedy, claimed he could recall nothing of the crime. (See also key study opposite.)

Evaluation

Repression is hard to prove or disprove. Someone may simply say they can't recall something (though it is there), or their eventual recall may be inaccurate.

AQA (A) Key study: Repressed memories

Myers and Brewin (1994) Repression

Aims Some individuals are classed as 'repressors'. They are characterised by having low anxiety and high defensiveness, i.e. they tend to use repression as a coping strategy and that is why they are low on anxiety. Truly non-anxious people score high on tests of defensiveness. Do repressors have restricted access to negative childhood memories?

Procedures This was a natural experiment using semistructured interviews. A psychological test was used to classify 27 female undergraduates as repressors, or other types such as defensive high-anxious. The participants were asked to recall unhappy childhood memories as quickly as possible, and were also questioned about the quality of parenting experienced (to check that the repressors did have something to repress).

> What makes this a natural experiment? You can read about natural experiments on page 161.

Findings The repressors took about twice as long to recall unhappy memories but not positive ones. The repressors free-recalled fewer negative childhood memories than nonrepressors, and the age of first memory was older in both free recall and cued recall conditions. Repressors were more likely to report poor or negative relationships with their fathers.

Conclusions This suggests that individuals with anxiety-provoking memories are more likely to repress such memories. The reason why repressors took longer to recall unhappy childhood memories and fewer were recalled was repression rather than a lack of unhappy memories.

Criticisms Repression in this study was probably 'inhibited recall' rather than total forgetting. On the other hand, participants may have been reluctant to report certain memories in the experimental situation.

Speed of recall does not necessarily mean that a memory was repressed, only that it may be more difficult to *report* a painful memory. McGinnies (1949) showed lists of words to participants, including emotionally toned words such as 'raped'. Participants were significantly slower at recognising these words, showing the effects of emotion on perception.

Emotional factors in forgetting

Repressed memory

> What flashbulb memories can you recall? Many people have a clear picture of exactly what they were doing when they heard the news of Princess Diana's death. But flashbulb memories need not involve major public events – they might be related to some special personal moment which was either intensely happy or sad.

As seen above, this *inhibits* recall. It is an example of lack of accessibility, or restricted access due to emotion.

Flashbulb memories

Key Term A **flashbulb memory** is a long-lasting and vivid memory of the context in which a person heard about an important and/or dramatic event. The memory is for the context and not the event itself. It is as if a flash photograph was taken at the moment of the event and every detail indelibly printed in memory. Brown and Kulik (1977) first coined the term, after noting that many people were able to vividly recall what they were doing at the time of President Kennedy's assassination.

Empirical support

Are flashbulb memories accurate? McCloskey *et al.* (1988) interviewed people shortly after the explosion of the space shuttle *Challenger* and then re-interviewed the same people nine months later, finding that recall was not particularly accurate. However, Conway *et al.* (1994) felt that the *Challenger* explosion lacked distinctiveness for many people and therefore would not evoke flashbulb memories. Using the incident of Mrs Thatcher's resignation as the flashbulb event, Conway *et al.* tested people a few days after the event and again later, finding that 86% of their UK participants still had flashbulb memories after 11 months compared with 29% in other countries.

An experimental attempt to produce flashbulb memories had mixed success. Johnson and Scott (1978) arranged two experimental conditions:

• high stress – a 'witness' watches as a confederate runs through the room carrying a letter-opener covered in blood
• low stress – the confederate holding a pen covered in grease.

When later asked to identify the culprit, some participants in the high-stress condition did have better recall but it was not true for all participants.

Evaluation

It is difficult to test the accuracy of flashbulb memories without affecting later recall. Immediate testing may enhance subsequent recall.

AQA (A) Key study: Flashbulb memories

Schmolck *et al.* (2000) O.J. Simpson verdict

Aims	To investigate the recall of the context in which an individual heard about an emotionally arousing event. Previous research has found that the length of time after the event has little effect on the accuracy of such memories, supporting the concept of a flashbulb memory. This study set out to investigate how such memories change over time.
Procedures	This was a natural experiment, using a naturally occuring event (the announcement of the verdict in the O.J. Simpson murder trial). Psychology students were interviewed 3 days after the verdict to record their flashbulb memories associated with this event.
	The participants were divided into two groups, matched on the emotional significance of the event to them, and whether they agreed or not with the verdict. Group 1 was re-interviewed 15 months later, and group 2 were re-interviewed 32 months later.
Findings	After 15 months, 50% of the recollections were highly accurate, and 11% contained major errors or distortions. After 32 months, 29% of the recollections were highly accurate, more than 40% containing major distortions.
Conclusions	The findings show that retention interval is important in the recall of flashbulb memories. They do decay and are not accurate over a long period of time.
Criticisms	The big issue is whether the event (trial verdict) was significant enough to produce a flashbulb memory. It may not have been significant for all participants, which challenges the validity of these findings. The sample used was restricted (students) and it is not reasonable to generalise to the whole population, i.e. the study lacked population validity.

Progress check

1 What effect can emotion have on memory?
2 Name one study of flashbulb memory.

2 E.g. McCloskey *et al.*, Conway *et al.*, Johnson and Scott.
1 It can inhibit or enhance recall.

2.4 Critical issue: Eyewitness testimony

After studying this topic you should be able to:

- *assess the accuracy and value of eyewitness testimony*
- *use the concept of 'reconstructive memory' in relation to eyewitness testimony*
- *discuss the effects of language on recall*
- *discuss the effects of emotion on recall*
- *discuss research into memory for faces*

LEARNING SUMMARY

How accurate is eyewitness testimony?

AQA A	U1
AQA B	U2
EDEXCEL	U1
OCR	U1, U2

The concept of a 'schema' is fundamental to cognitive psychology. The concept may not, at first, seem to be easy to understand, but it is important that you grasp it.

Defining terms

Key Term Eyewitness testimony (EWT) refers to the descriptions given in a criminal trial by individuals who were present during the crime. This includes identification of perpetrators, details of the crime scene (such as how fast a car was travelling in an accident), and/or peripheral information (such as the weather that day).

Key Term Reconstructive memory describes how memory is more than passive recall. It is the active process of building up a memory using fragments of an event plus expectations (schema). These schema are socially constructed so that the way we alter memory is socially (culturally) determined.

Schema (or schemata) are organised packets or clusters of information which facilitate understanding and generate expectations. For example, we each have a schema for what a 'mother' is like, or what a football game will be like.

Why is eyewitness testimony so unreliable?

AQA A	U1
AQA B	U2
EDEXCEL	U1
OCR	U1, U2

'Schema theory' is a general approach to understanding cognitive processes and doesn't just apply to memory. Here, it is used to explain the reconstructive nature of memory.

There are many answers to this question, some of which are examined below.

Reconstructive memory

Bartlett (1932) suggested that recall is not simply a matter of accessing a piece of information and 'reading it'. Instead, memory involves active reconstruction. Prior knowledge, or schema, leads to distortions of memory during both storage and recall. Bartlett demonstrated this (see key study on page 44).

Initial learning

Past experience or schema affect what you 'see'. For example, Cohen (1981) described a woman in a videotape as either a waitress or a librarian, and showed her doing a variety of things. When participants were later asked a series of questions, such as 'What was she drinking?' they tended to remember those features which were consistent with their stereotypes.

Subsequent recall

Schema affect recall. Bransford and Johnson (1972) found that ability to understand a passage and subsequent recall were greater if participants were told the title ('Washing clothes') before rather than after reading a passage. The title generates schema which are helpful in interpreting the meaning of otherwise meaningless text and this comprehension facilitates recall.

Evaluation

- In terms of EWT, this evidence suggests that, when people try to recall what

they witnessed, their recall is likely to be affected by previous experience.
- However, the reconstructive theory of memory does not explain why memory is sometimes very accurate, as when an actor has to learn his or her lines.

AQA (A) Key study: Reconstructive memory

Bartlett (1932) War of the ghosts and other stories

Aims To investigate how a person's memory for stories is affected by his or her attitudes, beliefs, motivation and general cognitive style. Bartlett's hypothesis was that memory is largely a reconstructive process. When we store and retrieve data we reconstruct it according to our expectations or schema.

Procedures Bartlett used a technique he called 'repeated reproductions'. This involved showing a story, or simple drawing, to a participant and asking them to repeat it shortly thereafter (e.g. 15 minutes later) and then repeatedly over weeks, months and years. One of the best-known stories was a legend about North American Indians, 'The War of the Ghosts'. The tale belongs to a culture very different from ours, with unexpected concepts. This makes it ideal for persistent transformation.

Bartlett used a number of participants for each story and, for each one, kept a record of successive recall (a protocol).

Findings Participants distorted the story rather than remembering it exactly. The distortions (or transformations) were consistent with the participants' Western expectations. The distortions included omissions, using a dominant theme to organise the story, and transformation of information into more familiar terms. The stories become more dramatic, and more stereotyped (according to the stereotypes of the tellers). Each retelling was different.

Conclusions The process of remembering is not a passive recording but rather active processing, altering material to a form that can be readily dealt with. This is done by making connections with existing schemas.

Criticisms The study may lack ecological validity because the findings don't apply to more naturalistic conditions. Wynn and Logie (1998) tested students' recall of real-life events over a 6-month period. Recall was relatively accurate and little transformation took place, suggesting that there was very little use of reconstruction.

There was a lack of rigorous methodology. For example, participants were not given very specific instructions and therefore some of the distortions may be a result of conscious guessing. Gauld and Stephenson (1967) found that when accurate recall was stressed at the outset, then errors fell by almost half.

Effects of language on the accuracy of memory

The language that is used by police, when interviewing witnesses, and by court officials, during a trial, may influence the answers given by witnesses. Language may affect initial perception and subsequent recall. Both of these effects are shown in the study on page 45 by Loftus and Palmer (1974).

Initial perception

Carmichael *et al.* (1932) gave two groups of participants different descriptions for the same set of drawings, e.g. a picture which looked as follows: C was described as a 'crescent moon' or 'the letter C'. Subsequent recall was related to the labels provided. It is likely that the labels affected initial encoding, though they may also affect subsequent recall.

Subsequent recall

A leading question is one that prompts the desired answer. Loftus and Zanni (1975) showed how the use of 'a' or 'the' in a question changes the way people answered a question. 'Did you see the broken headlight?' assumes that there was a broken headlight whereas 'Did you see a broken headlight?' is more open-ended. Participants were shown a short film of a car accident. There was no broken headlight in the film, but 17% of those asked about *the* broken headlight said there was one, whereas only 7% of those asked about *a* broken headlight said there was.

Effects of emotion on the accuracy of memory

We have seen that emotion may enhance recall (flashbulb memories) or suppress it (repressed memories). Loftus (1979) was called as an expert witness on the psychology of memory in a trial where a shop assistant, Melville, had identified a robber, José Garcia. One of the points she made, in relation to memory research, was about the effects of emotion. Melville was in a state of extreme distress after seeing a colleague shot, and psychologists have found that arousal and stress have a negative effect on recall – especially short-term memory (the memory trace may not be consolidated).

Progress check

1 What is a schema?
2 How do schema affect memory?

2 They lead to predictable distortions in initial learning and in subsequent recall.

1 A packet or cluster of related concepts.

OCR core study and AQA (A) Key Study: Eyewitness Testimony

Loftus and Palmer (1974) Reconstruction of automobile destruction

Aims Eyewitnesses are often asked to provide details of a complex event. This study aimed to investigate the effects of leading questions on recall, using a situation where participants are asked to estimate speed – a task that most people find difficult and therefore, one where where accurate recall is more likely to be affected.

Part I

Procedures This was a laboratory experiment using an independent groups design. Participants (students) were shown film clips of automobile accidents, and asked a set of questions, one of which was a *critical* question: 'About how fast were the cars going when they [hit] each other?'. Participants were in one of 5 conditions determined by the word used in the critical question, 'hit' was replaced by: smashed, collided, bumped, hit or contacted.

The 'critical question' contained the independent variable – a word was expected to affect memory. All other questions were there to distract the participant from guessing the experiment's purpose.

Findings Participants in the 'smashed' group reported the highest speeds, followed by collided, bumped, hit and contacted groups.

Conclusions Some words imply speed more than others and act as leading questions, i.e. the questions influenced the answers given by participants, demonstrating how recall can be biased by language/schema.

Part II

Procedures A one-minute film was shown which contained a 4-second multiple car accident. The participants were divided into 3 experimental groups:

- Group 1 were asked: 'How fast were the cars going when they *hit* each other?'
- Group 2 had the words 'smashed into'
- Group 3 were asked no question about the speed of the vehicles.

A week later the participants were asked some further questions including the critical question 'Did you see any broken glass?'

Findings   The group with the word 'smashed' were twice as likely to answer 'yes' to seeing broken glass (though there was none) than either of the other two groups.

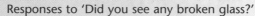

Responses to 'Did you see any broken glass?'

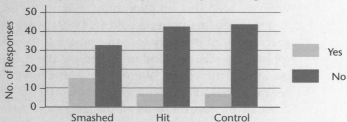

Conclusions   Post-event information (information supplied after an event) was shown to affect later recall of the video.

Criticisms   The experiment lacked ecological validity because participants only witnessed a video clip. This would lack the emotional effects of witnessing a real-life accident. Foster *et al.* (1994) found that if participants thought they were watching a real-life robbery and also thought that their responses would influence the trial, their identification of a robber was more accurate than if they didn't think it was real-life.

The findings may be due to demand characteristics – participants in an experiment are uncertain about how to behave (especially on questions about speed) and therefore look for cues about what answer to give. This leads to systematically similar responses from all participants.

OCR Revision question   The study on eyewitness testimony by Loftus and Palmer includes two experiments. In the second experiment, the use of the verbs 'smashed' and 'hit' led to different responses from the participants.

a) Outline one of these differences. [2]

b) Give one explanation of why these differences were found. [2]

(January 2002 Core Studies 1, question 1)

Memory for faces

Key Term Memory for faces refers to an individual's ability to recall and recognise faces. This is important in EWT where there is an obvious problem in that the perpetrator of a crime may only be glimpsed in poor lighting. What other aspects of memory for faces influence our ability to identify someone at a later time?

Recognising configuration

People may recognise individual features but the overall arrangement is more important. Young *et al.* (1987) constructed faces by combining the top half of one person's face with the bottom half of another's. When these combined pictures were aligned as closely as possible, participants found it harder to identify the two contributing people than when they were not as closely aligned. Presumably the close alignment produced a new configuration which interfered with face recognition.

Evaluation

EWT often involves the use of identikit pictures which require feature detection not configuration. Feature-by-feature recognition is less accurate than configuration.

Faces in motion

Identikit pictures are also motionless whereas most 'face knowledge' is related to faces in motion which, for example, shows emotional states. Bruce and Valentine (1988) showed faces in motion only, rather than the facial features. They did this by attaching lights to a face and filming the face in the dark. They found that participants were able to identify the facial expressions (e.g. smiling or frowning) and sometimes could identify the person on the basis of the movements only.

Evaluation

In EWT people have to match identikit pictures (no motion) to the real thing (motion), and there is a less good match. In research studies of EWT, participants are likely to be matching a motionless stimulus face with a subsequently motionless picture, and therefore face recognition appears to be better than it is in real life.

Recognition of familiar and unfamiliar faces

In EWT people have to recognise unfamiliar faces, which is a very different task from recognising familiar faces. People have excellent memories for familiar faces. For example, Bahrick *et al.* (1975) demonstrated that people, 35 years later, can still recognise the school photographs of their class mates (see page 33). But this is different from recognising the face of someone you have only seen once.

Burton *et al.* (1999) examined participants' ability to identify familiar and unfamiliar people on video. Psychology students, non-psychology students and police officers were shown video clips of psychology lecturers, and warned they would be asked to identify the individuals later from a selection of face photos. They were also asked to score how certain they were that they recognised the faces. The psychology students performed well, assigning high scores to seen targets, and low scores to unseen targets. There was no difference in performance between the unfamiliar student and police groups, but both were significantly poorer than the familiar group.

Other studies show that recognition of unfamiliar faces is poor: Kemp *et al.* (1997) tested recognition of faces on identity cards. Supermarket cashiers were asked to identify shoppers from a small (2cm square) photograph on a credit card. Even when the picture bore no particular resemblance to the bearer they accepted the likeness.

Evaluation

Bruce and Young (1986) proposed a model for face recognition that suggested that there are two *different* mechanisms for familiar and unfamiliar face recognition – a distinction supported by the study of brain-damaged patients. The recognition of unfamiliar faces probably involves feature detection (as in identikit photographs) whereas familiar-face recognition involves recognition of configuration (Yin, 1969).

AQA (A) Key Study: Memory for faces

Bahrick *et al.* (1975) Recalling names and faces
This study is described on page 33.

Progress check

1 Suggest one way that memory for faces might be unreliable.
2 Name one study to support the suggestion you gave.

1 E.g. normally we see a face in motion but in EWT we have to identify a motionless, unfamiliar face.
2 Bruce and Valentine; Bruce and Young.

Sample question and student answer

(a) Outline **two** factors that may influence the likelihood of information being retrieved from long-term memory. [3 + 3]

(b) Describe **one** model or theory of memory. [6]

(c) 'A lot of psychology has very little relevance to everyday life.' To what extent is memory research relevant to our everyday lives? [18]

The candidate has provided one detailed and accurate response but the second one is in name only, and it isn't entirely clear in what way familiarity might increase or decrease retrieval from LTM. (3+1 marks)

The candidate has identified and described the essential details of the model. The answer is generally accurate but limited. The candidate might have been a bit more careful in explaining the transfer between stores, and the rehearsal loop. (4 marks)

The candidate has presented a wealth of material that is all relevant to the question. The slight inaccuracy (e.g. in relation to Loftus' research) is balanced by the focus on the question and the range of arguments presented (regarding kinds of memory, kinds of stimulus material, EWT, and the effect of language and schemas on recall). A number of studies have been described although the detail is rather thin; a bit more on findings and/or conclusions would have helped (AO1=4 marks). The answer is well structured, demonstrating good skills of analysis and the commentary is reasonably informed. The material has been used in an effective manner (AO2=10 marks).

(a) One factor that might influence retrieval from LTM is the availability of a suitable cue. Many memories are available, i.e. they are there, but they aren't accessible. A second factor is familiarity.

(b) One model of memory is the multi-store model. This suggests that memory consists of more than one kind of store – specifically a sensory memory, short-term memory and long-term memory. The way information is passed from one store to another is as a result of verbal rehearsal. If material is not rehearsed then it disappears and is not remembered.

(c) A lot of memory research has been conducted in laboratories. For example, the classic research by Peterson and Peterson was in a laboratory and, furthermore, it simply tested individual's recall of nonsense syllables. Some psychologists have suggested that this kind of memory (called episodic or explicit) is not representative of all memory.

There is psychological research which has looked at implicit memory, that is the memory which is stored when a person is not aware that they will be tested. Traditional memory experiments involved telling participants that they were going to have to remember a list of words and then asking them to recall the list. In research into implicit memory the participants' memories are not tested in this way. For example, Tulving et al. (1982) asked participants to complete a 'fill in the blanks' one week after being given word lists. They were better with words from the original list – showing there was something there in memory.

Perhaps the most important way that memory research can be applied to real-life is by using it in relation to real-life problems such as eyewitness testimony (EWT). Psychologists can be asked to advise courts on the reliability of such evidence. For example, Loftus has done lots of studies which show how the language that is used (leading questions) can influence what a person remembers. In one study, she asked participants whether 'a headlight was smashed' or 'the headlight was smashed'. People said yes more often when the word 'the' was used (even though it wasn't) because 'the' implies that there was one.

Bartlett's idea of reconstructive memory also shows how memory isn't reliable. What we remember in the first place, and what we later recall, is affected by our schemas and cultural expectations.

TOTAL: 21 out of 30 marks

Practice examination questions

1

(a) Describe **two** differences between short-term and long-term memory.   [3 + 3]

(b) Describe the procedures and findings of **one** study on the capacity of short-term memory.   [6]

(c) Outline **one** theory of forgetting in long-term memory and evaluate this theory.   [18]

AQA A style question

2

(a) Identify **three** factors which have been found by psychologists to affect the reliability of eye-witness testimony.   [3]

(b) The cognitive interview is a technique used to improve the reliability of eye-witness testimony. Describe **one** feature of the cognitive interview.   [3]

(c) Psychologists have used pictures of famous people in studies of face recognition.

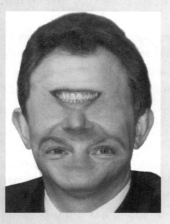 

Jumbled face of Tony Blair   *Normal face of Tony Blair*

Studies have shown that participants take longer to recognise a jumbled face like the face on the left than they do to recognise a normal face like the face on the right.

Explain what the results of these studies may tell us about the processes involved in the recognition of faces.   [4]

(d) Discuss strengths and limitations of **one** theoretical explanation for face recognition.   [10]

AQA B paper specimen

3

The term 'identify' requires you to simply name these assumptions and offer no further elaboration.

(a) Identify **two** general assumptions of the cognitive approach to psychology.   [2]

(b) Psychologists have conducted many investigations into the accuracy of eyewitness testimony. Describe **three** factors that have been shown to influence the accuracy of eyewitness testimony.   [6]

(c) Give **one** criticism of psychological research into eyewitness testimony and assess this criticism.   [4]

Edexcel specimen paper Unit Test 1 question 2

Chapter 3
Developmental psychology

The following topics are covered in this chapter:

- The developmental approach
- Cognitive development
- Attachments in development:
  The development and variety of attachments
- Attachments in development:
  Deprivation and privation
- Critical issue: Day care

3.1 The developmental approach

After studying this topic you should be able to:

- define the concepts of nature and nurture
- describe the key assumptions of the developmental approach in psychology
- evaluate the developmental approach in terms of its advantages and limitations
- outline some of the methods used in the developmental approach

LEARNING SUMMARY

Key assumptions of the developmental approach

AQA A	U1
EDEXCEL	U1
OCR	U1, U2

You can think of nature and nurture in terms of a plant. One seed (nature) may thrive when planted in a sunny corner of garden with fertile soil (nurture). Another seed may not do as well despite enjoying the same conditions (nurture) due to genetic differences (nature).

The term 'development' refers to the changes that take place over a person's lifetime. These changes may be the result of:

- inherited factors (**nature**), which include events that occur as a result of maturation, such as puberty
- lifetime experiences (**nurture**), which include interactions with other people.

Psychologists used to talk about 'nature *versus* nurture', meaning that development could be explained in terms of either nature or nurture. They now recognise that all behaviour is a result of an *interaction between* both nature and nurture. But they still argue about which has the greater influence.

There are many aspects to a person's development:

- *Cognitive* (mental abilities). Your thinking changes as you get older (we look at cognitive development later in this chapter, p.53–59); your knowledge increases, and your language develops.
- *Social*: for example, gender development, making friends, and learning pro- and anti-social behaviour
- *Personal*: for example, development of your emotional self (this is considered later in the chapter under 'Attachments in development' see p.60–74) and your self-concept generally (self-esteem, self-efficacy, and so on).

The cognitive-developmental approach focuses on the development of cognitive activity, and explanations of how behaviour changes in terms of cognition. So, for example, moral behaviour could be explained in terms of how a child's *thinking* about right and wrong changes over time.

Evaluation of the developmental approach

Weaknesses of this approach

Until recently, developmental psychology focused on childhood as the only time when changes took place, describing life thereafter as a plateau with little change. Psychologists are now increasingly aware of the cognitive, social and personal development that takes place *after* the age of 18.

Strengths of this approach

- Developmental psychology is a dynamic view of behaviour, emphasising the changes that occur over time and the factors that influence those changes.
- Developmental psychology has many applications, ranging from providing advice about education (see p.59), to providing information on the effects of day care on cognitive and socio-emotional development (see p.75–77) and better ways to raise children.

Methods used in the developmental approach

The experimental approach

The experimental method is unsuitable for developmental psychology for two reasons:

- Children are not ideal participants in experiments because they tend to behave very unnaturally in an artificial situation and they are highly sensitive to an experimenter's unconscious cues (**demand characteristics**). It is better to observe children in a naturalistic environment.
- In any developmental study the independent variable (IV) is likely to be age. For example, in a typical study, you want to know in what way a 5-year-old's behaviour differs from that of a 10-year-old. Age is the IV and the differences in behaviour are the DV (dependent variable). We cannot manipulate age directly (i.e. you cannot make one participant a 5-year-old and another a 10-year-old) and therefore the study is called a quasi-experiment, which is longitudinal or cross-sectional.

The methods which *are* suitable for the developmental approach are as follows:

Naturalistic observation

In this method, behaviour is observed in a natural environment. All variables are free to vary (unlike in an experiment) and interference is kept to a minimum. The participants may not be aware that they are being observed (undisclosed observation can be used, e.g. one-way mirrors, though this raises ethical concerns). On the other hand, if participants know they are being observed, this can affect their behaviour.

Evaluation

This method gives a more realistic picture of spontaneous behaviour but one cannot infer cause and effect. There are also problems with observer bias.

Controlled observation

Some observational studies, such as the Strange Situation (see p.62), involve observations made within a set of strict guidelines.

Evaluation

This means that the environment may still be fairly natural but some degree of control is exerted – which increases comparability from one participant to another, and from one observer to another (observer reliability).

Longitudinal studies

One group of individuals is studied over a period of time, taking periodic samples of behaviour. This makes it possible to determine what factors may influence development – see, for example, the study by Hodges and Tizard (p.74).

Demand characteristics are those features of an experiment which cause participants to try to work out what is expected of them, and lead them to behave in certain predictable ways.

Some of these methods are discussed in Chapter 7, along with a look at their strengths and weaknesses.

Evaluation

The main strength of these are that they use a repeated measures design (see p.167) and therefore personal variables are well controlled. The main weakness is that such studies take a long time, requiring a large investment of time and money. A further problem is that some participants 'drop out' and this may bias the results because one is left with a particular kind of sample (e.g. one which has lost all the 'difficult' participants because they couldn't be bothered to reappear continuously).

Cross-sectional studies

An alternative approach is to compare different age groups at the same point in time, as in the study by Samuel and Bryant (see p.57).

Evaluation

This is a cheaper method but one that offers less control of personal variables. One particular problem is that different age groups may not be comparable because of the **cohort effect** (social changes at certain points in time result in cohorts of children who are unique – such as those who grew up in the 1960s hippie culture).

Twin and family studies

The word 'zygote' means fertilised egg, so 'monozygotic' means the twins come from one egg and therefore share the same genetic material.

An obvious way to make comparisons between nature and nurture is to look at identical and non-identical twins – called monozygotic (MZ) and dizygotic (DZ) twins respectively. MZ twins share 100% of the same genes and therefore in terms of nature they are the same – so any differences in their behaviour must be due to environment. There are cases of twins brought up in different homes and in this instance any *similarities* are presumed to be due to nature. The term **concordance rate** is used to express the extent to which a certain trait in both twins is in 'concord' or agreement.

Evaluation

Twins who are reared together also share the same environment, so it isn't always possible to claim that any behaviour is due to similar nature or shared nurture.

Progress check

1 Give another word for the terms 'nature' and 'nurture'.
2 What is the difference between a longitudinal and a cross-sectional study?
3 What is a MZ twin?

3 This refers to monozygotic twins who come from one egg and who are therefore genetically identical.
2 In a longitudinal study the same participants are compared at different ages, in a cross-sectional study different participants are compared of varying ages.
1 E.g. innate (nature) and experience (nurture).

3.2 Cognitive development

After studying this topic you should be able to:

- *outline and evaluate Piaget's theory of cognitive development*
- *outline and evaluate Vygotsky's theory of cognitive development*
- *discuss the empirical evidence related to both theories*
- *describe and evaluate practical applications of these theories*

Piaget's theory of cognitive development

EDEXCEL U1
OCR U1, U2

Cognitive development is the study of how mental activities develop.

The essence of Piaget's theory

The essence of this theory of cognitive development is as follows:

- There are **qualitative** differences between child and adult thinking. Before Piaget the view was that children simply knew less than adults and cognitive development involved quantitative changes.
- It is a **biological** approach: cognitive development is mainly a consequence of physical maturation. Progress occurs only when the child is *ready* and then appropriate experiences will enable cognitive development to occur.
- **Language** is the outcome of a generalised cognitive ability. Language does not create cognitive development, it is the *result of* general cognitive maturity.

The structure of the intellect

Variant cognitive structures develop with age:

- **Schemas (or schemata)** are cognitive representations of things or activities. A child is born with innate schema. These are reflex responses, such as grasping schema or sucking schema. These schema integrate with each other, and new ones form in response to the environment.
- **Operations** are things that involve physical or symbolic manipulations (as in pre-operational thought – see p.54).

Invariant cognitive structures: The process of adaptation (learning) remains the same through life:

- **Assimilation.** A new object or idea is understood in terms of existing schema. For example, you see a furry thing and realise that it is a dog. You have understood the new experience in terms of existing schema.
- **Accommodation.** Schema are modified to fit new situations or information. For example, you realise the furry thing is not a dog nor does it belong to any other group of animal with which you were familiar. It is in fact a llama and you must modify your existing schemas to cope with this new information.
- **Equilibrium.** If existing schema are inadequate, a state of disequilibrium occurs, and this drives the person to accommodate the schema – thus ensuring cognitive development.

> Piaget's theory is sometimes called an 'ages and stages theory' because of the concept of stages. However, the structure of the intellect and the way development takes place (through disequilibrium and accommodation) is just as important.

Stages in cognitive development

A child moves from one stage to the next as a consequence of maturity. **Horizontal décalage** describes the fact that not all aspects of the same stage appear at the same time – for example, the ability to conserve number and volume.

- **Sensorimotor stage** (0 to approximately 2 years). Early reflex activities

Note the use of the word 'operational' which refers to the kind of mental logic which the child is using. Addition is an example of an 'operation'.

(e.g. sucking) are built up into more complex routines through **circular (repetitive) reactions**. The infant co-ordinates sensory and motor activity. By the end of this stage symbolic activity has started (e.g. language).

- **Pre-operational stage** (2–7 years). Using symbols but not adult logic (i.e. logic that is internally consistent). Pre-operational children use **transductive reasoning** (logic which is centred on one particular aspect of a thing and therefore cannot be transferred to other situations), e.g. 'if a thing has four legs and a dog has four legs, the thing must be a dog'. The stage is subdivided into:

  - **Pre-conceptual** (2–4 years). Concepts not fully formed, e.g. Daddy owns a blue car – therefore all blue cars are called 'Daddy's car'.
  - **Intuitive** (4–7 years) e.g. child displays animism, egocentric behaviour (as in the three mountains experiment described on p.55), and cannot conserve (see also below).

- **Concrete operational stage** (7–11 years). Children now use logical mental rules, but only for concrete rather than abstract tasks, e.g. they cannot cope with the transitive interference task problem 'Mary is taller than Susan, Susan is taller than Anne, who is tallest?' unless the problem is presented using dolls (i.e. in concrete form). The child can cope with conservation, class inclusion, and using numbers to perform calculations. However, problem solving still tends to be random rather than systematic (scientific).

- **Formal operational stage** (11+ years). Abstract and systematic thought possible, organised deduction/induction, more scientific approach.

Empirical evidence

Piaget's methods involved naturalistic observation and semi-structured interviews, using small samples of (often) his own children. However, he did spend over 50 years amassing a detailed record of individual behaviour (idiographic approach). Piaget also conducted research with Inhelder of a more experimental nature, which did involve large samples of children. Piaget's research led him to several conclusions, as outlined below.

Object permanence (sensorimotor stage)

This refers to a child's realisation that objects continue to exist even when they cannot be seen. Piaget claimed that this developed after the age of 8 months.

- However, Baillargeon and DeVos (1991) showed that infants aged 3–4 months demonstrated object permanence when tested on various tasks. In the rolling car task (see below) there was a large or small carrot sliding along a track and hidden at one point by a screen with a large window. The track is arranged so that the large carrot should be visible as it passes behind the window whereas the small carrot (not as broad) should remain hidden. The infants looked longer at the large carrot presumably expecting the top half to be visible behind the window.

- It would seem that children develop object permanence before the age suggested by Piaget but that it is still a developmental stage.

The rolling car task

Small carrot is invisible behind window – child expects this.

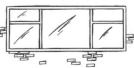

Large carrot remains invisible because window contains opaque glass – child shows surprise.

Piaget's three mountains scene

Egocentrism (intuitive pre-operational stage)

Pre-operational children find it hard to take the perspective of another.

- In the three mountains experiment Piaget and Inhelder (1956) asked children aged 4–12 to say how a doll, placed in various positions, would view a model of a mountain range (see diagram). The youngest children could only work from their own perspective, but by the age of nine they were sure of the doll's perspective.
- However, Hughes (1975) achieved better performance by hiding a doll from a toy policeman and Borke (1975) used the character Grover from Sesame Street driving along in his fire engine, again finding that younger children were not as egocentric as Piaget suggested.

Conservation (intuitive, pre-operational stage)

This refers to the ability to understand that quantity is not changed even when a display is transformed.

- In the number conservation experiment, Piaget showed a child two identical rows of counters and asked whether they were both the same. He then made one row longer by moving the counters in it further apart and again asked whether they were the same. A child over 7 (concrete operational stage) recognises that quantity can not change and says 'yes'. Similar experiments were done with volume (water in a jar) and mass (balls of clay).
- Rose and Blank (1974) and Samuel and Bryant (1984 see p.57) found that using two questions confuses younger children. If one question was asked younger children performed better, but there were still age differences.
- McGarrigle and Donaldson (1974) found that a less artificial task led to success at a younger age. They used 'naughty teddy' to rearrange a row of counters. However, subsequent research (Moore and Frye, 1986) has suggested that the naughty teddy may have unduly distracted the children and they didn't realise that any transformation had taken place and that's why they were not 'fooled' by the transformation.

Formal operational thinking

- Bryant and Trabasso (1971) showed that difficulty on transitive inference tasks (see p.54) may be due to memory failure rather than lack of ability. They trained children until they could perform a transitive task successfully, and found that they could then perform a more lengthy series of comparisons.
- Piaget and Inhelder (1956) tested deductive reasoning using the beaker problem. Children are given four beakers of colourless, odourless liquid and asked to find which combination turns yellow. They found that concrete thinkers try to solve the problem randomly whereas formal thinkers are systematic.

The influence of language on thought

Sinclair-de-Zwart (1969) produced evidence that the inability to conserve was related to linguistic development (i.e. children who could conserve had more extensive vocabularies using words such as 'larger' instead of absolute terms such as 'big'). However, training in verbal skills did not increase the ability to conserve (i.e. teaching the children to use other words for 'small' such as 'short', 'thin' or 'few'). 90% of the non-conservers remained unable to conserve, which supports the view that children only move from one stage to the next when they are ready – not when given extra practice.

Criticisms of Piaget's theory and the empirical evidence

- **Age.** Many studies have found that children develop certain cognitive structures earlier (or later) than Piaget claimed but the *stage sequence* remains unchallenged by this evidence.
- **Appropriateness of the task.** Piaget's tasks may have confused children, e.g. the three mountains task.
- **Form of questioning.** Children aim to please and so they respond to demand characteristics and/or experimenter bias, e.g. the conservation experiment.
- **Practice.** If the development of cognitive structures is related to maturity then practice should not improve performance. Danner and Day (1977) coached students aged 10, 13 and 17 in three formal operational tasks. The effects were limited with the younger participants but very marked at 17 years, showing that training does make a difference although it is still related to cognitive maturation.
- **Effects of language.** Frank (1966) claimed that language can help overcome concrete thinking. He tested 4–6-year-olds on the volume conservation task with a screen in front of the beakers so the level was not visible. Almost all the older children coped, and half the 4-year-olds. However, Sinclair-de-Zwart (see p.56) did not find that language training led to improved performance.

Evaluation

The strengths of Piaget's theory are as follows:

- Piaget's theory was the first comprehensive account of cognitive development.
- It changed the traditional view of the child as passive and stimulated an enormous amount of research.
- It had a large impact on education, particularly in primary schools.

Weaknesses of Piaget's theory have been identified as follows:

- Piaget's evidence often lacked scientific rigour. The samples were small and open to experimenter bias. Bryant (1995) claimed that Piaget's experiments lacked control (which means that he did not rule out other possible explanations for the behaviours he observed).
- Piaget suggested that disequilibrium would be the driving force in cognitive development. However, although conflict would create a sense that something is wrong it does not tell a child how to solve the problem.

OCR core study: Conservation

Samuel and Bryant (1984) Asking only one question

Aims Do younger children fail to cope with Piaget's conservation task because they are not sufficiently mature, or is it because they find being asked two questions is confusing? The child may well think that the reason the experimenter asks the same question again is because he wants a different answer. This would be especially *true* because children are susceptible to demand characteristics.

Procedures This was a laboratory experiment, with a cross-sectional design. The children (252 boys and girls aged between 5 and $8\frac{1}{2}$ years) were divided into four age groups, whose mean ages were: 5 years 3 months, 6 years 3 months, 7 years 3 months, 8 years 3 months. Each group was further subdivided into 3 subgroups.

- *Standard*: Traditional conservation task, asked two questions.
- *One judgement*: Only one question asked, after the display was changed.
- *Fixed array control*: Only saw one display, the post-transformation one.

A control group was necessary in order to be able to explain the performance of the other two groups in terms of the information they had from the pre-transformation display. If the control group couldn't cope with the task then failure might be due to problems understanding just the one question.

The children were tested on:

- *Mass*. Two equal plasticine cylinders. One cylinder is squashed so it looks like a sausage or a pancake.
- *Number*. Two rows of 6 counters each, arranged identically. One row was either spread out or bunched up so the two rows were not of equal length.
- *Volume*. Two identical glasses, with the *same* amounts of liquid. The liquid from one glass is poured into a narrower or wider one.

Findings The table below shows the mean number of errors for each child (rounded to the nearest whole number). An error is a failure to give a conserving response.

Age	Standard	One question	Control
5	8	7	9
6	6	4	6
7	3	3	5
8	2	1	3

Table of results from Samuel and Bryant's study

Conclusions Younger children did cope better with the one question task but there were still age differences.

Criticisms The younger children may still have felt intimidated by the experimental situation and been less able to cope.

OCR Revision question a) In the study by Samuel and Bryant on conservation, in the 'one question condition' children are asked a question about number, mass or volume, only after they have seen the substance changed in front of them. Identify the **two** other conditions of this experiment. [2]

b) In addition to these conditions, **two** other factors affected the children's ability to conserve. Identify **both** these factors. [2] (June 2001, Core Studies 1, question 3)

Vygotsky's theory of cognitive development

EDEXCEL   U1

The essence of his theory is as follows.

- Cognitive development is the result of the **child's active construction** of their knowledge rather than passive conditioning (Pavlov's view).
- The **social construction of knowledge**: Social and cultural influences, especially *language* and other cultural symbols (e.g. mathematics), are the driving force behind cognitive development. Vygotsky's theory grew out of the political world he lived in (Marxist Russia) which believed that the only way to bring about psychological change was by altering social conditions.
- The **guidance of experts** (people with greater knowledge) is the main reason why children move forward in their thinking (as opposed to Piaget's notion of biological readiness).
- The role of **scaffolding** (see p.59) in constructing a framework to promote effective learning.

The structure of the intellect

- **Elementary mental functions:** these are innate capacities (such as attention and sensation) that will develop to a limited extent through experience. This kind of thinking is not dissimilar to that of other primates.
- **Higher mental functions.** In the main it is cultural influences that are responsible for transforming elementary functions into higher mental functions, such as problem solving and thinking. Culture is transmitted via language, shared symbol systems such as mathematics, and the help of 'experts'.
- The **zone of proximal development (ZPD)** is the distance between a child's current and potential abilities. The aim of instruction is to stimulate those functions which lie waiting in the ZPD.

Stages in cognitive development

Vygotsky's theory was not a stage theory in the same way that Piaget's was, nevertheless he did identify certain phases of development:

- **Pre-intellectual, social speech** (age 0–3 years). Language serves a social function. At the same time, thought is pre-linguistic.
- **Egocentric speech** (3–7 years). Language is used to control one's own behaviour but often spoken aloud.
- **Inner speech** (7+ years). Self-talk becomes silent and differs in form from social speech. Throughout life, language serves these dual purposes – for thought and social communication.

Empirical evidence

- Gredler (1992) argued that if higher mental functions depend on cultural influences, we would expect to find different higher mental functions in different cultures. One example of this can be seen in the children of Papua New Guinea who are taught a counting system which begins on the thumb of one hand and proceeds up the arm and down to the other fingers, ending at 29 (which means that it is very difficult for them to add and subtract).
- Shif (Vygotsky, 1987) asked pupils to complete sentences which ended in 'because' or 'although' and found that they were better able to finish the sentences which dealt with scientific rather than everyday concepts. Vygotsky argued that this demonstrates a greater understanding of scientific concepts – because these are learned through instruction with expert guidance, whereas everyday concepts are assimilated through self-directed activity.

- Freund (1990) arranged for one group of children to play on their own with a doll's house, and another to play with their mothers. At the end, the children who worked with experts (mothers) showed a dramatic improvement in their ability to perform a furniture sorting task.

An evaluation of Vygotsky's theory

- Vygotsky's approach has produced comparatively little empirical support (so far), but lots of interest from psychologists and educationalists.
- The central role of language and culture in cognitive development has important implications for education.

Piaget and Vygotsky need not be seen as opposites. Glassman (1999) argues that in fact the two theories are remarkably similar, especially at their central core. An attempt to integrate the two approaches would be productive.

Practical applications to education

EDEXCEL U1

'Each time one prematurely teaches a child something he could have discovered for himself, that child is kept from inventing it and consequently from understanding it completely' (Piaget, 1970).

Piaget's theory

- **Readiness.** Children advance their knowledge because of biologically regulated cognitive changes. Children should be offered stimuli which are moderately novel only when they are ready.
- **Self-discovery and self-motivation.** If you tell a child how to do something you prevent their complete understanding.
- **Individualised.** Since each child matures at a different rate and has different schema, their learning programme should be unique.
- **Discovery learning.** The teacher should set tasks which are appropriate for pupils and intrinsically motivating. The teacher's role is not to impart knowledge but to ask questions or create situations which 'ask questions', thus creating disequilibrium and forcing children to make accommodations.
- **Logic** is not an innate mental process, it is the *outcome* of cognitive development. Logic, maths and science should be taught in primary schools.
- Use of **concrete materials** in teaching children, in the stage of concrete operations.

Vygotsky's theory

'What a child can do with assistance today he/she can do by him/herself tomorrow' (Vygotksy)

- **Expert intervention** (by peers or adults) should be most effective when the expert is aware of the limits of the ZPD. Thus, the more sensitive an adult is to a child's competence the more the child should improve.
- **Scaffolding.** An adult advances children's thinking by providing a framework (scaffolding) on which children can climb. Wood *et al.* (1976) observed mothers and children (aged 4–5 years) working together. When the learner ran into difficulty, the mothers gave specific instructions. When the learner is coping well only general encouragement is needed. The learner is given a scaffold by those more expert and the scaffold enables them to 'climb higher' i.e. achieve more. In time, we all learn to scaffold ourselves (self-instruction).
- **Peer tutoring.** Peers can also be experts and co-operative group work successful in schools. Bennett and Dunne (1991) found that children who were engaged in co-operative group work were less competitive, less concerned with status and more likely to show evidence of logical thinking than those who worked alone.

Progress exercise

1 What is the difference between elementary and higher mental functions?
2 Whose theory of cognitive development emphasises the role of experts?

2 Vygotsky's.

1 Elementary functions are innate, higher mental functions develop as a result of cultural influences

3.3 Attachments in development: The development and variety of attachments

The nature and consequences of attachment

Key Term **Attachment** is a mutual and intense emotional relationship between two individuals. It is especially used to describe the relationship between an infant and his/her caregiver(s). There are four characteristic behaviours associated with attachment:

- seeking proximity, especially at times of stress
- distress on separation (**separation anxiety**)
- pleasure at reunion
- general orientation of behaviour towards primary caregiver.

The purposes of attachment are as follows:

- **Safety.** It may be no accident that attachment bonds develop at the time when the infant becomes mobile.
- **Secure base.** Provides an emotionally safe place from which to explore.
- **Anxiety reduction.** The presence of the attachment figure reduces anxiety.
- **Promoting emotional and self-development** – an attachment figure may act as a model for later emotional relationships.

> *Notice that some benefits of attachment are short-term ones while others are long-term.*

The development of attachments

Schaffer and Emerson (1964) and Bowlby (1969) have identified the following key phases in the development of attachment.

Phase 1 Pre-attachment: Indiscriminate social responsiveness (Birth–2 months)
In this phase infants behave in characteristic and friendly ways towards other people but their ability to discriminate between them is very limited, e.g. they may just recognise familiar voices. They are equally friendly to inanimate objects, though towards the end of this period infants are beginning to show a greater preference for social stimuli (such as a smiling face).

> *The words 'mother' and 'maternal' are used to refer to a 'mother-figure' – this need not necessarily be a woman.*

Phase 2 Attachment-in-the-making: Recognition of familiar people (2–6/7 months)
Infants continue to be generally social but there is beginning to be a marked difference of behaviour towards one primary caregiver. They continue to be relatively easily comforted by anyone, and do not yet show anxiety with strangers.

> *Separation protest and stranger anxiety are both forms of distress displayed by an infant who can now distinguish between known and unknown people. Both behaviours are related to the formation of attachments.*

Phase 3 Specific attachments: Separation protest and stranger anxiety (7 months–2 years)
The infant shows attachment to one special person by protesting when that person puts them down (**separation protest**), and showing especial joy at reunion with that person. Around the same time, the infant begins to display **stranger anxiety** and also starts to be mobile. The infant will follow his or her caregiver and use this person as a safe base for exploration.

Phase 4 Multiple attachments (8 months approximately)
Very soon after the main attachment is formed, the infant also develops a wider circle of attachments depending on how many consistent relationships he or she has. The quality of these attachments is a matter of some debate. Some

Monotropy means 'turning towards one person'. Monotropy doesn't exclude multiple attachments but is the view that there is one special relationship that is at the top of the hierarchy of the infant's other relationships.

psychologists believe that there remains one special attachment figure (**monotropy** is the term used to represent this view). Bowlby felt that this was important for emotional development. Other psychologists have suggested that all attachments are equivalent though qualitatively different (for example, mum is used for comfort, older brother for play, dad for encouragement).

Phase 5 Formation of a goal-corrected partnership (From age 2 onwards)
The child develops insight into the mother-figure's behaviour and this opens up a whole new relationship where the infant can consciously influence what the caregiver does. This is the beginning of a real partnership.

An evaluation of the sequence of development
More recent research suggests that very young infants are far more social and discriminating than was once thought. For example, Bushnell *et al.* (1989) found that infants who were less than 24 hours old looked longer at their mother than at another woman. They could discriminate between people and showed a preference for one special person.

Progress check

1 Name one consequence of being attached.
2 What behaviours indicate that an infant is attached?

2 E.g. separation protest or stranger anxiety.

1 E.g. safety, emotional security or development.

Variation in attachment: Individual differences

AQA A ▸ U1

Secure and insecure attachment

One of the ways in which children differ is in terms of how securely they are attached to their primary caregiver.

Key Term Secure attachment is the optimal form of attachment, which is associated with healthy emotional, social and cognitive development. A securely attached child shows mild protest (separation anxiety) on their caregiver's departure. On the caregiver's return the child seeks out the caregiver and is relatively easily comforted. Securely attached children are more likely to display stranger anxiety than insecurely attached children.

Key Term Insecure attachment is associated with less optimal emotional, social and cognitive development. There are two main forms of insecure attachment: avoidant (child avoids contact with caregiver at reunion) and resistant (child resists contact with caregiver at reunion). These are described in more detail on page 62.

Measuring security of attachment

Ainsworth and Bell (1970) developed the Strange Situation as a method of measuring an infant's attachment. This method has been revised so that it can be used with older children as well. The study and its findings are reported below.

Explaining security of attachment

• **Bowlby's theory** (see page 67). Secure attachment is the result of sensitive and responsive caregiving.
• **Temperamental hypothesis.** Kagan (1982) suggested that some children are innately more vulnerable to stress due to inherited temperamental differences. Such differences mean that some children are less easy to care for and maternal rejection leads to insecure attachment.

AQA (A) Key study: Secure and insecure attachment

Ainsworth and Bell (1970) The Strange Situation

Aims To establish a method of assessing strength of attachment. The theory of attachment suggests that one of the functions of attachment is to provide a secure base. If you place young children in situations of mild stress, how do they respond? Are there individual differences? This study aimed to test how different children respond to stranger anxiety and separation anxiety.

Procedures The method used was a controlled observation, called the **Strange Situation**. The procedure consists of seven 3-minute episodes designed to be used with children aged 12–18 months old:

1. Parent (or caregiver) and infant enter a room, infant plays.
2. Stranger enters and talks with caregiver, gradually approaches infant.
3. Caregiver leaves. Stranger leaves child playing unless appears distressed and then offers comfort.
4. Caregiver returns, stranger leaves.
5. Caregiver leaves, after the infant has again begun to play.
6. Stranger returns and behaves as described in 3.
7. Caregiver returns and the stranger leaves.

The Strange Situation provides a measure of the security of a child's attachment on the basis of four behaviours:

- **Separation anxiety**. This is the unease the child shows when left by its caregiver.
- **Infant's willingness to explore**. A more securely attached child will explore more widely.
- **Stranger anxiety**. Security of attachment is related to greater stranger anxiety.
- **Reunion behaviour**. Insecurely attached children often greet their caregiver's return by ignoring them or behaving ambivalently.

Findings When separation anxiety, willingness to explore, stranger anxiety and reunion behaviour were examined, certain patterns of behaviour emerged. The infants could be classified within one of these three groups:

- **Secure attachment** (Type B). 71% of infants showed mild protest on their caregiver's departure. On the caregiver's return the infants sought the caregiver and were relatively easily comforted.
- **Insecure/avoidant attachment** (Type A). 12% showed indifference when their caregiver left, and did not display stranger anxiety. At reunion they actively avoided contact with their caregiver, and the caregiver generally ignored the infant during play.
- **Insecure/resistant attachment** (Type C). 17% were seriously distressed when their caregiver left and not easily consoled when the caregiver returned. The infant sought comfort and rejected it at the same time. The caregiver was also inconsistent: either rejecting and angry toward the infant, or overly responsive and sensitive.

Conclusions The distinct patterns of behaviour observed suggest that this is a valid method of assessing individual differences. Secure attachment was regarded as the optimal type of attachment and is associated with healthy socio-emotional development.

Criticisms On the positive side, there is support for the validity of this measurement. A number of studies have found that children who were classified as secure in infancy do show more positive social and emotional development. For example, Sroufe (1983) found that infants rated as secure in their second year were later

The concept of validity refers to the extent to which a measurement is actually assessing something that is real. Reliability concerns the extent to which a measure is consistent – the test should give the same result every time it is used.

found to be more popular, have more initiative, and were higher in self-esteem, less aggressive and more likely to be social leaders.

On the other hand there is evidence that this method of assessment lacks validity. The Strange Situation may test the child's relationships rather than some characteristic that has developed in the child (as a result of caregiver interaction). Children can have different attachment classifications with different caregivers, e.g. Lamb (1977) found that some children were securely attached to their mothers but avoidantly attached to their fathers. This makes the Strange Situation classification meaningless (lacking validity).

Cross-cultural variation

Key Term **Cross-cultural variation** refers to the differences that exist between people from different cultures. A culture is all the rules, customs, morals and ways of interacting that bind together members of a society or some other collection of people. These rules affect the way we behave and, in relation to attachment, lead to different methods of child-rearing – and these may lead to differences in kinds of attachment.

To what extent does security of attachment vary across cultures? Van Ijzendoorn and Kroonenberg (1988) compared results from studies using the Strange Situation with the results shown below:

Country	Number of studies	Percentage of each attachment type (to the nearest whole number)		
		Secure	*Avoidant*	*Resistant*
West Germany	3	57	35	8
Great Britain	1	75	22	3
Netherlands	4	67	26	7
Sweden	1	74	22	4
Israel	2	64	7	29
Japan	2	68	5	27
China	1	50	25	25
United States	18	65	21	14
Overall average		65	21	14

A comparison of results from Strange Situation studies

The noteworthy features are:

- **Considerable consistency across cultures:** Bee (1995) concluded that it is likely that the same caregiver–infant interactions contribute to secure and insecure attachments in all cultures.
- **Some differences.** In Japan, infants very rarely leave their mother (Miyake *et al.*, 1985). Therefore, the Strange Situation is a particularly stressful event for them, which might explain the large number of insecure-resistant children. Using a 'tool' developed in one culture and applied to another culture may produce meaningless results – see also study by Grossman and Grossman in the key study on p.64.
- Van IJzendoorn and Kroonenberg found that the variation of attachment within cultures was $1\frac{1}{2}$ times greater than the variation between cultures. This means that the Strange Situation may also be an **imposed etic** (i.e. meaningless form of assessment) for many sub-cultures in the Western World.
- Some of the studies involved **small samples** and in some countries there were only a few studies that were analysed. This would bias the results.

AQA (A) Key study: Cross-cultural variations

Grossmann and Grossmann (1991) Study of attachment in Germany

Aims • The aim of this study was to investigate whether the Strange Situation can be used in a different cultural context and whether similar attachment types exist in another culture. The study also explored the relationship, proposed by Ainsworth, between maternal sensitivity and attachment type.

Procedures This was a longitudinal study following 49 'normal' German families over a period of time using controlled observation (the Strange Situation) and naturalistic observation (observing the children with their parents).

Findings More of the infants were insecurely attached (anxious and avoidant) than securely attached.

Maternal sensitivity was positively related to secure attachment.

There was high stability in attachment over a 10-year period (80% of the children were classified the same).

Early attachment experiences with mothers showed a stronger influence on the child's socio-emotional development than attachments to fathers.

Children who were securely attached to their mothers as infants enjoyed close friendships later in childhood, whereas those who were avoidant or anxious reported either having no friends or few friends.

Conclusions The findings suggest that there are important cross-cultural similarities (maternal responsiveness) but also there are important differences in attachment. The different distribution of attachment types, compared to Ainsworth and Bell's findings, suggests that secure attachment is not always optimal. In other cultures other attachment types are associated with preferred outcomes.

Criticisms As suggested on page 64, it may not be appropriate to use the Strange Situation in a culture other than the one it was designed in (the US). German culture requires keeping some interpersonal distance between parents and children, therefore the norm would be for infants who appear to be insecurely attached within the Strange Situation classification scheme. The scheme does not have the same meaning in Germany.

This study provides a useful cross-cultural perspective for interpreting studies of attachment in the US and Britain. It shows that there are many similarities, which suggests that some aspects of attachment and parent–child relationships may be universal, whereas others are related to child-rearing methods specific to the culture.

Progress check

1 Name two types of insecure attachment.
2 Why is it inappropriate to use the Strange Situation in a culture other than the one it was designed for?

2 E.g. infants in different cultures experience different child-rearing styles so the Strange Situation has different meaning for them.

1 Avoidant and resistant.

Explanations of attachment

AQA A ▶ U1

What factors determine the formation of attachments? Why do infants become attached to one person rather than another?

Learning theory

Learning theory is described in Chapter 1, but as a reminder: learning theorists (behaviourists) believe that all behaviour is acquired through conditioning.

Classical conditioning

Food (the unconditioned stimulus) produces a sense of pleasure (unconditioned response). The food becomes associated with the person doing the feeding, who then becomes a conditioned stimulus also producing a sense of pleasure.

> According to behaviourists, infants become attached to the person who feeds them, or gives them pleasure.

Operant conditioning

Dollard and Miller (1950) adapted the principles of operant conditioning to incorporate the concept of mental states. The hungry infant feels uncomfortable and this creates a drive to lessen the discomfort. Being fed reduces the discomfort and the drive. Drive reduction is rewarding and the infant learns that food is a reward or primary reinforcer. The person who supplies the food is associated with the food and becomes a secondary (or conditioned) reinforcer, and a source of reward in their own right.

Social learning theory

This proposes that learning can take place indirectly through vicarious reinforcement and modelling. Hay and Vespo (1988) suggested that attachment occurs because children learn to imitate the affectionate behaviour shown by their parents. Parents/caregivers also teach children in an explicit way to show affection.

Evaluation

Learning theory accounts suggest that infants should become most attached to the person who feeds them. However, Schaffer and Emerson (1964) found that fewer than half of the infants in their study had a primary attachment to the person who usually fed them. Harlow's (1959) classic study of rhesus monkeys also showed that feeding was less important than contact comfort. In this study each monkey was given two 'mothers', a wire one and a cloth one. Milk was provided through a nipple in one of the mothers. Half of the monkeys received milk from the wire mother, the other half from the cloth mother. Harlow found that all of the monkeys spent more time with the cloth mother, whether or not this 'mother' provided milk. When the monkeys were frightened they went to the cloth mother (a secure base). This appears to indicate that physical contact is more important than feeding with regard to attachment. In addition, it would seem that 'contact comfort' alone is not sufficient for healthy development because later in life the monkeys had difficulty mating and became rejecting mothers.

> There may have been a confounding variable in the study, insofar as the shapes of the "mothers'" heads were different: a possible confounding variable.

Progress check

1 How does the caregiver become a conditioned reinforcer?
2 In what way does Schaffer and Emerson's research provide evidence against the learning theory explanation of attachment?

2 They found that the person who fed the child was more often *not* the primary attachment figure.

1 By being associated with drive reduction and providing a reward.

Psychodynamic theory

Freud's psychodynamic theory of development (see Chapter 1) suggests that an infant is born with innate drives to seek pleasure. Love has its origins in the attachment formed with the person who first satisfies those needs. If the infant is deprived of such satisfaction, he or she will become fixated on the earliest stage of development – the oral stage.

Evaluation

This account also suggests that it is the person who provides food that will become the primary attachment object, but the evidence does not support this.

Ethological theory

Ethology is the study of animal behaviour in its natural environment, focusing on the importance of innate capacities and the functions of behaviours.

Imprinting

Imprinting is the process of learning an indelible impression of another individual. The imprint thus formed has both short-term consequences (for following and safety) and long-term consequences (for reproduction).

- **Following response (short-term):** Lorenz (1937) divided a clutch of gosling eggs into two groups: one group was left with their natural mother, and the others were hatched in an incubator and saw Lorenz when they hatched, following him around thereafter.
- **Reproduction (long-term):** Imprinting acts as a template for future reproductive partners. For example, Immelmann (1972) arranged for zebra finches to be raised by Bengalese finches, and vice versa. In later years, when the finches were given a free choice, they preferred to mate with the species which they had imprinted on.

Critical period

Biological (innate) characteristics tend to have a 'window' for development. If the characteristic does not develop at a particular time, then it won't happen. Hess (1958) found that ducks showed the strongest following response (imprinting) about 16 hours after hatching and that, after this period, the imprint was irreversible. Furthermore, 32 hours after hatching, the ducklings showed almost no ability to acquire a following response if they hadn't acquired one already.

Sensitive period

Sluckin (1961) found that some birds will imprint beyond the normal critical period, and suggested that it might be more appropriate to use the concept 'sensitive' instead of 'critical'. Imprinting is possible at all times but happens more easily and effectively during a certain window of time.

Imprinting in humans

Imprinting research generally involves non-human animals though some psychologists have applied the same principles to humans. For example, Klaus and Kennell (1976) argued that there is a sensitive period immediately after birth in which bonding (an initial part of the attachment process) can occur through skin-to-skin contact (thus it has been called the skin-to-skin hypothesis). To test this, they arranged for a group of mothers to have extra contact time with their newborn babies, including skin-to-skin contact. A year later these infants and mothers had stronger attachments. However, Goldberg (1983) reviewed a number of studies and concluded that the effects of early contact are neither large nor long lasting.

Evaluation

- There is some question as to whether imprinting is any different from learning in general. This suggests that it is a superfluous concept.
- Using the concept of a sensitive rather than critical period means that learning can actually occur at any time, though perhaps less easily.

Bowlby's theory of attachment

Bowlby developed the most influential theory of attachment which drew on both psychoanalytic theory (he was a trained psychoanalyst) and ethological theory.

The main strands of Bowlby's theory

- **Attachment is adaptive:** Attachment behaviour promotes survival because it ensures safety and food for offspring. This makes it an adaptive behaviour because it enables the individuals with this characteristic to be better adapted to the environment and more likely to survive to reproduce themselves.
- **Social releasers:** Infants are born with innate social releasers, such as crying and smiling, which elicit caregiving.
- **Critical period:** Bowlby claimed that if attachment does not take place before the age of $2\frac{1}{2}$, then it is not possible thereafter.
- **Quality rather than quantity of care:** Ainsworth *et al.* (1974) proposed the **caregiving sensitivity hypothesis.** Secure attachments are the result of mothers being responsive to children's needs. Isabella *et al.* (1989) found that mothers and infants who were more responsive to each other at one month were more likely at twelve months to have a secure relationship. Those that had a more one-sided pattern of interaction tended to have insecure relationships. Schaffer and Emerson (1964) also found that responsiveness was important, as did Grossmann and Grossman (1991).
- **The internal working model:** Infants have many mental models (schema) of their environment, one of these 'internal working models' represents the infant's knowledge about his or her relationship with the primary caregiver. The model generates expectations about other relationships so that, whatever this child's primary relationship was like, will lead the child to have similar expectations about other relationships and serve as a template for all future relationships. Hazan and Shaver's (1987) research provided support for this hypothesis. They devised a 'Love Quiz' and analysed over 600 responses, classifying individuals (1) as secure, ambivalent, or avoidant 'types' based on their description of their childhood experiences, and (2) in terms of their adult style of romantic love. They found that secure types had happy, trusting and lasting love relationships; anxious-ambivalent types worried that their partners didn't really love them and experienced love as extremes of high and low; and avoidant lovers typically feared intimacy, and believed that they did not need love to be happy. This suggests that there is a consistent relationship between early attachment type and later, adult styles of romantic love, supporting the concept of the internal working model. However the data is correlational and relies to some extent on recall of childhood experiences.
- **Monotropy:** Bowlby claimed that infants need one special attachment relationship, which is qualitatively different from all others, because this intense emotional relationship forms the basis of the internal working model and underlies the ability to experience deep feelings.

Evaluation

- **Influential:** This theory has had an enormous effect, which will be examined in the next topic on deprivation and privation.
- **Evolutionary argument:** The notion that attachment is adaptive is unfalsifiable (can't be proven wrong) though it is highly plausible insofar as being close to a caregiver is protective and helps the infant find food.
- **Critical period:** The concept of a critical period may be too strong. Ethologists now prefer the idea of a **sensitive period**, which would lead us to believe that children might well be able to form attachments at any time if the opportunity presents itself (this will be discussed in the next topic).
- **Internal working model:** This would lead us to expect children to form similar sorts of relationships with all people because they are always working from the same template. However, the correlations among a child's various relationships are actually quite low (Howes *et al.,* 1994). Even if there are positive correlations there could be an alternative explanation to that of the internal working model – namely that some infants may simply be better than others at

> According to Bowlby, attachments are to those individuals who are most responsive to the infant's social releasers.

> All psychologists agree that an infant has multiple attachments. The issue is about whether there is one primary attachment which serves a special purpose in emotional development and that it is qualitatively different from all others.

forming relationships, and they do this as infants and again later in life.

- **Monotropy:** Some psychologists believe that the infant's many attachments are **qualitatively equivalent**. Thomas (1998) suggested that a network of close attachments provides an infant with a variety of social and emotional interactions that meet their various needs.
  Bowlby agreed that the infant had multiple attachments but he believed that one attachment was at the top of the hierarchy. Support comes from various studies – for example, Fox (1977) studied infants raised on Israeli kibbutzim, and found that they remained most attached to their mothers despite the fact that they spent more time with their metapelet (nurse or childminder). The fact that there is quite a high turnover rate of metapelets might explain the low attachment there.
- **Secure base for exploration:** Attachment is important for cognitive as well as emotional development because secure attachment promotes independence. Hazen and Durrett (1982) found that securely attached young children were more independent explorers of their environment and more innovative.

Progress check

1 How is a 'sensitive period' different from a 'critical period'?
2 Identify two key features of Bowlby's theory.

1 A sensitive period means that behaviour can be acquired at any time in development but may happen most easily during a 'window', whereas the concept of a critical period is that behaviour must be acquired at that time or it will never happen.
2 E.g. adaptiveness, internal working model, monotropy, social releasers, responsiveness.

3.4 Attachments in development: Deprivation, separation and privation

After studying this topic you should be able to:

- explain Bowlby's maternal deprivation (separation) hypothesis
- distinguish between the concepts of deprivation (separation) and privation
- describe and evaluate research into the effects of both deprivation (separation) and privation
- assess the impact of both deprivation (separation) and privation on development

LEARNING SUMMARY

Defining deprivation and privation

AQA A | U1
OCR | U1, U2

Again, note that the use of the term 'maternal' was to describe mothering – this does not necessarily have to be done by a woman.

Key Term Deprivation occurs when something is taken away. In the context of attachment, deprivation occurs when a child who has experienced attachment, is separated for a period of time from their primary attachment figure. Short-term effects of deprivation have been described by the protest–despair–detachment model (see page 69). The maternal deprivation hypothesis describes the long-term effects of deprivation.

Key Term Separation occurs when a child is physically separated from his/her primary caregiver, for example when attending a nursery. The child may receive suitable replacement emotional care during this separation, in which case emotional bonds are not disrupted and no harm may occur. When there is no suitable substitute emotional care there may be short- and/or long-term developmental effects.

Key Term Privation occurs when a child has never been able to form any attachments. Rutter (1981) suggested that one important distinction is between deprivation (loss of an attachment figure) and privation (lack of any attachment figure). It is privation that may have permanent consequences.

The effects of deprivation

AQA A | U1

Short-term effects of deprivation: separation protest

The protest–despair–detachment (PDD) model

Robertson and Bowlby (1952) observed young children who were separated from their mothers, often as a result of hospitalisation (mother or child). They noted three stages in the child's response to separation:

1 Protest: crying but able to be comforted, inwardly angry and fearful.
2 Despair: calmer, apathetic, no longer looking for caregiver, may seek self-comfort through, for example, thumb-sucking.
3 Detachment: if the situation continues for weeks or months, the child may appear to be coping but is unresponsive, caregiver may be ignored on return.

AQA (A) Key study: Short-term effects of deprivation

Robertson and Robertson (1952) Young children in brief separation

Aims Husband and wife, James and Joyce Robertson, sought to demonstrate how brief separations were extremely emotionally damaging for young children but that this damage can be reduced if substitute emotional care is offered.

Procedures James Robertson filmed children during periods of short separation. It was important that he used a rigorous sampling method when filming because otherwise he could be accused of just filming when the children were distressed. He used a method of time sampling where he took films at regular intervals.

Findings The details of two of the cases are:

John, 17 months, spent 9 days in a residential nursery. He gradually broke down under the cumulative stresses of the loss of his mother, the lack of mothering care from the nurses, the strange foods, institutional routines, and the attacks from the other toddlers. He refused food and drink, stopped playing, cried a great deal, and rejected his mother when reunited.

Jane, 17 months, in foster care for 10 days. Food and routines were kept similar to those at home, her father visited daily, and the foster mother (Joyce Robertson) was fully available to meet her needs. She showed signs of missing her mother but she slept and ate well and related warmly to the foster family. Jane's reunion with her natural mother was not difficult.

Conclusions The observations suggest that good physical care is not sufficient to help a child cope with separation/deprivation; loss of emotional care during short-term separation (deprivation) has profound effects. However, the films show that substitute emotional care (avoiding **bond disruption**) can compensate for this.

Criticisms These are case histories. Even though there were a number of children filmed they may have had unique characteristics. This means it may not be reasonable to generalise to all children from these findings.

Barrett (1997) re-examined the original films, and noted that there were significant individual differences – securely attached children coped relatively well, whereas the insecurely attached children did become despairing.

Long-term effects of deprivation

Bowlby's maternal deprivation hypothesis

Before Bowlby formulated his theory of attachment he proposed the **maternal deprivation hypothesis**. This stated that deprivation of attachment during a critical period of development would result in permanent emotional damage. Bowlby (1953) said 'prolonged deprivation of a young child of maternal care may have grave and far reaching effects on his character … similar in form … to deprivation of vitamin(s) in infancy'.

Supporting evidence came from Bowlby's own study (1946, see key study p.71).

Material deprivation reassessed

Rutter (1981) wrote a book *Maternal deprivation reassessed* in which he offered support for Bowlby's hypothesis but felt that refinements were needed. He identified three key criticisms:

- **Bowlby had confused 'cause and effect' with correlation:** Early separation and later maladjustment may be linked but that doesn't mean that one caused the other. Rutter suggested that early separation and maladjustment may both be caused by family discord. Rutter *et al.*'s 'Isle of Wight study' (1976) involved interviews with over 2,000 boys, aged between 9 and 12, and their families. They found that boys were four times more likely to become delinquent (i.e. emotionally damaged) if separation was related to family discord rather than through illness or death of their mother.

- **Deprivation is not a homogeneous concept**: It includes a variety of different experiences including short- and long-term deprivation and also privation.
- **Individual differences are important**: Some children are harmed by early deprivation/privation, whereas others are quite resilient.

Anaclitic depression

Spitz (1945) used this term to describe the severe depression found in institutionalised infants as a result of prolonged separation from their mothers. Spitz and Wolf (1946) studied 100 apparently normal children who were hospitalised. They became apathetic and sad but recovered quickly when restored to their mother if the separation lasted less than three months. However, longer separations were rarely associated with complete recovery. It is possible that other factors associated with being in hospital were also distressing.

The term 'anaclitic' means 'arising from emotional dependency on another'.

Effects of hospitalisation

Douglas (1975) used data from a longitudinal study of all the children born in Great Britain during one week in 1946. The children were tested every two years over the next 26 years. He found strong evidence that a hospital admission of more than a week, or repeated admission in a child under 4, was associated with an increased risk of behaviour disturbance and poor reading in adolescence.

However, Clarke and Clarke (1976) reanalysed Douglas' data and found that many of the children were in hospital because of problems associated with disadvantaged homes, and felt this might explain the children's subsequent problems rather than early separations (deprivation).

AQA (A) Key Study: Long-term effects of deprivation

Bowlby (1944) Forty-four juvenile thieves

Aims   To test the maternal deprivation hypothesis by looking at the possible causes of habitual delinquency. Individuals who are delinquent (thieves) lack a social conscience, which may be due to early experiences of separation that would damage the child's emotional development.

Procedures   Children and parents attending a child guidance clinic were interviewed about the children's early experiences. The group consisted of: 44 'thieves' or delinquents, children referred to a child guidance clinic who had been involved in stealing. There was also a control group of 44 emotionally-disturbed teenagers, seen at the child guidance clinic. Their ages ranged from 5 to 16 years. It was presumed that the 'thieves' lacked a social conscience (i.e. lacked emotional sensitivity) whereas the control group were disturbed but remained emotionally functional.

Findings   There were two distinctive features of the children studied.

- Some displayed an 'affectionless' character, a lack of normal affection, shame or sense of responsibility.
- Many of these affectionless children (86%) had, before the age of 2, been in foster homes or hospitals, often not visited by their families.

Conclusions	Bowlby termed this disaffected state **'affectionless psychopathy'** and concluded that it was caused by attachment bonds being disturbed in early life. This supports the maternal deprivation hypothesis.
Criticisms	The key data were collected retrospectively, and may be unreliable because people do not recollect past events accurately.
	The evidence is correlational, we cannot be certain that the cause of affectionless psychopathy was maternal separation.

The effects of privation

AQA A   U1
OCR   U1, U2

> In Chapter 4, we will see that stress causes certain hormones to be produced and these can affect physical health.

Case studies

Genie

Curtiss (1989) reported the case of Genie, who spent most of her childhood locked in a room at her home in Los Angeles. She came to the attention of the social services department when she was $13\frac{1}{2}$. She looked like a child half her age, could not stand erect, and could not speak. She never fully recovered, socially or linguistically. This may have been due to her extreme early emotional privation, as suggested by Bowlby. It may also have been for a variety of other reasons, such as that she might have originally been retarded.

Czechoslovakian twins: PM and JM

Koluchová (1976) studied twins who had spent the first seven years of their lives locked up. When they were discovered, they couldn't talk. They were then looked after by two loving sisters and by age 14 had near normal intellectual and social functioning. By the age of 20, they were of above average intelligence and had excellent relationships with the members of their foster family (Koluchová, 1991).

Other case studies

Isabelle (Mason, 1942), Anna (Davis, 1947), sisters Mary and Louise (Skuse, 1984), and a Japanese brother and sister (Fujinaga *et al.*, 1992). All these children, when discovered, were extremely underdeveloped physically (deprivation dwarfism, a lack of physical development resulting from emotional deprivation) and showed cognitive, social and emotional delays. If they were relatively young when discovered, they were able to recover reasonably well.

Conclusions

- **Age matters:** Those children who were discovered early enough appeared to have a better chance to recover. Genie may have been too old.
- **Experiences during privation:** Some of the children were able to form attachments with peers or siblings, protecting them from total privation.
- **Subsequent care:** Some children had good care after discovery which assisted their recovery. Without this they might not have recovered.

Evaluation

It is difficult to draw any real conclusions from these cases because:

- they are small samples
- the data about the children's early childhood were collected retrospectively
- any lack of development might be due to innate backwardness
- it is difficult to separate emotional from physical deprivation.

Reactive attachment disorder

This is a mental disorder with symptoms such as being unable to form relationships, showing little emotion, and engaging in very aggressive and controlling behaviour. Children with this disorder have often been adopted after the age of 6 months, subsequently experiencing multiple foster homes or institutional care. This means that they have little or no early experience of attachments.

Institutionalisation

Research by Skeels

Privation may affect cognitive development (remember that attachment is important for both emotional and cognitive development).

- Skeels and Dye (1939) observed how two apparently retarded children developed near normal IQs when transferred from their orphanage to a women's ward in an institution for the mentally retarded. The increased attention (attachments) presumably helped.
- Skodak and Skeels (1949) tested this by transferring 13 mentally retarded infants aged under 2 from their orphanage to an institution for the mentally retarded. After 19 months in the new institution the transferred infants' mean IQ had increased from 64 to 92, whereas another group who had stayed in the orphanage showed a decrease in IQ from 87 to 61 over the same period.
- Skeels (1966) assessed the children 20 years later and found that the differences between the groups remained.
- One criticism should be considered: the children may have been responding to the researcher's expectations and it was this, as much as the increased stimulation, which led to the intellectual improvements of the two.

Research by Hodges and Tizard

Classic longitudinal study is described on page 74.

Research by Rutter

Recovery from extreme privation can be achieved given adequate care. Rutter *et al.* (1998) studied 111 Romanian orphans adopted in the UK before the age of two. By the age of 4 they had recovered to normal levels of cognitive and physical development. There was a negative correlation between age at adoption and rate of recovery (the later the adoption, the slower was recovery). This suggests that the longer children experience emotional deprivation, the longer it will take for them to recover. Alternatively, the more damaged children may not be so readily adopted because they are less appealing.

Conclusions

Children who suffer early deprivation are also likely to continue to experience disruption, and later maladjustment may be due to this rather than early privation. When children have better experiences later, they may cope well. Triseliotis (1984) recorded the lives of 44 adults who had been adopted late and whose prognosis had been poor. However, these adults showed good adjustment.

Progress check

1 What is the 'maternal deprivation hypothesis'?
2 What is 'privation'?

2 The lack of any attachment figures.
1 The theory that early deprivation of attachment leads to permanent emotional damage.

OCR core study and AQA (A) Key Study: Long-term effects of privation

Hodges and Tizard (1989) Social relationships of ex-institutional adolescents

Aims To investigate the long-term effects of early institutionalisation, further exploring the maternal deprivation hypothesis. If this hypothesis is correct, children who experience early privation should experience permanent emotional damage.

Procedures This was a longitudinal study and a natural experiment, following 65 children placed in care before the age of four months. There was an institutional policy against the 'caretakers' forming attachments with the children. They were physically well cared for but, it was assumed, emotionally privated. Some of the children remained in the institution, some were adopted and some returned to their natural homes.

Findings Early follow ups at age 4 and 8 (Tizard and Rees, 1975, and Tizard and Hodges, 1978) found that the adopted children were doing best in virtually every way when compared with those who returned home ('restored' children), although they were having more social and cognitive difficulties than a control group of children who had never been in care. This shows that some recovery is possible after the age of 4 and that a child's natural home may not necessarily be best.

> Bowlby had claimed that bad homes were better than good institutions but this study suggests he was wrong.

> Five of the original children had remained in the institution but were not included in the final analysis because their behaviour could tell us little about recovery from the effects of institutionalisation.

At age 16 twenty-three adopted children and eleven 'restored' children were again assessed, and compared with a matched 'normal' control group:

- Those who were adopted formed close bonds with their adoptive parents, whereas the 'restored' group were much less likely to be closely attached.
- Both groups of children (adopted and restored) had problems with relationships in school, both with adults and peers. They were less likely to have a special friend, to be part of a crowd, or to be liked by other children.

Conclusions *At home* the adopted children maintained good relationships because their parents presumably put a lot of effort into the relationship, whereas in the 'bad' homes the children still had ongoing problems.

Outside the home, the adopted children and the restored children had the same difficulties. This may be for a number of reasons.

- The adopted children may have suffered from poor self-esteem stemming from being adopted, which affected their relationships outside the home.
- The ability to form and maintain peer relationships is especially affected by early emotional deprivation, more so than family relationships.
- It may be that all the ex-institutional children lagged behind their peers in emotional development and that is why they couldn't cope.

This suggests that recovery is possible up to a point, but it depends on having continuing supportive relationships.

Criticisms Only some of the children were included in the final sample because of 'drop out' (some participants couldn't be found or refused to take part). This results in a biased sample. Hodges and Tizard reported that those adopted children who were left in the study were the ones who, at age 4, had fewer adjustment problems. In contrast, the restored children who remained in the study had earlier shown somewhat more adjustment problems than the restored children who dropped out. This left a 'better' sample of adopted children.

As this is a natural experiment we can comment on an association between early privation and later maladjustment but cannot conclude that one causes the other because the IV was not directly manipulated, and participants were not randomly allocated to groups.

OCR Revision question a) Hodges and Tizard's study on social relationships is an example of a natural experiment. What is a 'natural experiment'? [2]

b) What was the independent variable in this study? [2] (June 2001 Core Studies 1, question 4)

3.5 Critical issue: Day care

After studying this topic you should be able to:

- *outline different forms of day care*
- *describe and assess research into the effects of day care on cognitive, emotional and social development*
- *explain individual differences in relation to the effects of day care*
- *recommend ways of improving day care in terms of attachment*

LEARNING SUMMARY

Forms of day care

 U1

Key Term Day care refers to situations where children are regularly looked after by temporary caregivers during the day and thus separated from their main caregivers for regular periods. Children in day care do not stay overnight, as in a residential nursery or hospital care. The maternal deprivation hypothesis would predict that such separations could have permanent consequences for both cognitive and socio-emotional development.

Day nurseries

Large numbers of children are cared for in a specially designed environment. Kagan *et al.* (1980) studied 33 infants over a two-year period while they attended a day-care centre in Boston, and 67 control infants cared for by their mothers in their homes. The staff at the school each had special responsibility for a small group of children, thus ensuring close emotional contact. Kagan *et al.* found no consistently large differences between the two groups of children on social, emotional or cognitive variables.

Childminding

A person registered with the local authority cares for a small number of children in his or her own home. Mayall and Petrie (1983) observed and interviewed 66 pairs of mothers and minders in London. The children were under 2. They found that the quality of care was very variable. They concluded that the things which moderate the effects of child-care arrangements are: (1) the quality of the care, (2) the stability of the arrangement, (3) the original attachment bond.

The effects of day care

 U1

Three features of the day-care environment are especially important for development:

- stimulation – affects cognitive development
- attachment with substitute caregiver(s) – affects cognitive, emotional and social development
- interaction with peers – affects social development.

Effects of day care on cognitive development

Key Term Cognitive development describes the changes that occur as a child gets older in terms of their cognitive (mental) abilities. This includes the development of the child's intelligence and abilities at school such as in reading and maths.

Day care may harm cognitive development

Day care may affect the security of attachment between child and caregiver because of bond disruption, resulting in insecure attachment and impaired cognitive development. Bus and van Ijzendoorn (1988) found that children who were securely attached at age 2 showed more interest in written material three years later than did the insecurely attached children, regardless of their intelligence and the amount of preparatory reading instruction.

Tizard (1979) found that the conversations between mother and child were more complex, had more exchanges and elicited more from the children than conversations between the child and their nursery school teachers. This is in part due to a teacher's lack of time and divided attention but also because they inevitably know the children less well.

Day care may boost cognitive development

Operation Head Start was an enrichment programme begun in 1965 in the USA. The rationale was that some children begin school at a disadvantage and therefore are destined for failure. If they were given an early boost through intensive preschool care, involving both health and education, this might break the cycle of failure. When the Headstart children did start school, they showed IQ gains in comparison to those disadvantaged children who had not attended daycare programmes, but these differences soon disappeared. Follow up studies, e.g. Lazar and Darlington (1982) found that participants were less likely to, for example, need welfare assistance, and become delinquent; and/or to continue in further education.

Andersson (1992) studied Swedish children in day care and assessed their performance at age 8 and 13. School performance was rated highest in those children who entered day care before the age of one. School performance was lowest for those who did not have any day care. This suggests that day care is not harmful in terms of development and may even be beneficial. It should be remembered that day care in Sweden is high in quality.

Broberg *et al.* (1997) compared Swedish children in nursery care with those looked after by a childminder and those who remained at home. When these children were assessed at the age of 8, the children who had been in day care were consistently better than other groups on tests of verbal and mathematical ability.

Effects of day care on emotional development

Day care disrupts attachment

Belsky and Rovine (1988) found that there was an increased risk of an infant developing insecure attachments if they were in day care for at least four months and if this had begun before their first birthday.

Day care has no ill effects on attachment

Clarke-Stewart *et al.* (1994) compared security of attachment in 15-month-old children who spent a lot of time in day care (30 hours or more a week from age 3 months) with children who spent less time (less than 10 hours a week). There was no difference between the groups in terms of attachment security.

Effects of day care on social development

Key Term Social development describes the changes that occur as a child gets older in terms of their relationships with others ('social' refers to interactions between two or more members of the same species). This includes the number of friendships they form, their popularity with peers, their abilities to negotiate in social situations and their desire to be with others.

Why might nursery care be good for cognitive development whereas childminding has been associated with a 'failure to thrive'?

All studies assess attachment using the Strange Situation. However, children who are used to separations because of day care may react differently in this controlled observation to children who spend most of their time with one caregiver.

Day care increases sociability

Shea (1981) videotaped play times at nursery school and found that the children became more sociable from the start of the year. The children stood closer together and engaged in more rough-and-tumble play and peer interactions. They were less aggressive and had less need to cling to the teacher.

Clarke-Stewart *et al.* (1994) studied 150 children attending school for the first time and found that those who had attended day care could cope better in social situations and negotiate better with peers.

Individual differences in social development

Not all children benefit. Pennebaker *et al.* (1981) found that the nursery experience was threatening for those children who were shy and unsociable.

Individual differences in response to day care

The reason why some of the studies have contradictory findings may be because:

• some children are insecurely attached and they cope less well with day care
• some day-care provision is poor – the children lack stimulation and/or lack close emotional contact with substitute caregivers.

An NICHD (The National Institute of Child Health and Human Development) study (1997) looked at about 1,000 infants and their mothers at age 6 months and again at 15 months. In general, there were no differences between children looked after at home or in day care, but children whose mothers lacked responsiveness and who were in low-quality day care were less secure.

Egeland and Hiester (1995) studied about 70 children either at home or in day care. The children all came from poor backgrounds and were assessed at age one and again at $3\frac{1}{2}$ years, using the Strange Situation procedure. Day care appeared to have a negative effect for secure children but had a positive influence on the insecure children.

Improving day care

The evidence generally indicates that day care need not be harmful and can be positively beneficial, given the right circumstances, which are as follows.

• **Consistent care:** avoid high staff turnover, low adult : infant ratio, assign each child to one member of staff. The institutionalised children in Hodges and Tizard's study (see p.74) experienced high staff turnover and the staff were told not to form attachments with the children.
• **A stimulating environment.**
• **Increased emotional sensitivity to avoid bond disruption.** The NICHD study (1997) found that one fifth of the caregivers were 'emotionally detached' from the infants under their care.
• **Trained staff.** Howes *et al.* (1998) found that a short course aimed at improving caregiving practices of day-care providers led to increased attachment in the two-year-old children they cared for, as compared with caregivers who received no extra training.

Sample question and student answer

AQA A style question

(a) Identify **two** factors that are associated with secure attachment.   [3 + 3]

(b) Outline **one** explanation of attachment.   [6]

(c) 'Bowlby claimed, in his maternal deprivation hypothesis, that children who experience repeated separations for their main caregivers during their early years may suffer permanent emotional consequences.' To what extent has research into deprivation and privation supported Bowlby's maternal deprivation hypothesis?   [18]

The candidate has been able to identify two things that are associated with secure attachment. The description of each factor contains some detail and is generally accurate but not as full as would be expected for full marks. The candidate might have explained how the secure base is related to secure attachment (as in the next answer). (2 + 2 marks)

(a) A child who is securely attached has a secure base from which to explore the world. The child is likely to have a sensitive and responsive caregiver. Securely attached children are likely to form good adult relationships.

The candidate wisely chose Bowlby's theory because there is so much that can be written. The description of the theory is both accurate and well detailed, and covers various features of the theory. It clearly deserves full marks. (6 marks).

(b) Bowlby proposed a theory of attachment which explained how attachment is an adaptive behaviour because it helps survival and also acts as a basis for emotional development. The child's first main attachment relationship provides a template for later relationships in the form of an internal working model. Bowlby also claimed that attachments have to form before the child is $2\frac{1}{2}$ years old, otherwise it will be too late and the child will be forever emotionally scarred. A further part of his theory was that attachment acts as a secure base for exploration. For this reason good attachment is important for cognitive development because otherwise the child won't be able to wander from its caregiver, and this affects cognitive development.

(c) The first thing to realise is that deprivation and privation are different. When Bowlby wrote the maternal deprivation hypothesis he was referring to his own study on juvenile delinquents. These children experienced temporary breaks in their attachments and this loss of attachments was said to lead to affectionless psychopathy.

However, other research, such as another study by Bowlby into children in a TB sanatorium, showed that separations need not cause permanent damage as long as bond disruption is minimised. If children are given adequate emotional care when they are away from their main caregiver then they may be alright. This was also the finding of the Robertsons who looked after two little girls while their mother was in hospital. The fact that they were allowed to maintain links with their normal lives, reduced their separation anxiety and bond disruption.

The answer covers a large range of different studies with plenty of detail (AO1=6 marks). The evidence, presented clearly, could be used to support (or challenge) Bowlby's theory but the AO2 links are not always explicitly made. The final paragraph does usefully link the research studies to a conclusion about the maternal deprivation hypothesis. AO2 credit can also be awarded for any evaluative comments throughout the answer, such as the final sentence about the Czech twins. Overall there is a limited analysis and reasonably effective use of material, close to 'slightly limited' (AO2=8 marks).

Rutter pointed out that some children who might be called 'deprived' in fact were 'privated' because they have never been able to form any attachments. This might have more serious consequences. Though research has shown that even here children are quite resilient and, if they are given adequate substitute care, they recover well. For example, the study of the Czech twins showed that they went on to lead quite normal adult lives despite extreme early privation. However, in their case it is possible that they were able to provide some attachment experience for each other so maybe they were not so isolated.

Tizard's study of institutionalised children showed that those children who were adopted could cope well, though they did have more difficulties with peer relationships than normal children. This suggests that there may be some emotional damage arising from the early lack of attachments.

Children with reactive attachment disorder may behave like this because they were not able to form attachments with a mother when they were young. They might have been rejected at an early age and then they are unwilling to put their trust in anyone afterwards.

This research does support Bowlby's hypothesis because it appears that some children do not fully recover from early deprivation (privation): although in some circumstances they may appear to be doing OK, this is only as long as the other people are giving them quite a lot of support.

TOTAL: 24 out of 30 marks

Practice examination questions

1

(a) Explain what is meant by secure and insecure attachment. [3 + 3]

(b) Outline findings from research into the effects of day care on cognitive development. [6]

(c) To what extent are there cross-cultural variations in attachments? [18]

AQA A style question

2

(a) The following table describes Piaget's four developmental stages. Give the correct name for each stage of cognitive development. [4]

Name of stage	Brief description
	Recognises self as agent of action and begins to act intentionally – for example, pulls a string to set a mobile in action or shakes a rattle to make a noise.
	Learns to use language to represent objects by images and words. Thinking is still egocentric.
	Achieves conservation of number, mass and weight.
	Can think logically about abstract propositions and test hypotheses systematically.

(b) Outline **two** research methods used in the cognitive-developmental approach to psychology. [6]

(c) Evaluate **one** of the methods you have outlined in (b) above, in terms of one of its strengths and one of its weaknesses. [6]

Edexcel specimen paper

Chapter 4

Physiological psychology

The following topics are covered in this chapter:

- *The physiological approach*
- *Genetic explanations of behaviour*
- *Bodily rhythms*

- *Stress: Stress as a bodily response*
- *Stress: Sources of stress*
- *Critical issue: Stress management*

4.1 The physiological approach

After studying this topic you should be able to:

- *outline the key assumptions of the physiological approach in psychology*
- *evaluate the physiological approach in terms of its strengths and weaknesses*
- *discuss some of the methods used by the physiological approach*
- *describe the usefulness of split-brain studies in understanding the human brain*

LEARNING SUMMARY

Key assumptions of the physiological approach

AQA A	U2
AQA B	U1
EDEXCEL	U2
OCR	U1, U2

Biology refers to the study of living organisms, **physiology** is concerned with the functioning of body parts. Genetic explanations are biological but not physiological.

Behaviour and experience can be reduced to the functioning of physiological systems.

The nervous system

The nervous system consists of the central nervous system and the peripheral nervous system – which is further subdivided into the somatic nervous system and the autonomic nervous system (ANS).

Central nervous system (CNS)

This comprises the brain and spinal cord, containing about 12 billion nerve cells (neurons). The brain consists of the following parts:

- The **forebrain**: the **cerebral cortex**, the outer, much-folded grey matter responsible for higher cognitive functions. It is divided into two halves (hemispheres) joined by fibres, including the corpus callosum. Each half has 4 lobes: **frontal** (fine motor movement, thinking), **parietal** (bodily senses, e.g. pain), **occipital** (vision), **temporal** (hearing, memory, emotion, language) lobes. The forebrain also contains various subcortical structures such as the **hypothalamus** (which integrates the ANS, and is important in stress and emotion).
- The **midbrain** contains, e.g., the reticular activating system (**RAS**) (which deals with sleep, arousal, consciousness and attention).
- The **hindbrain** contains, e.g., the **cerebellum** (controlling voluntary movement) and the **medulla** (controlling heart beat, respiration).

Somatic nervous system

(soma = body) Messages are sent out to control voluntary movement and sent back regarding sensations.

The autonomic nervous system

Controls involuntary muscles, such as the stomach and the heart, and the endocrine system which produces and distributes hormones. The ANS is largely self-regulating (automatic or autonomous). There are two branches of the ANS that work in a correlated but antagonistic fashion to maintain internal equilibrium (homeostasis):

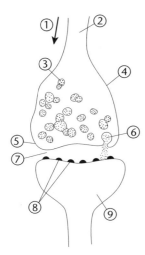

1 Direction of neural impulse
2 Axon
3 Vesicles containing neurotransmitter
4 Synaptic knob
5 Axon terminal
6 Neurotransmitter
7 Synaptic gap
8 Receptors
9 Receiving neuron

A synapse

- the **sympathetic branch**, which activates internal organs for vigorous activities and emergencies, 'fight or flight'
- the **parasympathetic branch**, which conserves and stores resources, monitors the relaxed state, promotes digestion and metabolism.

See p.93–95 for more details of the ANS.

Communication in the nervous system

Neurons

A nerve is a bundle of neurons.

- **Electrical transmission** occurs along the **axon** due to changes in potassium and sodium ions.
- **Chemical transmission** occurs at the **synapses** (see diagram opposite). Each neuron ends in numerous **dendrites** where it is connected to many other neurons across the synapse. The electrical signal stimulates **presynaptic vesicles** which release chemical messengers (**neurotransmitters**) – these may be excitory or inhibitory. Some common neurotransmitters are: dopamine, serotonin (sleep and arousal), adrenalin, GABA (decreases anxiety), endorphins (pain blockers).

Hormones

These are chemical substances produced by the **endocrine system** – a group of ductless glands controlled by the ANS. Hormones are secreted directly into the bloodstream and have a profound effect on behaviour and development. They are present in very small doses and the individual molecules have a very short life, so their effects quickly disappear if they are not secreted continuously.

The main endocrine glands and their functions are as follows:

- The **pituitary gland** in the forebrain controls much of the endocrine system by producing hormones, such as: growth hormone, prolactin (responsible for milk production), anti-diuretic hormone (ADH regulates the amount of water secreted by the kidneys), vasopressin (which acts on the kidneys and controls blood pressure) and adrenocorticotrophic hormones (ACTH).
- The **pineal gland** in the forebrain secretes melatonin, which regulates sleep and other bodily rhythms.
- The **adrenal gland** produces many hormones, especially adrenalin and noradrenalin (see p.93).
- Other glands include the thyroid (metabolism and growth), pancreas (insulin), gonads (sex hormones promote and maintain secondary sexual characteristics).

Progress check

1 What is the difference between the CNS and ANS?
2 What is a synapse?

2 The junction between neurons.

1 The CNS is the brain and spinal cord, the ANS controls involuntary muscles and the endocrine system.

Localisation of cortical function

Localisation refers to the fact that particular areas of the cerebral cortex are associated with specific physical or behavioural functions. Localisation of function allows more specialised development – for example, if an area of the brain is pre-set to interpret visual information, it reduces the amount of learning which is necessary.

- **Language** is directed by areas of the frontal and temporal cortex on the left side of the brain, as illustrated in Sperry's OCR core study on p.83. **Broca's**

area is in the anterior frontal lobe and is involved with language production. **Wernicke's area** is in the posterior temporal lobe and is mainly concerned with language comprehension. In some people the language centres are on the right or present in both hemispheres (which may lead to stuttering).

- **Vision** is controlled bilaterally by the visual cortex in the occipital lobe.

Evaluation of the physiological approach

Weaknesses of this approach

> The term 'reductionist' means that one is reducing something to its most basic components.

- Physiological explanations offer an **objective**, **reductionist** and **mechanistic** (machine-like) explanation of behaviour, which is oversimplified. There are, however, positive aspects of this oversimplification (see below).
- It overlooks the **experiential aspect** of behaviour.
- Physiological explanations are more appropriate for some kinds of behaviour (such as vision) than other kinds where higher order thinking is more involved (e.g. emotion) – although all human behaviour, even vision, involves some higher order mental activity. Therefore physiological explanations on their own are **usually inadequate**.
- Physiological explanations are also very **deterministic**, suggesting that all behaviour is entirely predictable. We may not yet be able to explain everything in physiological terms, but this approach suggests that such explanations are theoretically possible and then *everything* can be described in terms of biology.

Strengths of this approach

- The objective, reductionist nature of physiological explanations **facilitates** experimental research.
- Physiological explanations can be used to **treat behavioural problems**, as in drug therapies (see p.101).

Methods used in the physiological approach

Brain-scanning

> Non-human animals are often used in physiological research because of the ethical problems involved with human participants. The methods listed here are the 'more' ethical approaches.

X-ray tomography (CAT and PET scans). Brain tissue is dyed using radioactive substances which are injected into the bloodstream. Active areas of the brain take up more of these substances. One can determine what part of the brain is working and relate this to concurrent behaviour, such as learning activity. MRI and NMR (which are types of brain scanner) use magnetic fields and radio waves to construct a picture of the brain.

Evaluation

These methods cause no permanent damage, and allow one to observe the brain in action.

EEG (electro-encephalogram)

Micro-electrodes are attached to the patient's scalp to detect electrical activity in specific parts of the brain.

Evaluation

This is useful in understanding states of awareness but cannot tell us much about precise regions of the brain.

Lesioning

Cutting connections in the brain and therefore 'functionally' destroying a section of the brain. Temporary lesions can be created using sodium amytal, an anaesthetic, to deactivate a hemisphere for short periods in a fully conscious patient (the Wada test). For example, Jones (1966) used sodium amytal to establish where patients' speech centres were located so that he could operate on tumours (if they could still talk when the left side was paralysed, the centre must be on the right). He found that all patients with mixed dominance stuttered but after the left hemisphere centres were removed (with the tumour) their stuttering stopped.

Evaluation

You cannot be certain that a primary cause has been located. For example, if you sever a person's vocal chords they cannot speak but that doesn't mean the chords are central to speech.

Neurosurgery

Split brain operations (see Sperry's OCR core study below) have been used to demonstrate the functional asymmetry of the brain. Individuals may require surgery for removal of tumours which results in damage to specific areas, and indicates the function of that area. For example, HM (see p.29).

Evaluation

Patients may have suffered brain damage as a result of their condition and therefore their brains are atypical.

OCR core study: Split brains

Sperry (1968) Hemispheric deconnection and unity in consciousness

Aims   What happens when the two hemispheres of the brain are disconnected, and there are therefore two minds in one body?

Procedures   This was a natural experiment and controlled observation. The participants were a group of individuals who suffered from severe epileptic seizures, which were alleviated by a commisurotomy – an operation where all the connecting fibres between the two hemispheres are cut. This reduces the electrical storm which is the basis of an epileptic seizure.

Pictures were presented to the participants' left or right visual field. The participant covered one eye and looked at a fixed point in the centre of a projection screen. Slides were projected onto either the right or left of the screen at a very high speed. Below the screen there was a gap so that the participant could reach but not see objects.

Why do you think that Sperry had to project the slides at such a fast rate?

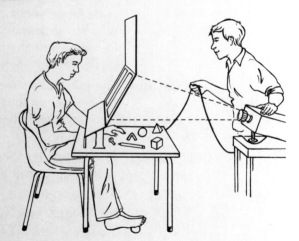

Split brain patient shown pictures to right and left visual fields and asked to identify objects manually, out of sight

Findings   The participant did not recognise a picture shown to the right visual field that had previously been shown to the left visual field.

OCR core study *(continued)*

Material in the right visual field could be described in speech and writing.

Visual material in the left visual field could be identified by the right but not left hand.

If visual material was presented to the left visual field the patient consistently *reported* seeing nothing or just a flash of light to their left. However, the participant could point to a matching picture or object with their *right* hand.

Conclusions These findings show that:

- The right visual field of both eyes feeds information to the right hemisphere.
- The left hand is connected to the right hemisphere and vice versa.
- The right hemisphere cannot speak or write.
- However, the right hemisphere can *comprehend* language, i.e. read and understand words.
- The left hemisphere is the 'major' hemisphere (because of its role in language functions) but the right or 'minor' hemisphere is not simply an automaton because it has a capacity for logical thought as well as language comprehension.

Other variations Sperry flashed $ to the left and ? to the right. Participants would draw a dollar sign with their left hand. Participants would *say* that they saw the question mark. If the patient was asked what he had just drawn he would say the question mark (which was the wrong answer).

Composite words were flashed on the screen so that, for example, 'key' was in the left visual field and 'case' in the right. The left hand would identify a key from a collection of objects and the right hand would spell out the word case.

If asked what their left hand was holding they would say something like 'This hand is numb', strategies for explaining their strange behaviour.

If two objects were placed one in each hand and then the participant was given a pile of objects containing the original object to search through, each hand would locate its own object.

The right hemisphere is not totally word blind. Some split-brain patients, when shown words to their left visual field, could identify the item with their left hand (right hemisphere). However, they were still not able to say what it was.

The right hemisphere demonstrates more appropriate emotional responses. If a nude figure was shown in amongst a series of geometric shapes, the participant typically denied seeing anything (left hemisphere is talking) but at the same time the participant might blush or display a cheeky grin (controlled by right hemisphere).

Criticisms The participants were not normal: they may have suffered brain damage from the severe epileptic seizures, or the seizures were the result of brain damage. However, the findings of Sperry's study have been confirmed in studies using the Wada test.

OCR Revision question In the study by Sperry (split brain) patients had problems with material presented to their left visual field.

a) Give **one** example of these problems. [2]

b) Suggest **one** way in which patients could overcome these problems in everyday life. [2] (January 2002, Core Studies 2, question 3)

4.2 Genetic explanations of behaviour

Key assumptions underlying genetic explanations of behaviour

AQA A U2
AQA B U1
EDEXCEL U2
OCR U1, U2

This is an example of a contemporary debate on a biological topic.

The question is to what extent is intelligence due to genetic factors (nature) and to what extent environmental factors (nurture)?

- All behaviour can be explained in terms of genetic determination. **Genes** are the units of inheritance.
- Genetically determined traits evolve through **natural selection**. A behaviour that promotes survival and reproduction will be 'selected' and the genes for that trait survive. As the environment changes (or an individual moves to a new environment) new traits are needed to ensure survival. New genetic combinations produce adaptation and the individual who best 'fits' the environmental niche will survive (**survival of the fittest**).

The inheritance of intelligence

Genetic factors

Twin studies

Monozygotic (MZ) twins have more similar IQs than dizygotic (DZ) twins, which indicates a genetic component. Through an appeal on the BBC, Shields (1962) gained access to a sample of 44 sets of twins, some of whom were reared apart and some together. The concordance for MZ twins reared apart was 0.77, and for those reared together was 0.76. This suggests little environmental influence. Bouchard *et al.* (1990) used data from over 100 twins in the Minnesota Study of Twins Reared Apart. They found that about 70% of the variation in IQ scores is due to genetic factors.

Evaluation

Kamin (1974) criticised Shield's study and twin studies generally on the grounds that:

- the samples were relatively small
- in reality the twins had often spent a substantial amount of time together. In Shields' study 14 sets of MZ twins were only separated after the age of one year and many were raised by relatives, often visiting each other
- those twins who were genuinely adopted might still have had similar environments because adoption agencies try to match backgrounds
- if intelligence was entirely inherited, the MZ correlations should be +1.00 – the fact that scores are lower shows a significant environmental component
- a correlation is not evidence that one factor **caused** another. A third (or more) factor may have been involved.

Family studies

Bouchard and McGue (1981) surveyed over 100 studies looking at familial correlations of IQ, and found that the closer the genetic link, the higher the correlation between IQ. For example, siblings reared together had a correlation of 0.45 and adopted siblings had a correlation of 0.31.

Evaluation

- This would seem to support the genetic position, but it could be taken equally as evidence for environment, as genetically related people usually also live in the same environment.
- Comparisons from one study to another involve grouping together many different tests.

Adoption studies

To compare a child and its natural parents, Skodak and Skeels (1949) followed 100 adopted children and their natural mothers. At the age of 4 the IQ correlation was 0.28 and at 13 it was 0.44. It appears that the effects of environment become less with age, and that the decline of environmental influence may be due to early enrichment and extra attention levelling out, and genetic factors showing through. Horn (1983) reported on the Texas Adoption Study which looked at about 300 families with adopted children. The biological mothers had all given the children up within one week of birth. The children at age 8 had a correlation of 0.25 with their biological mother (genetic link) and 0.15 with their adopted mother (environmental link). Plomin (1988) reported on the same children at age 10. They had a correlation of 0.02 with their adoptive siblings.

Evaluation

- There is usually a higher correlation between children and their biological rather than adoptive parents.
- Adoptions are often made to similar environments. Any differences tend to be in a positive direction.

Environmental factors

Adoption studies

The concept of a 'reaction range' proposes that genetically there are certain upper and lower limits for your development. You are born with certain genetic predispositions (genotype), such as your potential height. You might have the potential to grow six feet but even with the best diet in the world you would never have become taller. This is the upper end of your reaction range for height.

Schiff *et al.* (1978) found that children born to low socio-economic status (SES) parents who were subsequently adopted by high SES families, showed significant IQ gains when compared with siblings who had remained at home. Scarr and Weinberg (1977) found that, on average, adopted children have IQs that are 10 to 20 points higher than those of their natural parents.

Evaluation

- Adoptive families are generally smaller, wealthier and better-educated than natural families. This means that adopted children develop the higher end of their reaction range and become more similar to better-educated adopted parents. This would cause environmental factors to appear stronger.
- Early adopted children do better, favouring the idea that environment is important under suitable circumstances.

Social class

Bernstein (1961) introduced the notion of restricted language (code) as opposed to elaborated code. He argued that children from low SES groups learn a limited form of language which lacks, for example, abstract concepts. This affects their cognitive development and verbal intelligence. Labov (1970) rejected this idea and claimed that Bernstein was confusing social and linguistic deprivation, and had failed to recognise the subtleties of non-standard English. Sameroff *et al.* (1987, 1993) conducted the Rochester Longitudinal study, which has followed over 200 children from a range of socio-economic backgrounds since birth, keeping a record of IQ and life events. They found a clear negative (about 0.60) association between number of risk factors and IQ; (risk factors include: parental mental health, education, occupation, family support, stressful life events, and family size).

Evaluation

- It is factors associated with low social class that cause low IQ, not social class *per se.*

- It is possible that low socio-economic parents are biologically less intelligent: those with more intelligence become better educated and are able to have higher living standards.

Family influences

- **Stimulation:** Yarrow (1963) found a correlation of 0.65 between IQ at six months and the amount of time the mother spent in social interaction with her child.
- **Birth order:** Zajonc and Markus (1975) examined the IQ data of 40,000 Dutch males born in 1944 and found that IQ declines with family size and birth order. In larger families each child has a smaller share of parental attention, less money and more physical deprivation.
- **Diet:** Harrell *et al.* (1955) gave low income, expectant mothers supplementary diets. When their children were tested at three years they had higher IQs than those whose mothers had been given placebos. Benton and Cook (1991) demonstrated that IQ scores increased by 7.6 points when children were given vitamin supplements rather than a placebo.

Evaluation of the genetic approach

The genetic approach is deterministic and assumes a 1:1 correspondence between genes and behaviour. In reality, there is a difference between genotype and phenotype.

- **Genotype:** an individual's genetic constitution, as determined by the particular set of genes it possesses.
- **Phenotype:** the observable characteristics of an individual, which results from interaction between the genes he or she possesses (i.e. the individual's genotype) and the environment.

You can think of your height in terms of genotype and phenotype. What environmental factors influence your height?

An example of this would be hair colour. Your genes determine the colour of your hair, but the fact that you live in a sunny country may mean that your hair is bleached in the sun and this produces your phenotype: your observable hair colour which results from your genetic make-up and an environmental influence.

Progress check

1 What is a 'gene'?
2 Name three kinds of study used to demonstrate the genetic inheritance of intelligence.

2 Twin, familial, adoption.
1 The units of inheritance.

Methods used in the genetic approach

Twin and family studies

(See p.85).

Adoption studies

As described on p.86, these enable comparisons between nature and nurture.

Selective breeding

Animals are identified for certain characteristics, such as a dog who is good at hunting. These individuals are bred together to produce offspring with the same behavioural traits, which is evidence of the inheritance of behavioural characteristics.

OCR core study: IQ testing

Gould (1982) A nation of morons

The text provided here summarizes a review by Gould which considers the history of intelligence testing, aiming to indicate the flaws in IQ tests.

A new age for Psychology

Mental testing offered a way to help psychology appear more scientific. Yerkes saw the potential usefulness of such tests and the advent of World War I gave him an ideal opportunity to develop them. Army recruits could be tested so that the most able could be given jobs with greater responsibility. Yerkes and other psychologists wrote a set of mental tests which aimed to test innate abilities. The kind of questions they used were:

- *Analogies*, such as 'Washington is to Adams as first is to ...' [second, because Washington was the first US president and Adams was the second]
- *Number sequences*, such as 'What number comes next: 1, 3, 6, 10, ...'
- *Multiple choice*: 'Crisco is a: patent medicine, disinfectant, toothpaste, food product?' [It is a food product]

> What would you say is wrong with these questions? What skills are being tested?

The alpha and beta tests

Yerkes and his team tested 1.75 million recruits using two forms of the test.
- The *Army alpha* test was a written exam.
- The *Army beta* test was a set of pictures. This was given to any recruit who failed the Alpha test or who could not read – though even this test involved *writing* the answers.

Problems
- The standards varied from camp to camp.
- The large numbers of illiterate recruits meant there were huge queues for the Beta test and therefore some of these men had to do the alpha tests!
- The pressure for results meant that the re-testing of men who failed the beta test was not possible. This was especially true for the Black 'failures' who were treated with less concern. When such individuals *were* recalled their scores improved dramatically.
- Exam anxiety was also a problem. It is very likely that a foreign or an illiterate Black recruit would feel especially anxious at the strange experience of taking an exam, especially if they didn't understand English very well.

After the war

Once the war was over and Yerkes' tests became widely known, inquiries flooded in from schools and businesses to use the tests to select students and employees. The army data was also used politically. Another psychologist (Boring) analysed the test results from 160,000 men and concluded that:

- *White Americans* had an average mental age of 13, just above being a 'moron'
- *European immigrants* were all 'morons' but those from northern Europe (fair-skinned) were better than were those from the south ('darker' people).
- *Negroes* were at the bottom of the scale, scoring an average of 10.41.

It was concluded that cultural/racial differences in IQ were due to innate differences. Politicians argued that immigration laws should be passed to limit people coming from abroad because they were intellectually inferior.

Criticisms

Yerkes admitted that those who could not speak English inevitably were penalised. He also noted that test scores rose in relation to the number of years an immigrant had lived in the US. This strongly suggested that learning, not innate intelligence, was involved – familiarity with American ways (learning) was related to higher IQ.

OCR Revision question

In the paper on IQ testing, Gould identified three 'facts' that were created from the data collected by Yerkes.

a) Identify **one** of these 'facts'. [2]

b) Outline a difficulty with accepting this 'fact'. [2] (1998 Paper 1, question 18)

4.3 Bodily rhythms

After studying this topic you should be able to:

- describe and evaluate research into the sleep/wake cycle, and outline sleep stages
- describe and evaluate theories of sleep
- critically consider theories of dreaming

The sleep/wake cycle

Edexcel — U2
OCR — U1, U2

Biological rhythms are periodically repeated behaviours. The sleep/wake cycle is an example of a circadian rhythm. A circadian rhythm repeats itself once a day.

Causes of the sleep/wake cycle

External stimuli: zeitgebers

This is a German word meaning 'time-giver'. Light is the dominant zeitgeber, but meal times can also affect sleepiness, as can learned factors such as bedtimes.

Internal (endogenous) stimuli: the body clock

> This shows an interaction between the internal mechanism or 'clock' and external stimuli such as light.

The suprachiasmatic nucleus (SCN) generates circadian rhythms from protein synthesis and is 'fine tuned' by light and other stimuli, receiving information about light directly from the retina. The SCN regulates production of melatonin in the pineal gland – increases in melatonin are associated with decreases in arousal.

Research into the sleep/wake cycle

Demonstrating an endogenous (internal) pacemaker

- **Cave experiments:** Siffre (1972) spent 6 months in an underground cave finding that his sleep/waking cycle settled down to a naturally (endogenously controlled) cycle of 25–30 hours.
- **Transplanting the SCN:** Morgan (1995) transplanted SCNs from mutant hamsters who had a different circadian rhythm into non-mutant animals. The recipients quickly changed their rhythm to that of the donor, mutant hamster.
- **Different light conditions:** Luce and Segal (1966) recorded that people living near the Arctic circle still sleep the normal 7 hours a day despite the fact that in winter the sun doesn't rise.

Demonstrating the effects of external cues

- **Cave experiments:** Folkard *et al.* (1985) used artificial light to reduce the clock cycle – participants coped at a 23-hour cycle, but when it was reduced to 22 hours their bodies reverted to an endogenously controlled natural cycle. It appears that light can have a profound influence.

Stages of sleep

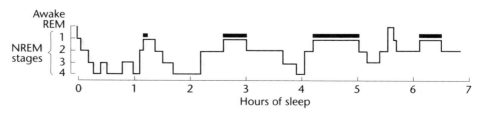

Sleep stages alternate through the night, starting with a rapid descent into deep sleep, followed by progressively increased episodes of lighter sleep and REM sleep (coloured area)

Theories of sleep

Edexcel U2

Restoration theory

Sleep allows various physiological and psychological states to be recovered. During slow-wave sleep the body makes repairs – for example, removing waste products. Certain metabolic processes also increase at night – for example, there is increased protein synthesis, particularly in REM sleep.

Evaluation

If restoration was the only function of sleep we would expect to observe deprivation effects, and increased sleep in relation to increased activity.

- **Case studies of sleep deprivation:** Dement (1972) reported the cases of a disc jockey, Peter Tripp, and a student, Randy Gardner, both of whom went for days without sleep. Towards the end, Tripp experienced hallucinations and profound delusions but Gardner wasn't affected except finding it difficult to perform some tasks. At the end Gardner only slept for 15 hours but this sleep consisted of mainly **core sleep** (stage 4 and REM). It's possible that Gardner benefited from episodes of **micro-sleep** (staring into space for a moment).
- **Controlled studies:** Webb (1985) found that sleep loss over 48 hours had little effect on precision and cognitive-processing tasks, whereas subjective and attention measures suffered. Depressed performance may be more due to motivational factors than cognitive components. Hüber-Weidman (1976) found that after 1 night there was an increased urge to sleep, after 4 nights increased episodes of micro-sleep, and after 6 nights a loss of identity and sense of reality (sleep-deprivation psychosis).
- **Increased activity:** Shapiro *et al.* (1981) found that marathon runners did require extra sleep, whereas Horne and Minard (1985) tried to exhaust their participants with numerous activities and found that they went to sleep faster but not for longer.

Conclusion

Empson (1989) reports that it is impossible to go without sleep and remain okay and Horne (1988) points out that sleep-deprived participants do show a rebound effect. It may be that only core sleep is essential and that some recovery can take place during relaxed wakefulness and micro-sleep.

Evolutionary theory

Sleep is an adaptive response to environmental and internal demands, akin to hibernation. There are two evolutionary theories:

- **Protection from predation** (Meddis, 1975). Animals have evolved an innate programme to protect them when they can't be gathering food and at times of danger (such as darkness). The more dangerous your world, the less time you should spend sleeping.
- **Hibernation theory** (Webb, 1982). Sleep is adaptive because it is a means of conserving energy in the same way that hibernation enhances survival by reducing physiological demands. An animal who is constantly active requires more food, and this is likely to decrease survival.

Evaluation

- If protection was the only function of sleep we would expect an inverse relationship between the time needed to search for food and the time needed for sleep. This is true for cows which graze all the time and sleep little, and cats who eat rapidly and sleep a lot.
- We would also expect that animals likely to be attacked will sleep little and

Infant sleep could be explained as an adaptive behaviour to help exhausted parents cope with finding food and other things.

lightly. Predators do sleep more than animals who are preyed upon, and animals who are preyed upon often sleep in burrows and feed at night, such as rabbits. But, taken to its logical conclusion, this would mean some animals shouldn't sleep at all in order to ensure their safety.

Beware of evolutionary arguments which sound as if the animal has made some deliberate choice about behaviour, the 'choice' is made through natural selection.

- Support for the evolutionary theory comes from looking at how species adapt their mode of sleep to suit their lifestyle. For example, dolphins sleep one hemisphere at a time which probably is related to the fact that they need to remain partly conscious to breathe.

A combined approach

Neither theory accounts for why animals lose consciousness when sleeping. It is not necessary for restoration, and from a safety (adaptive) point of view it makes little sense. The fact that all animals sleep means that it must perform some restorative function. The fact that each species evolves a particular style suggests an adaptation.

Progress check

1 What is a circadian rhythm?
2 What is restored during slow-wave sleep?

2 E.g. neurotransmitters, bodily repairs.

1 A biological rhythm that is repeated once a day.

Theories of dreaming

Edexcel   U2
OCR   U1, U2

The classic study by Dement and Kleitman (see OCR core study on p.92) demonstrated the link between dreaming and REM sleep.

Reverse learning

Many theories make the assumption that REM sleep = dreaming. This assumption in part comes from the study by Dement and Kleitman, reported on p.92. But the two are not necessarily equivalent.

Crick and Mitchison (1983) used a computer analogy to liken dreams to updating memory files and discarding redundant data, processes which are necessary to avoid wasted space. We dream to forget. The actual content of dreams is an accidental by-product and has no meaning.

Evaluation

- Animals that have a large cortex, such as a dolphin, don't appear to have REM sleep. This could be because they don't need to discard vast quantities of redundant data because they have plenty of room. However, the lack of folding of their cortical surface means there may not actually be as much storage space as is apparent.
- This theory doesn't explain dreams such as the common dream of falling, and why we have bizarre dreams that contain 'novel' experiences.
- The idea of wasted space doesn't fit with modern connectionist ideas. There are plenty of potential connectionist pathways in the brain.

Emotional catharsis

Freud (1900) suggested that dreams are 'the royal road' to the unconscious and enable repressed desires or memories to become known. Dreams are not accidental by-products but important ways of coping with anxieties. Dreams have manifest content (i.e. how one would describe the dream) which is arbitrary and meaningless but also have latent content (i.e. features of the dream symbolise deeper meanings such as a cave representing female sexual anatomy).

Evaluation

- This approach cannot explain why animals dream, if they do.
- The interpretation of a dream is entirely subjective.

> One of the main issues is the extent to which dreams have real meaning.

Activation-synthesis

Hobson and McCarley (1977) suggested that the brain is activated during REM sleep and this random activation is interpreted in a meaningful way.

Evaluation

- This account can explain common experiences like feeling one is falling, and explains both why we dream and why the dream contains a particular content.

Progress check

1 What theory of dreaming suggests we need to save wasted space?
2 What is the latent content of a dream?

2 The underlying meaning.
1 Reverse learning theory.

OCR core study: Dreaming

Dement and Kleitman (1957) The relation of eye movements during sleep to dream activity

Aims To what extent are dreams related to REM activity? Does the length of the dream and movements of the eye relate to the content of the dream?

Procedures This study involved a controlled observation. Each participant reported to the sleep laboratory on a number of occasions just before their usual bedtime. Electrodes were attached around the participant's eyes to measure eye movement, and to their scalp to record brain activity as a measure of depth of sleep.

Findings REM activity was accompanied by a relatively fast EEG pattern, compared with the slower activity during deeper sleep.

REM periods lasted between 3 and 50 minutes. During that time the eyes were not constantly in motion but there were bursts of activity.

REM activity occurred at regular intervals for each individual. For one participant they were every 70 minutes, for another every 104 minutes.

Most (but not all) dreaming occurred during REM sleep.

It proved difficult for participants to estimate the length of their dream. Therefore participants were woken after 5 or 15 minutes of REM and asked to state how long it felt like. All but one participant gave very accurate responses.

> Dreams are subjective experiences and it is difficult to study such things empirically.

Relationship of type of eye movement to imagery of dream. There did appear to be some support for a relationship – for example, when one participant displayed horizontal eye movements (which were quite rare) they dreamt they were watching two people throwing tomatoes at each other!

Conclusions It appears that REM activity is roughly equivalent to the experience of dreaming. Without this objective measure the study of dreaming would be difficult.

Criticisms It may be that people do dream in NREM sleep but it is deeper sleep and therefore the dreams are forgotten when a person is woken, or wakes up.

OCR Revision The study by Dement and Kleitman (sleep and dreaming) involved participants' self reports of dreams and the use of equipment to measure REM and NREM.
a) Outline **one** finding of the relationship between sleep and dreaming. [2]
b) Give **one** reason why the conclusions of the study might not be valid. [2]
(January 2002, Core Studies 2, question 5)

4.4 Stress: Stress as a bodily response

The body's response to stress

You can think of stress in engineering terms – it is a force placed upon a system which may lead to some modification of form.

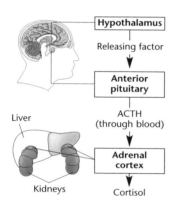

The hypothalmic–pituitary –adrenal axis
(Source: Kalat, J.W. (1998)

Americans use the terms **epinephrine** and **norepinephrine** for adrenaline and noradrenaline respectively.

Definitions

Key Term Stress is an emotion, a state of psychological tension and physiological arousal produced by a stressor which makes the individual ready to respond. It is an adaptive response because it enables the individual to cope. It becomes maladaptive if the stressor persists.

Key Term A stressor is a physiological or psychological stimulus that threatens an individual's well-being. It may or may not lead to a stress response.

The role of the autonomic nervous system

See pages 80–81 for a description of the autonomic nervous system (ANS).

- **The hypothalamus** is in the midbrain. It produces hormones in response to stress, e.g. **corticotrophin-release factor (CRF)** which stimulates the anterior pituitary gland to secrete its hormones.
- **The pituitary gland** is called the 'master gland' because it directs the endocrine system. The anterior pituitary gland releases **adrenocorticotrophic hormone (ACTH)** which stimulates the **adrenal cortex.**
- **The adrenal glands** are located just above the kidneys. They are divided into the:
  - **adrenal cortex** which secretes different hormones, including **cortisol**. (The function of cortisol is to maintain a steady supply of blood sugar for continued energy and also to reduce the immune response.) This is the **HPA system** (hypothalamus → pituitary → adrenal cortex);
  - **adrenal medulla**. Immediate (acute) stressors arouse the ANS, leading to a 'fight or flight' response – physiological arousal ready to fight or take flight. The sympathetic branch of the ANS is activated and this, in turn, arouses the adrenal medulla leading to the production of adrenalin (and noradrenalin). Adrenalin leads to: increased blood flow to the muscles, increased heart and respiration rate, reduced activity in the digestive system, etc. Parasympathetic activity is decreased, such as slowing down digestion. This is the **SAM system** (sympathetic → adrenal medulla).

Evaluation of the role of the ANS in stress

- **Support for the explanation:** People without adrenal glands have to be given additional quantities of glucocorticoids in order to survive (Tyrell and Baxter, 1981). This shows that the ANS stress response is vital for survival.
- **Weakness:** The straightforward physiological account doesn't explain how the stress response varies depending on the type of stressor and individual differences. Mason (1975) found adrenaline and noradrenaline secretion varied in different individuals when exposed to situations.

The General Adaptation Syndrome (GAS)

Key Term General adaptation syndrome is a model outlined by Selye (1936). Selye observed that all animals produce the same sequence of responses to all stressors: cold, pain, physical trauma. This response (outlined below) is adaptive because it enables the individual to cope under stress. The three phases of the response are:

1 Alarm reaction

The stress response is adaptive because it prepares the animal to respond to environmental demands. The hypothalamic–pituitary–adrenal system is activated: the sympathetic branch of the ANS is aroused, and ACTH and adrenal hormones are released in readiness for fight or flight.

2 Resistance

If the stressor persists, the body adapts by returning to a normal level of functioning while coping with the stressor. Hormone production is maintained but at a lower level.

3 Exhaustion

Eventually the body's resources are depleted. Adrenal glands are not functioning properly, leading to a drop in blood sugar levels and various psychosomatic disorders such as high blood-pressure and ulcers.

Evaluation of GAS

Strengths

- Empirical support: Selye (1936) observed stress reactions in rats and later confirmed this in studies of hospital patients with various injuries and illnesses.
- Selye's contribution was to alert medicine to the importance of stress.

Weaknesses

- It ignores the role of **emotional and cognitive factors**, possibly because the research is based on non-human animals. Lazarus *et al.* (1965) showed that people experienced a film as stressful, or not, depending on what they had been told beforehand. This means that cognitive appraisal affected the stress experienced.
- Selye thought that GAS was a nonspecific response to any stressor, but different stimuli lead to different responses (**stimulus differences**). Also, no two people respond in the same way (**individual differences**) nor does the same person always respond in the same way (**situational differences**).

> Note the use of the word 'adaptive'. This is a feature of the **theory of evolution** – a behaviour is adaptive if it promotes survival. In terms of stress, it is seen as an adaptive response, at least initially, because it promotes survival. Furthermore, it is adaptive because the body tries to return to a normal level of functioning as soon as possible.

Progress check

1 What is the effect of adrenaline?
2 Why is GAS adaptive?

2 It promotes survival because it helps the animal cope with a stressor.

1 It activates the sympathetic branch of the ANS.

Stress and illness

AQA A   U2

> Psychoneuroimmunology (PNI) is the field of research which investigates the link between stress and other psychological states.

Stress has been linked with a range of physical illnesses

How does stress cause illness?

- **Directly**, by reducing the body's ability to fight illness.
- **Indirectly**, by leading the stressed individual to adopt an unhealthy lifestyle (e.g. increased smoking and drinking).

The effects of stress on cardiovascular disorders

Key Term Cardiovascular disorders are any disorder of the heart heart disease) and circulatory system (e.g. hypertension – high blood pressure).

- **Coronary heart disease (CHD)**: The link with stress was demonstrated in a study by Friedman and Rosenman (1959, see Key Study below).
- **Hypertension**: This is diagnosed when a person has experienced raised blood pressure for at least several weeks. It is a major risk factor for coronary heart disease. Cobb and Rose (1973) found that hypertension rates were several times higher in air-traffic controllers, and especially in those controllers working in busy airports, than other people working at the airport.

AQA (A) Key study: Stress and cardiovascular disorders

Friedman and Rosenman (1959, 1974, 1996) Type A and heart disease

Aims Friedman and Rosenman proposed that some individuals (Type A) are typically impatient, competitive, time pressured, and hostile. Type B individuals lack these characteristics and are generally more relaxed. Type Bs are nice, industrious, conventional, sociable but tend to be repressed and react to stress or threat with a sense of helplessness. Friedman and Rosenman predicted that Type As would be less able to cope with stress and therefore more likely to experience coronary heart disease (CHD). They set up the Western Collaborative Group Study to test the long-term effects of stress on certain types of people.

Procedures This was a longitudinal study. Participants (3,154 healthy men aged between 39 and 59, living around San Francisco) were assessed using a set of 25 questions that looked at how a person typically responds to everyday pressures that would create feelings of impatience, competitiveness or hostility. For example, they were asked how they would cope with having to wait in a long queue or working with a slow partner. The interview was conducted in a provocative manner to try to elicit Type A behaviour. For example, the interviewer might speak slowly and hesitantly, so that a Type A person would want to interrupt.

Both the participants' answers and the way they answered were recorded. Participants were then classed as A1 (Type A), A2 (not fully Type A), X (equal amounts of Type A and B), and B.

Findings Eight and a half years later (Friedman and Rosenman, 1974) 257 of the total sample had developed CHD, 178 of these had been assessed as Type A (69%), whereas half as many were Type B.

Twenty-two years later (Friedman, 1996) 214 men had died from CHD, 119 were Type A and 95 Type B – a rather less impressive difference.

Conclusions This offers strong support for the idea that aspects of a person's temperament are associated with CHD, in particular a link between Type A personality and CHD.

The fact that the death rate was lower in the second study may be because some people take preventive measures once they know they are ill.

Criticisms Hostility rather than stress may explain the findings. Matthews *et al.* (1977) suggested that high levels of hostility produce increased activity within the sympathetic nervous system.

The findings have been applied to improving health. Friedman *et al.* (1986, the Recurrent Coronary Prevention Project) found that, after 5 years, those CHD patients taught how to modify their behaviour had fewer second heart attacks than those who received just counselling or no treatment.

Someone with AIDS is suffering from an immunosuppressive effect because the HIV virus attacks T-helper cells. AIDS doesn't kill in itself but it prevents the body from protecting itself against other viruses and tumours.

The effects of stress on the immune system

Key Term The immune system protects us from disease. The main components are antibodies, and white blood cells (leucocytes and lymphocytes), which include T-cells. The presence of cortisol and adrenaline seem to inhibit the production of these components.

- **The common cold:** Cohen *et al.* (1991) exposed participants to the cold virus. Those who had highest stress levels (as measured in life change units, see p. 97) were twice as likely to become ill as those with lower levels of stress.
- **Tumours:** Riley (1981) created stress in mice by placing them on a turntable rotating at 45 rpm. After 5 hours of continual rotation their lymphocyte count was reduced. In another study cancer cells were implanted in mice. Those mice who were given 10 minutes of rotation per hour for 3 days (high stress) developed large tumours whereas mice exposed to no stress had no tumours.
- **T-cell activity.** See Kiecolt-Glaser *et al.* (1984, key study below).

Evaluation of link between stress and illness

- The functioning of the immune system in people who say they are very stressed is actually within the **normal range**.
- The link between illness and stress **oversimplifies** a complex system.
- The correlation between stress and illness doesn't mean one causes the other. There may be other indirect factors, such as **lifestyle**. Cohen and Williamson (1991) found that people who are stressed tended to smoke more, to drink more alcohol and take less exercise, than people who are not stressed.

AQA (A) Key study: Stress and the immune system

Kiecolt-Glaser *et al.* (1984) Immunocompetence in medical students

Aims One reason why stress may be associated with illness is because the immune system in a stressed individual is not functioning as normal. This study set out to test this hypothesis and also aimed to see if other factors such as loneliness were associated with lowered immune function.

Procedures This was a natural experiment, using a questionnaire. The participants were 75 first-year medical students who volunteered to take part. The researchers took a blood sample one month before the students' final examinations, and again during their exams. The samples were tested for T-cell activity. On both occasions the students were also given questionnaires on psychiatric symptoms, loneliness and life events.

Findings T-cell activity was significantly lower on the second occasion, when the students were presumably most stressed. It was particularly low for students who reported feeling most lonely, and those experiencing other stressful life events and psychiatric symptoms such as depression or anxiety.

Conclusions The findings suggest that stress arising from exams is associated with a lowered immune response. This effect is stronger where social support is lacking. This suggests that social support reduces the effects of stress.

Criticisms The study lacked population validity as only students were tested and, in addition, it lacked ecological validity as stress was tested in one setting (exams) and the findings may not generalise to other settings.

The findings are supported by many other studies. For example, Kiecolt-Glaser *et al.* (1987) analysed blood samples from married, separated and divorced women. Happily married women had better immune functioning than those who were dissatisfied. Separated and divorced women who found their separation hard to bear also had weaker immune functions.

4.5 Stress: Sources of stress

After studying this topic you should be able to:

- *outline research into the sources of stress*
- *discuss the effects of life changes and workplace stresses*
- *discuss the role of individual differences in modifying the effects of stressors*

Research into sources of stress

AQA A U2

To use the SRRS, you should circle events which have happened to you in the last 12 months. Each event is awarded a value measured in 'life change units' (LCUs). Your LCU total is an estimate of the amount of life stress you have experienced.

Life changes

Key Term Life changes are events in a person's life that cause stress because they require the person to make adjustments. It is said that they use 'psychic energy'. Such events may be positive (such as marriage) or negative (such as divorce).

Two doctors, Holmes and Rahe (1967), observed in their patients that poor health was associated with life events which involved change from of a steady state, even when the change was for the better. They developed the Social Readjustment Rating Scale (SRRS) as a means of measuring life change units (LCUs). They did this by analysing 5,000 patient records and identifying 43 life events which seem to precede illness. Then they asked people to rate the events using marriage as a reference point. Some examples are shown below.

Rank	Life event	Mean value
1	Death of spouse	100
2	Divorce	73
3	Marital separation	65
4	Jail term	63
5	Death of close family member	63
6	Personal injury or illness	53
7	Marriage	50

Evaluation

- The scale muddles different kinds of life events. Those over which you have least control may be most stressful (see 'lack of control' on p.99 and p.103).
- The scale does not allow for the fact that different people interpret the same event differently, and therefore a single value cannot be assigned for stress.
- Studies using the scale have found only a small correlation between life events and illness (see key study by Rahe *et al.* 1970 below).
- The importance of this scale is not in its usefulness but in its status as a breakthrough. It triggered off a wealth of research.
- Daily events. DeLongis *et al.* (1982) noted that most people do not often experience major life events, therefore the strains of everyday life might be a better measure of stress and a better predictor of physical illness.

Key study: Life changes

Rahe *et al.* (1970) Illness in navel personnel

Aims Are life events associated with physical illness? Rahe *et al.* set out to test the hypothesis that life events may lead to stress and illness, using the SRRS that had been designed to measure life events.

Procedures This was a correlational study using the SRRS to assess life events. The participants were 2,500 naval personnel.

Just before a tour of duty, participants were asked to fill in a questionnaire relating to significant changes in their life over the past six months. This meant that a LCU (life change unit) value could be calculated for each participant.

A health record was kept by the ship's physician for each participant during the six months tour of duty.

Findings   They found a small but significant positive correlation of 0.118 between LCUs and illness. This means that as life events increased so does illness. The fact that the findings were significant means that the relationship is not simply due to chance.

Conclusions   This seems to suggest that life events do cause physical illness, though since the study was correlational this means we cannot draw conclusions about cause and effect. We can only state that life events and physical illness are positively associated. The findings support the view that changes associated with major life events absorb 'psychic energy', leaving less available for other matters such as physical defence against illness.

Criticisms   The data collected about life events was retrospective. It is likely that individuals did not recall these events accurately. They might have forgotten which events had happened in the past 6 months, included ones from longer ago, and excluded ones they preferred to forget. This means the data might be unreliable.

The study lacked population validity because the sample consisted of American males (and in the Navy). This means we cannot justifiably generalise these findings to other cultures or to women.

Progress check

1   What is an LCU and what does it measure?
2   Give one criticism of the SRRS.

2 E.g. it assumes that life events mean the same thing to everybody.
1 Life change unit which measures amount of stress in terms of change experienced.

Workplace stressors

Key Term   **Workplace stressor** is any feature of the workplace that creates stress. This can affect paid workers, volunteers, students or housewives, and may be due to the factors described below.

- **Effects of workplace stress:** absenteeism; high job turnover; alcohol and drug abuse; and poor performance in terms of quantity and quality.
- **Causes of workplace stress:** job uncertainty; organisational change; work overload; under-utilisation of skills; difficult tasks; decision-making and dangerous, unpleasant or uncomfortable work environments.

Further causes of workplace stress have focused on a number of areas:

Shift work

Having to adjust one's body clock to different sleep patterns results in considerable stress and has been associated with major industrial accidents. Czeisler *et al.* (1982) found that shift work amongst manual workers in an industrial setting in Utah, USA correlated with raised accident rates, absenteeism and chronic feelings of ill health.

Overcrowding

Calhoun (1962) placed a population of rats in a limited space. Once their population reached a certain level, their behaviour became pathological (males became hypersexual, and attacked females and young, females became poor mothers). The overcrowding created stress.

Remember that a stressor is any physical or psychological stimulus that threatens an individual's psychological and/or physiological well-being.

There is evidence that density also causes stress in humans. Freedman (1973) found correlations between urban density and pathological behaviour such as admissions to mental hospitals. However, in other situations, such as a football match, density can be an uplift rather than a hassle.

Noise

Glass *et al.* (1969) arranged for participants to complete various cognitive tasks, such as number work and letter searches, while listening to noisy tapes. Later the participants had to complete four puzzles. Two of them were insoluble. Frustration was measured in terms of the time that participants persisted at these tasks and stress was measured throughout using galvanic skin response (GSR). Participants did adapt to the noise as shown by the fact that their GSR levels and number of errors were considerably reduced by the end of the first set of tasks. However, if the noise was intermittent, participants made more errors and showed less task persistence.

One comment that is made about many psychological experiments is that they involved American male undergraduates – a population sample that is by no means typical of the rest of us. Glass' research involved *female* students, different but still potentially biased.

Lack of control

Glass *et al.* (1969) tried a further variation where some participants were given a button to ostensibly control the noise. These participants showed greater task persistence than those who thought they had no control. Perceived control avoids a sense of helplessness and anxiety, which would increase stress and frustration. In Cohen *et al*'s. study (1991 see p.96) those participants who felt their lives were unpredictable and uncontrollable were twice as likely to develop colds as those suffering low stress.

Responsibility

In contrast with 'lack of control' studies, other research has found that increased responsibility (greater control) is linked to higher stress. Brady's (1958) classic study which showed that control was associated with increased stress is described below.

AQA (A) Key study: Workplace stressers

Brady (1958) Ulcers in executive monkeys

Aims

If you use this study in an exam make sure you link it to workplace stress.

Brady conducted research where monkeys were strapped in a chair and given electric shocks unless the monkey pressed a lever every 20 seconds. Many of them died and postmortems showed they had stomach ulcers. The question was whether these ulcers were due to the physical restraint and electric shocks (physiological stress) or to psychological stress (the task they had to perform).

Procedures

The study with monkeys may be considered unethical, though we should weigh up the costs versus the benefits. Do you think that usefulness of the findings 'excuses' the harm done to the participants?

This study used non-human animals and was a laboratory experiment. Brady used a yoked control technique – the executive monkey received the shocks but had control over the lever, a yoked control was also restrained but had no control over the shocks and received the shocks whenever the first monkey failed to press the lever regularly.

A number of variations were tried: 6 hours on and 6 hours off; 18 hours on, 6 hours off; 30 minutes on, 30 minutes off.

Findings After 23 days the executive monkey died due to a perforated ulcer. The control monkey had no ulcers nor any gastrointestinal abnormalities. This happened when using the 6 hours on, 6 hours off schedule. None of the other timings produced ulcers. An investigation of stomach secretions showed that stomach acidity increased during rest periods when in the 6 on, 6 off schedule, and such acidity was related to the development of ulcers.

Conclusions First, these findings show that the ulcers were due to psychological stress not physiological stress. Second, they suggest that it is being in control that creates the psychological stress. Third, the study of stomach acidity suggests that the greatest danger period for an individual under stress is during rest.

Criticisms It may not be reasonable to draw conclusions about human behaviour. However, research with humans has supported Brady's findings. For example, Margolis and Kroes (1974) found that foremen (more responsibility) were seven times more likely to develop gastric ulcers than shop-floor workers.

Subsequent research on ulcers found that a bacterium (helicobacter pylori), not stress, is a major cause of ulcers (Marshall *et al.*, 1985).

Progress check

1 What is GSR?
2 In what ways is a managing director likely to suffer different levels of stress to a shop-floor worker?

2 A managing director probably has a greater sense of control (less stress) but increased responsibility (higher stress).

1 Galvanic skin response: a test of skin conductivity, sweating and ANS activity.

Individual differences in modifying the effects of stress

 AQA A ▶ U2

Personality

- **Type A** individuals are more likely to be affected by stress, as indicated in a study by Friedman and Rosenman (see key study on p.95).
- **Hardiness:** Kobasa *et al.* (1982) found that managers for large companies who were psychologically 'hardy' suffered less illness. Hardiness characteristics are:
  - greater sense of commitment to work and personal relationships, seeing stressful situations as a challenge and an opportunity, a stronger sense of personal control.

Culture

Black-African Americans are more likely to have cardiovascular problems than White Americans. This may be due to:

- **Biological factors** arising from racial differences. However, Cooper *et al.* (1999) compared hypertension rates of Africans living in Western and African countries. They were highest in urban societies, suggesting that hypertension is due to social factors and not to race.
- **Social factors.** Different cultural groups learn to manage stress differently. Wade and Tavris (1993) note that the Japanese deal with stress by trying to accept problems; westerners try to control a stressful problem.
- **Cognitive factors.** Black Americans experience high levels of prejudice.

Gender

Men are more likely to have cardiovascular problems than women. This may be due to:

- **Biological factors:** Women appear to be less affected by stress than men. It may be that women's hormones (such as oxytocin and oestrogen) protect them. Hastrup *et al.* (1980) found that women had lowered stress responses at the time in their menstrual cycle when their oestrogen levels were highest.
- **Social factors:** It may be that women engage in fewer unhealthy behaviours than men. Carroll (1992) reported that women are now smoking and drinking more, and their CHD rates have risen, which suggests that lifestyle could be important.
- **Cognitive factors.** Females may think differently about stressful situations. Vögele *et al.* (1997) suggest that females learn to suppress anger and therefore show low reactivity in stress situations.

4.6 Critical issue: Stress management

After studying this topic you should be able to:

- *describe and evaluate physiological approaches to stress management*
- *describe and evaluate psychological approaches to stress management*
- *explain the role of control in the perception of stress*

Physiological approaches to stress management

 AQA A. ▷ U2

> There is no clear distinction between physiological and psychological therapies since all physiological treatments have psychological effects.

Key Term Stress management refers to techniques for coping with the negative effects of stress. One group of techniques is physiological and the other is psychological.

Key Term Physiological approaches to stress management are techniques that aim to reduce stress by altering the body's natural stress responses. Examples include the use of drugs and biofeedback.

Drugs

What are they?

Anxiolytic drugs reduce anxiety. These include:

- **Benzodiazepines:** (e.g. Valium and Librium). These are most common today. They act on synapses and neurotransmitters, especially by promoting **GABA** (the body's natural form of anxiety relief). GABA reduces **serotonin** levels, a neurotransmitter related to arousal and aggression. The common side-effects of benzodiazepines are sleepiness and dependence.
- **Buspirone** enhances the effects of serotonin, thus reducing anxiety, but also has side effects (e.g. depression).

How do they work?

All drugs are related to the bodily processes involved in the stress response, i.e. they intervene in the activity of the ANS.

Evaluation

- Drugs can be effective in reducing stress in the **short term**.
- They do not tackle the **real problem**.
- Drugs often have unpleasant **side-effects** and problems of **dependence**.

Biofeedback

What is it?

This is a technique to learn voluntary control of involuntary muscles that control, for example, blood pressure and heart rate. Learning occurs through:

- **feedback** – a patient is connected to various monitoring devices and a light or tone signals when a correct alteration occurs
- **relaxation** – in order to reduce blood pressure the patient is told to relax, and this leads to changes in muscle tone and ANS activity.

How does it work?

> Remember that operant conditioning involves a behaviour being 'stamped in' as a result of rewards or reinforcement.

There are two possible explanations.

- **Operant conditioning** occurs. Certain behaviours are reinforced because they result in a desirable state of affairs. Miller and DiCara (1967) demonstrated this by paralysing rats with curare (they had respirators to keep them breathing).

This was to ensure that the rats could not use any form of voluntary control. Half of the rats were rewarded whenever their heart rates slowed down by electrically stimulating the pleasure-centre in the brain. The other half were rewarded when their heart rates speeded up. In both groups there were significant changes in heart beats after repeated reinforcement.

- Relaxation leads to restoration of **homeostasis** (the body's normal state of balance). Selye's GAS model suggested that stress disrupts the body's normal state, so relaxation helps the body to regulate the various physiological activities that are out of control, e.g. high blood-pressure.

Empirical support

- Dworkin and Dworkin (1988) used biofeedback to teach sufferers of scoliosis (curvature of the spine) to control their back muscles and alter their posture.
- There are reports of its usefulness with asthma, hypertension, migraine, circulatory problems, pain control, and bed wetting (Underhill, 1999).

Evaluation

- Biofeedback certainly works with **voluntary** responses. However, apparent changes in **involuntary** control may be due to relaxation and control of unused voluntary muscles.
- Such strategies are costly, time-consuming and require effort and commitment.
- On the other hand, biofeedback is non-invasive, has virtually no side-effects, and can be effective over the long term.

Psychological approaches to stress management

AQA A ▶ U2

Key Term Psychological approaches to stress management are techniques that aim to reduce stress by helping to cope better with stressors now and/or in the future. Such techniques require considerable effort on the part of the 'patient' but offer long-term solutions.

Meichenbaum: Stress inoculation therapy

> The term 'cognitive' refers to mental activity, so cognitive therapies are those techniques concerned with thinking.

What is it?

Meichenbaum (1985) proposed a form of therapy to protect an individual ('inoculate') *before* dealing with stress rather than coping with it afterwards. This is a form of cognitive therapy because it aims to change the way the individual *thinks* about their problem rather than changing the problem itself.

How does it work?

- **Assessment:** therapist and patient discuss potential problem areas.
- **Stress reduction techniques** are taught, e.g. relaxation and using self-coping statements (such as 'Stop worrying, because it's pointless').
- **Application and follow-through:** patient practises stress-reduction techniques in role play, and then uses them in real-life situations.

Empirical evidence

Fontana *et al.* (1999) found that students benefited from a 6-week peer-led stress inoculation programme. They had lower heart rate and state-anxiety levels than did controls even 6 months later.

Meichenbaum (1977) compared stress inoculation with desensitisation (a form of learning therapy where patients learn to relax with their feared object). Patients had both snake and rat phobias, one of which was treated with one of the methods. Meichenbaum found that both methods were effective but stress inoculation also greatly reduced the non-treated phobia, showing that the patient had learned general strategies for coping with anxiety.

Evaluation

- Stress inoculation therapy is good for coping with **moderate stress** but not as effective for severe stress.
- **Not all individuals** are able to use this method effectively.

Kobasa: Increasing hardiness

What is it?

Kobasa (1986) suggested that people who are psychologically more hardy find it easier to cope with stress.

How does it work?

- **Focusing:** People often are unaware that they are stressed, so they should become more aware of signs of stress, such as tight muscles.
- **Reconstructing stress situations:** Think of a stressful situation and write down how it could have turned out better and worse.
- **Compensating through self-improvement:** Find tasks that can be mastered. This reassures you that you can cope.

Empirical evidence

Wiebe (1991) found that individuals rated high in hardiness showed lower rates of heart rate when performing a stressful task.

Maddi (1999) found that hardy individuals had lower blood pressure and reported less stress than individuals who measured low in hardiness.

Evaluation

Some people find this sort of strategy doesn't work. It requires **considerable effort** and determination – the characteristics of a hardy personality.

The role of control in the perception of stress

Key Term **Control** refers to the extent to which an individual feels able to direct his/her life. Research indicates that control may either reduce (e.g. Glass *et al*, see page 99) or increase stress (e.g. Brady, see page 100). In addition it is the perception of control that is significant, not whether an individual *is* actually in control.

Seligman (1975) proposed that individuals acquire **learned helplessness** when placed in situations where they have no control. In one experiment animals were placed in a cage and given shocks which were impossible to escape from. Later, when placed in a cage where there were opportunities to escape the animals didn't try. They had learned to be helpless.

Rotter (1966) introduced the concept of **locus of control**. People who have an internal locus of control believe they are responsible for the things that happen to them. They control their world. People with an external locus of control blame someone or something else. Locus of control moderates the perception of stress. For example, Kim *et al.* (1997) found that children with an internal locus of control showed fewer signs of stress when parents divorced.

Progress check

1 Give one drawback to using drugs to manage stress.
2 What did Kobaso mean by 'hardiness'?

2 The ability to cope with stress.

1 Side effects, may mask the problem.

Sample question and student answer

AQA A style question

(a) Describe **two** sources of stress [3 + 3]

(b) Explain how the body responds to stress. [6]

(c) To what extent are stress management techniques successful for coping with stress? [18]

(a) Two examples of things that make a person feel stressed are: noise and lack of control.

The candidate has named two sources of stress but the question requires a little more than this. Some more detail might have been provided by, for example, saying that noise is stressful when it is unpredictable and that the stress is due to the extra load put on your attentional system, leaving less psychic energy. Just to say 'noise' is a very limited answer. The same comments apply to 'lack of control'. (1 + 1 marks)

(b) When an animal is exposed to a stressor the brain sends signals to the pituitary which releases a hormone which activates the adrenal glands to produce adrenaline and noradrenaline. These activate the ANS ready for fight or flight. After a while, if the animal remains in a state of stress, the body recovers some balance so that normal metabolic functioning can take place. The levels of stress hormones are reduced but the body remains in a state of alertness. After a long period these hormones are depleted and a state of exhaustion occurs.

The answer outlines the essential features of the General Adaptation Syndrome. The candidate has a good grasp on the process but has omitted some useful details, such as the name of the pituitary hormone (adrenocorticotrophic hormones, ACTH) and reference to Selye's concept of GAS. The description of the body's response is accurate but lacking in some detail and therefore would receive 4 marks.

(c) There are both physiological and psychological methods for managing stress. Two examples of physical methods are drugs and biofeedback. The common drugs are barbiturates and benzodiazepines (such as Valium and Librium). These have offered a great deal of help to individuals who are suffering stress but they are better seen as short-term solutions because of their potential side effects. They may cause people to feel drowsy, which will affect their ability to cope with day-to-day life. People may also become addicted to drugs. Drugs also do not help people to cope if they get stressed again but they mean that the individual does not have to make a great effort to get better themselves. Other methods of stress management require much more active involvement.

Biofeedback is another physiological method. The aim is to learn through conditioning to control involuntary muscles and therefore reduce, for example, headaches or high blood-pressure. Miller and DiCara (1967) showed how rats could learn to control involuntary muscles when they were paralysed with curare. However, this research has never been replicated and it is not clear that people actually do learn to control involuntary muscles or are just learning relaxation and the control of voluntary muscles that they couldn't control before. Nevertheless, the method appears to be quite effective, for example Dworkin and Dworkin treated teenagers with curvature of the spine. The method of biofeedback has the benefit of no side-effects and being non-invasive, but it is very time-consuming and expensive and requires effort and commitment from the patient.

This is an extensive and very well-informed essay covering four different methods of stress management. There is no requirement to provide such a comprehensive answer and many students would create problems for themselves in doing this. The problem is that if you try to cover too many methods, you don't leave enough time for the 12 marks worth of evaluation. In this case the candidate has managed to provide ample description of methods (AO1=6) and evaluation of them (AO2=12).

Two psychological methods are stress inoculation and increasing hardiness. Meichenbaum's stress inoculation aims to teach people to be able to cope with stress before it comes, rather than trying to treat stress where it already exists. This should enable them to cope better. The individual is taught how to relax and to use self-coping statements. These are first tried out in role play and later applied in real life. One study by Meichenbaum showed the stress inoculation was better than other forms of therapy for coping with phobias and their associated anxiety. Even though a patient was only treated for one phobia they were able to cope better with other phobias as well. It seems that stress inoculation therapy

Sample question and student answer (continued)

is good for coping with moderate stress but not as effective for severe stress. Also, it requires a lot of effort on the part of the patient but again has no side-effects.

Kobasa suggested that people could learn to be more 'hardy' and therefore cope better with stress, in the same way as other people who are just naturally better at coping with stress. She said you should recognise that you are stressed (people often just get used to being slightly stressed and fall apart when stress levels get too high), then you should rethink the stress situation by writing a list of how it could have turned out better and worse. This allows one to focus on the positive and see that it could have been worse. This method appears to be effective and certainly Kobasa's own research has shown that people who are more hardy are better able to cope with stress.

It is clear that there are many ways to manage stress and each has its own advantages and disadvantages. The effectiveness of any technique is related to individual differences and the kind of stress. If the stress is extreme it may be necessary to use drugs to reduce the anxiety levels first. Some individuals could never cope with the level of commitment required by the psychological techniques.

TOTAL: 24 out of 30 marks.

Practice examination questions

1

(a) Describe the main features of Selye's General Adaptation Syndrome. [6]

(b) Describe the findings and conclusions of **one** study relating to workplace stressors. [6]

(c) To what extent does research support a link between stress and the immune system? [18]

AQA A style question

2

A number of the core studies take a biological approach to psychological processes. This approach attempts to explain human behaviour in terms of the biological structures and chemicals that make us up.

Take any **one** of the following studies presented in the core specification and answer the following questions.

Sperry (split brain)

Raine, Buchsbaum and LaCasse (brain scanning)

Dement and Kleitman (sleep and dreaming)

(i) Outline the procedures that were used to investigate physiological processes. [6]

(ii) Evaluate what this research tells us about the affect of physiological processes on behaviour. [12]

(iii) Suggest one change to your chosen study and evaluate how it would affect the results. [8]

OCR style question

Chapter 5

Individual differences

The following topics are covered in this chapter:

- *The individual differences approach*
- *Studying gender*
- *Abnormality: Defining psychological abnormality*

- *Abnormality: Biological and psychological models of abnormality*
- *Critical issue: Eating disorders*

5.1 The individual differences approach

After studying this topic you should be able to:

- *outline key assumptions of the individual differences approach*
- *distinguish between nomothetic and idiographic approaches in psychology*
- *evaluate the individual differences approach in terms of its strengths and weaknesses*
- *discuss some of the methods used in the study of individual differences*

Key assumptions of the individual differences approach

AQA A	U2
EDEXCEL	U2
OCR	U1, U2

This approach focuses on the way that people differ. Traditionally, this has involved the study of personality and intelligence. However, clearly, there are many other ways in which individuals differ: for example, in terms of hair colour, skin colour, gender, willingness to conform, and mental health.

The nomothethic approach to individual differences:

- aims to make **generalisations** about the differences between people;
- involves the study of **a large number of people** and then seeks to make generalisations about them. For example, research on gender differences highlights the way that men **on the whole** and women **on the whole** differ from one another.

The idiographic approach to individual differences focuses on the unique characteristics of individuals – for example, research based on case studies. Many psychological theories are written in a way that assumes all people are the same: all men are the same, all Americans are the same and so on, i.e. a nomothetic view. The idiographic approach is different and emphasises the fact that there is considerable individual variation:

- within any group of people;
- between cultures. Many psychological theories are **eurocentric** in that they are based on White, middle-class Europeans and assumed to apply to all classes of people. Even more research is based on American sources – possibly as many as 90% of the research studies in psychology are conducted with American participants.

Evaluation of the individual differences approach

Strength of this approach

The aim of psychology is to explain behaviour and clearly individual differences are an important part of this explanation: both in terms of making generalisations about groups of people (nomothetic) and focusing on individual cases (idiographic).

Weaknesses of this approach

- The danger with the nomothetic approach is that individual variation is overlooked.
- The danger with the idiographic approach is that we can not make generalisations about human behaviour from the study of individuals.

Methods used in the individual differences approach

Psychometric testing

A psychometric test is an objective and standardised measure of a small but carefully chosen sample of some aspect of human psychological ability. A 'good test' must have **reliability** (consistency) and **validity** (it must measure what it claims to measure). Tests also need to be standardised so we know whether any score is within the normal range or outside it. This is achieved either by **norm referencing** (establishing norms for a target population) or **criterion referencing** (establishing objective criteria of what is expected).

Evaluation

The strength of such tests is that one can collect large amounts of data about people. The disadvantage is that they are inevitably biased (e.g. culture bias) because they are based on the views of the test designer. They also give an illusion of reality, i.e. each individual can be given a score such as their IQ score which makes it appear that this is a absolute thing (like their shoe size). However, there is little evidence that this single number provides an accurate overall picture of the individual's capabilities.

Different historical periods are examples of different cultures. Britain today is as different from Britain in the 1800s as it is from life in a Third World country.

Cross-cultural research

Research may be conducted in different cultures in order to make comparisons. This can demonstrate universal behaviours and/or the effects of specific cultural practices.

Evaluation

The problems are that often psychologists use measures designed for one cultural group that are inappropriate for another group. In addition, observers are culture-biased and are only able to *sample* behaviour in that culture, a sample that may be biased.

Progress check

1. What does 'idiographic' mean?
2. What is the aim of cross-cultural research?

1 An approach related to the unique characteristics of the individual.
2 To compare behaviour and practices in different cultures and determine what human behaviours are universal and what are due to social influences.

5.2 Studying gender

After studying this topic you should be able to:

- *distinguish between the terms sex and gender*
- *outline gender concepts*
- *describe factors affecting gender role identity and development*
- *discuss methods used to study gender differences*

Gender concepts

AQA B ▷ U1

Many people use the terms 'sex' and 'gender' as if they refer to the same thing, but this is not true.

Androgyny is defined as 'having a partly male, partly female appearance'. This can be applied to physical and psychological characteristics.

Can you think of an example of a behaviour which would be reinforced in boys but not in girls?

Sex and gender

- **Sex** is a biological fact – i.e. whether someone is male or female.
- **Gender** refers to being male or female, i.e. masculinity and femininity.

Androgyny

Bem (1974) proposed that it was not necessary to regard 'male' and 'female' as mutually exclusive categories. A person can be both male and female, i.e. androgynous. For example, a person might be independent (normally considered as masculine) and at times show vulnerability (normally considered as feminine).

Bem further proposed that a person who is androgynous will be psychologically more healthy than an individual who is tied to being like a male or a female. Individuals who are less sex-stereotyped are freer to do things which are appropriate for a *situation* rather than being appropriate to their *gender*.

Sex-role stereotype

This is a set of related concepts (**schema**) which tells us what behaviours are appropriate for our sex/gender, i.e. how males and females should behave. They are learned through direct and indirect reinforcement and exposure to role models.

Role and identity

A key feature of any individual's self-identity is their gender. Martin and Halverson's **gender schema theory** (1981) proposes that once a child has a basic gender identity they are motivated to learn more about gender and incorporate this information into their gender schema. Like all schemas, this serves to organise relevant information and attitudes, and will influence behaviour.

Nature and nurture

Some aspects of gender role are biologically determined (nature) whereas other aspects are learned (nurture).

- **Nature:** Hormones (e.g. testosterone in males and oestrogen in females) control many sex-related behaviours (such as puberty). Money and Ehrhardt (1972) found that girls who were exposed prenatally to male hormones were more tomboyish in later life.
- **Nurture:** Maccoby and Jacklin (1974) reviewed over 1,500 studies of gender differences and concluded that sex-role stereotypes are 'cultural myths' that have no basis in fact. They are perpetuated by expectations arising from gender stereotypes.

Cultural diversity

Williams and Best (1982) explored gender stereotypes in 30 different national cultures, finding that men were seen as more dominant, aggressive and autonomous, whereas women were more nurturant, deferent and interested in affiliation. Mead's classic studies (1949, described in the next section) found that, for example, in some cultures both men and women behaved in a way Westerners would regard as feminine. This must be due to social influences. At the same time, in all cultures men were always more aggressive, indicating the effects of nature.

Progress check

1 What does the term 'gender' mean?
2 What is meant by 'sex-role stereotype'?

2 The schemas you have about what is appropriate behaviour for males or females.

1 Your masculinity or femininity, not whether you are a male or female.

Methods used to study gender

 AQA B   U1

Case studies

Goldwyn (1979) described the case of Daphne Went. She was a married woman who sought help because she could not become pregnant. Internal examination revealed that she didn't have a womb and was in fact a male. Since she was content with her female role, she continued to live happily as a woman and adopted two children. This suggests that gender is a result of rearing not biological sex. However, any conclusion drawn from a single case history must be treated with caution as other unique factors may be involved.

Content analysis

Crabb and Bielawski (1994) compared children's books from 1938 and 1989 in terms of the way they represented how men and women use equipment such as washing machines and lawn mowers, and so on, and found relatively little change. Such stereotypes act as **social representations** of our culture. They reflect the way that society thinks, and they also shape the way people continue to think.

Observation

Lamb and Roopnarine (1979) observed the behaviour of 3–5-year-old children during free-play periods. They found that children generally reinforced peers for sex-appropriate play and were quick to criticise sex-inappropriate play, and that they responded more readily to reinforcement by the same sex rather than opposite sex peers. This suggests that children already know what is sex-appropriate, and that their peers are just reinforcing that knowledge. This supports gender schema theory.

Experiments

Laboratory experiment: Smith and Lloyd (1978) showed how reinforcement of gender stereotypes takes place very early on. Participants were asked to play with a baby who was referred to as a male or female. They were given toys to use while playing: e.g. a squeaky hammer (masculine); a doll (feminine); a rattle (neutral). If a participant thought she was playing with a boy, she verbally encouraged more motor activity and offered masculine toys.

Natural experiment: Williams (1985) studied the effects of television on sex stereotypes in a community that had recently got access to TV. The children's sex role attitudes became more traditional and sex-stereotyped. American television portrays men and women in traditional roles. This may considerably influence sex-attitudes in other cultures.

Cross-cultural research

Mead (1935) recorded observations of tribes from New Guinea.

- The Mundugumour tribe were all aggressive (masculine quality) regardless of sex. Neither gender gave much attention to childrearing.
- The Arapesh were all warm, emotional and non-aggressive (feminine qualities).
- The Tchambuli exhibited a reversal of our own gender roles. Women reared the children but also looked after commerce outside the tribe. The men spent their time in social activities, and were more emotional and artistic.

Mead (1935) initially concluded that gender was culturally determined. Later (1949) she changed her view to one of **cultural relativism**: in all tribes the men were more aggressive in comparison with the women. This suggests that some aspects of gender behaviour are innate. However, Freeman (1983) suggested that Mead was selective in reporting her results, and that the natives told her what she wanted to hear.

Ethical issues: socially sensitive research

Research that has direct social consequences creates particular problems because it often concerns issues where there is little agreement, much bias and serious implications. This applies to psychological research concerning 'alternative' sexuality. For example, Hamer *et al.* (1993) found evidence of a 'gay gene' by looking at the genes of homosexual brothers. If this is true, it could lead some people to testing unborn children.

5.3 Abnormality: Defining psychological abnormality

After studying this topic you should be able to:

- *describe ways of defining abnormality*
- *consider the strengths and limitations of attempts to define abnormality*
- *explain what is meant by cultural relativism*

LEARNING SUMMARY

Attempts to define abnormality

Key Term **Abnormality** means to deviate from what is usual or from some sort of standard. The problem lies in establishing a standard. Possible approaches are described below.

Statistical infrequency

Key Term The **statistical infrequency** approach suggests that the standard can be defined statistically, i.e. in terms of what most people in the population are like. We can test a population for any behaviour, such as depression, and plot its frequency. If only 10% of the population exhibit this behaviour then it is abnormal.

Advantages of this approach

It is relatively easy to determine abnormality using psychometric tests.

Limitations to this approach

- Many unusual behaviours, such as genius, are statistically uncommon but not aberrant, in fact they may be **highly desirable**.
- Some undesirable behaviours or disorders, such as chicken pox, anxiety, or depression, are **statistically normal**.
- What is **common at a certain age** or in a certain context, is not universally applicable. For example, thumb sucking is normal at a certain age but not later.

Deviation from social norms

Key Term The **deviation from social norms** approach proposes that abnormality can be defined in terms of certain standards of social behaviour. Many people who are labelled as clinically abnormal do behave in a socially deviant way, for example schizophrenics behave anti-socially and erratically.

Advantages of this approach

Includes some consideration of the **effect** of deviant behaviour on others.

Limitations to this approach

- This approach allows serious **abuse of individual rights**. Examples of deviation through history have been witchcraft, homosexuality and political dissent.
- Social deviation is related to **social and cultural context**. What is deviant behaviour in Britain may not be deviant elsewhere.
- Social deviation can be a **good thing**, as in the case of people who resisted German occupation during World War II.

Failure to function adequately

Key Term The **failure to function adequately** approach suggests that certain behaviours are distressing or dysfunctional for the individual. For example, they disrupt the ability to work and/or to conduct satisfying relationships. Rosenhan and

Seligman (1989) suggested that certain elements jointly determine abnormality – singly they may cause no problem but when several co-occur they are symptomatic of abnormality:

- psychological suffering
- irrationality and incomprehensibility
- vividness and unconventionality
- violation of moral and ideal standards
- maladaptiveness (personally and socially)
- unpredictability and loss of control
- observer discomfort.

Advantages of this approach

Using the concepts of dysfunction and distress acknowledges the subjective experience of the individual.

Limitations to this approach

- In some situations apparently dysfunctional behaviour **may be functional** – for example, depression can be an adaptive response to stress.
- Personal distress may **not be a good indicator** of an undesirable state. Although many people do seek psychiatric help because they feel distressed, not all mental disorders are accompanied by a state of distress.
- Diagnoses of dysfunction and distress require **judgements to be made by others**, which are inevitably influenced by social and cultural mores.

Deviation from ideal mental health

Key Term The **deviation from ideal mental health** approach likens mental health to physical health. Doctors use the concept of physical health as a yardstick to measure ill-health (for example, a body temperature outside the normal range indicates illness) so why shouldn't we do the same with mental health? Jahoda (1958) suggested that the key features would be:

- self-acceptance
- autonomy
- environmental competence
- potential for growth and development
- accurate perception of reality
- positive interpersonal relations.

Advantages of this approach

- This is a **positive approach**.
- It is preferable to have some **absolutes** (signs of healthiness) rather than relying on a reference population to establish norms.

Limitations of this approach

- Such approaches are influenced by **cultural attitudes** – for example, autonomy is not a universal ideal.
- The list is **idealistic**, and few people achieve most of the behaviours identified.
- It is possible to measure physical illness objectively (e.g. temperature and blood pressure) but the concepts for mental health are **vague**.

Progress check

1 Outline one disadvantage of the 'deviation from statistical norm' explanation.
2 Which of the four explanations takes the most positive approach?

2 The deviation from mental health model.

1 E.g. some behaviours which are undesirable are statistically common.

Limitations associated with attempts to define abnormality

Reliability

The aim of diagnosing abnormality is to offer treatment to those who might be considered abnormal. This only makes sense if the diagnosis is reliable, i.e. two people would give the same diagnosis. The study by Rosenhan (1973 on page 115) demonstrates how the diagnosis of mental illness may lack reliability.

Cultural relativism

Key Term Cultural relativism is the view that behaviour must be viewed in the cultural context in which it occurs otherwise it doesn't make sense. This is because the meaning and causes of any behaviour are relative to the culture of the person.

Cultural relativism was a key problem for all of the definitions outlined above. Each standard is relative to cultural context. However, if one considers Rosenhan and Seligman's list, there are some universal indicators of undesirable behaviour, such as distress to oneself or others.

OCR core study: Diagnosing mental illness

Rosenhan (1973) On being sane in insane places

Study 1 — **Aims** Can diagnoses of mental illnesses ever be reliable? If 'normal' people were diagnosed as mentally ill this would suggest that the diagnosis was unreliable.

Procedures A field experiment involving eight sane people who acted as pseudo-patients (i.e. not real). The pseudo-patients presented themselves in different US mental hospitals saying that they had been hearing voices (a symptom of schizophrenia). All other details were drawn from their real lives, i.e. were normal. If and when the pseudo-patient was admitted, they continued to behave entirely as normal. They spent their time making notes. To be released they had to convince staff that they had now recovered

Note that the participants in this study were not the pseudo-patients but were the staff in the mental hospitals.

Findings All but one pseudo-patient was admitted. When they were released it was with the label 'schizophrenia in remission'. The length of stay ranged from 7 to 52 days (average 19 days). Visitors and staff found that the pseudo-patients 'exhibited no abnormal indications'. Real patients were suspicious.

Conclusions It was possible that doctors were biased towards making type-two errors (making a false judgement to avoid failing to diagnose a real illness).

Study 2 — **Aims** To test whether the tendency to err on the side of caution could be reversed.

Procedures Field experiment. The staff in another mental hospital were told the results of the first study, and that during the next 3 months, one or more pseudo-patients would attempt to be admitted to the hospital.

Findings There were no pseudo-patients but of 193 patients admitted 41 were judged as such by at least one staff member.

Conclusions The staff were now making more type-one errors (calling a sick person healthy).

Study 3 — **Procedures** Rosenhan conducted a mini-experiment in four of the original hospitals. The pseudo-patient asked a staff member 'Pardon me, Mr/Mrs/Dr X, could you tell me when I am likely to be discharged?'

Findings Only 4% of the psychiatrists and even fewer nurses answered the question posed by the pseudo-patient. Whereas, in a control test, all people stopped.

Overall conclusions It is the setting (situation) as much as the individual's behaviour (disposition) which leads to the diagnosis. The medical model does not work with mental illness, partly because mentally ill individuals do not have objective symptoms and partly because people can recover from physical illnesses whereas mental illness carries a lifelong stigma.

OCR Revision question The study by Rosenhan (sane in insane places) broke a number of ethical guidelines.
a) Outline **one** way in which the hospital staff were treated unethically. [2]
b) If the study had been ethical, suggest what effect this would have on results. [2]
(June 2001, Core Studies 2, question 5)

5.4 Abnormality: Biological and psychological models of abnormality

After studying this topic you should be able to:

- *describe the assumptions (and implications for treatment) of the biological (medical) model of abnormality*
- *describe the assumptions (and implications for treatment) of psychological models of abnormality—including psychodynamic, behavioural and cognitive models*

LEARNING SUMMARY

The biological (medical) model of abnormality

AQA A   U2

Assumptions of the biological (medical) model

- Psychological symptoms are manifestations of an **underlying biochemical or physiological dysfunction**, which may or may not have a known cause.
- **Symptoms** need to be identified and **syndromes** diagnosed, followed by appropriate somatic treatment(s).

Explanations for the cause of mental illness

Infection

Mental illness is caused by a virus or bacteria. For example, general paresis (a mental disorder known since the 16th century) was found to be caused by the syphilis bacterium. Crow (1984) proposed that schizophrenia is caused by a retrovirus, which becomes incorporated into DNA.

Genetic transmission

> A 'concordance rate' is the extent to which two things are related, in this case how frequently both twins have the same disorder.

Mental illness is the result of an inherited gene. For example, Gottesman and Shields (1972) found that **concordance rates** for schizophrenia in non-identical twins is about 9% whereas it rises to 42% in identical twins, indicating some environmental influence but a larger genetic component. Other studies have used **gene-mapping** to demonstrate the location of the actual gene that caused the disorder. For example, Sherrington *et al.* (1988) found evidence of a link between schizophrenia and a gene located on chromosome 5.

Biochemical abnormalities

Teuting *et al.* (1981) who analysed the urine of depressed and normal people and found lower levels of products associated with noradrenaline in the former. Some forms of depression are related to disordered hormone levels, such as post-partum depression, premenstrual syndrome and seasonal affective disorder (SAD).

Neuroanatomy

Chua and McKenna (1995) reported that the brains of schizophrenic patients were smaller and had larger ventricles than the brains of normal individuals.

Implications of the biological (medical) model for treatment

> Until fairly recently the medical model was the dominant model for explaining and treating mental illness. It tends to be favoured by psychiatrists, whereas clinical psychologists favour psychological models.

If one believes that mental illnesses have a physical basis, then they can be treated using physical (or somatic) methods. Some such methods are described on p.115.

ECT (electroconvulsive therapy)

Today, this involves little physical discomfort, as the patient is given an anaesthetic

The diagnosis of mental disorder is officially done using a classification scheme. The DSM-IV is used in America and the ICD-10 in Britain.

and muscle relaxant. An electric shock is applied to the non-dominant cerebral hemisphere to produce a seizure. The individual awakens soon after and remembers nothing of the treatment (which is desirable).

Evaluation

- The method is **potentially dangerous** and there are ethical concerns about it.
- ECT appears to be **successful** for cases of severe depression. Janicak *et al.* (1985) found that 80% of all severely depressed patients respond well to ECT, compared with 64% recovery when given drug therapy.
- Some criticise the fact that we don't know **how ECT works** and therefore it shouldn't be used. It has been suggested that the seizure may re-structure disordered thinking or it may alter the biochemical balance of the brain.

Psychosurgery

Moniz (1937) introduced the practice of lobotomy. The operation involved removing large portions of the frontal cerebral cortex to make a patient more controllable. Today the technique is much refined, electric probes destroy specific nerve fibres and cause minimal intellectual damage.

Evaluation

- It is **used only rarely**, in cases of severe depression, obsessive-compulsive disorder or pain where all other treatment has failed (Griest, 1992).
- The effects are **not consistent** and it is **irreversible**.

Drug therapy (chemotherapy)

The main classes of drugs are:

- **Anxiolytic drugs** (anti-anxiety) such as Valium and benzodiazepines (see p.101).
- **Neuroleptic drugs** (anti-psychotic) such as chlorpromazine, used to treat schizophrenia. They block dopamine receptor sites. Possible side-effects include blurred vision and a decrease in white blood cells (which can be fatal).
- **Anti-depressant drugs** (stimulants), e.g. Prozac. They promote activity of noradrenaline and serotonin, which leads to increased arousal. Side-effects include heart problems.
- **Anti-manic drugs**, e.g. Lithium, used to control mania in bipolar depression.

Evaluation

- The use of drug therapies has offered **significant relief** to many sufferers.
- There are problems of **addiction** and **dangerous side-effects**.
- Drugs are **not cures** – they are short-term remedies.
- **Effectiveness varies** considerably between individuals; questions usefulness.

Evaluation of the biological (medical) model

Strengths

- The medical treatment of insanity was a move in the direction of **humaneness**: the illness rather than the patient was blamed. On the other hand, control is taken away from the patient, who relies on expert guidance.
- At least some disorders have a **biological basis**; however, an exclusive emphasis on biological bases may mean that other factors are overlooked.

Weaknesses

- In many cases it is not clear whether the physical factor is actually an **effect rather than a cause.**
- The medical model may be appropriate for **physical illness** but not for mental illness where symptoms are less objective.
- The medical approach purports to be **value-free** and scientific, but is just as subject to prevailing attitudes as other models.

A combined approach: The diathesis-stress model

It may be more realistic to combine the biological and psychological models. Mental illness arises:

- Diathesis – a genetic vulnerability or predisposition.
- Stress – some environmental event which triggers the predisposition.

This would explain why, when one identical twin develops a disorder, their twin does not always go on to develop the disorder. It also explains why we don't all develop eating disorders even though we are all exposed to slim models.

Progress check

1. Identify one assumption of the medical model.
2. Name one therapy derived from the medical model.

2 E.g. drug therapy.

1 E.g. mental illnesses have a physical cause, symptoms can be identified and diagnosed.

Psychological models of abnormality: The psychodynamic model

AQA A	U2
AQA B	U1
EDEXCEL	U2
OCR	U1, U2

Assumptions of the psychodynamic model

This model is largely based on Freud's psychoanalytic theory (see Chapter 1).

- Mental illness is the result of **psychological** rather than physical causes.
- Mental illness arises from **unconscious** and **repressed conflicts**.

Explanations for the cause of mental illness

- Behaviour can be explained in terms of the factors (dynamics) that motivate it.
- Unresolved, unconscious conflicts form in early childhood and create anxiety.
- Ego defences, such as projection and repression, form to protect the ego from anxiety.
- These defences lead to neurotic behaviour.
- Recovery depends on insight and working through past problems.

Implications of the psychodynamic model for treatment

Psychoanalytic theory implies that recovery can only take place if the unconscious is made conscious, and patients resolve their conflict. This is done through psychoanalysis which involves the following techniques.

Free association

The therapist asks a question and the patient is encouraged to talk freely about anything that comes into their mind, i.e. to verbalise their stream of consciousness so that the therapist can identify where the patient may be repressing material.

Rich interpretation

The therapist explains the patient's thoughts and feelings.

Analysis of dreams

Dreams are considered to express the innermost workings of the mind (see p.91).

Transference

The patient transfers their feelings about others onto the therapist which gives the therapist insight into the patient's other relationships, both past and present. This may have to be dealt with as an additional 'problem'.

Evaluation of psychoanalysis

- The emphasis on early conflicts means that **present conflicts** may be overlooked.
- Psychoanalysis has somewhat **limited applicability**, being suitable for motivated intelligent and verbally able patients.
- It is only suitable for those mental illnesses where some **insight is retained**.

Evaluation of the psychoanalytic model

Strengths

- It was the **first attempt** to explain mental illness in psychological terms.
  - It is supported by **extensive theory** and practice.

Weaknesses

- It is **not a scientifically rigorous** approach, the model is based on research with a limited sample (Freud's middle-class Viennese neurotic clients).
- It is a **reductionist** model, suggesting that the patient is controlled by instinctual forces and help must come from an expert.
- It is also a **determinist** model based on innate, biological mechanisms of psychosocial development with some room for cultural influences.
- Freud was overconcerned with **sexual factors**, and this may reflect the culture in which he lived. Subsequent psychoanalytic theories (e.g. Erikson) have replaced sexual with social influences.

Progress check

1 Identify one explanation for abnormality offered by the psychoanalytic model.
2 What is 'free association'?

2 The therapist says a word and the patient talks freely about whatever comes into their head.

1 E.g. unresolved conflicts create anxiety, ego defences against anxiety lead to neurotic behaviour.

Psychological models of abnormality: The behavioural model

AQA A   U2
AQA B   U1
EDEXCEL   U2
OCR   U1, U2

Assumptions of the behavioural model

- Behaviourists (see Chapter 1) suggest that **abnormal behaviours are learned**, like any other behaviours.
- Only behaviours which are currently **observable** are important, the patient's history doesn't matter.
- **Thoughts and feelings** are not relevant. There is no conscious activity involved in learning. It occurs through conditioning techniques:
- What can be learned can be **unlearned**.

Implications of the behavioural model for treatment

If abnormal behaviours are learned then these can be unlearned and/or new behaviours can be learned in their stead. The behavioural model suggests that this can be done with either classical or operant conditioning techniques.

Classical conditioning techniques (Behaviour therapy)

- **Aversion therapy:** For example, alcoholics are injected with a drug which makes them vomit when drinking, and eventually the nausea becomes a conditioned response to the presentation of alcohol (conditioned stimulus). Meter and Chesser (1970) found that at least half their patients abstained for a year after therapy. The use of an unpleasant stimulus is ethically questionable. The drop-out rate tends to be high and patients may become anxious.

- **Systematic desensitisation (SD)** is used to treat phobias. The patient learns to pair the feared thing with relaxation rather than anxiety. Wolpe (1958) described the following steps: (1) Patient learns deep muscle relaxation; (2) Patient constructs a hierarchy of increasingly threatening situations; (3) Patient is asked to imagine each scene while deeply relaxed. At any time, if the patient feels anxious, the image is stopped and relaxation regained.
- **Implosion therapy and flooding:** Both techniques aim to present the patient with maximum exposure to the feared stimulus, with exposure continuing until their fear subsides, thus extinguishing the conditioned response. This can be done in one's imagination (implosion therapy) where the person imagines a very fearful situation (such as being in a room full of spiders). There is evidence that real-life exposure (flooding) is more effective but it does involve placing the patient in an intensely anxiety-provoking situation.

Operant conditioning techniques (Behaviour modification)

- **Modelling:** The patient first watches the therapist experiencing the phobic situation calmly, then the patient does the same.
- **Token economy (TE):** Patients living in an institution are given tokens as secondary reinforcers when they engage in correct/socially desirable behaviours. The tokens can then be exchanged for primary reinforcers – food or privileges. The drawback to this therapy is that it often fails to transfer to life outside the institution. The effectiveness of tokens may be due to other factors, such as the fact that the system is being positively reinforcing for the nursing staff (because the patients respond to the rewards and the staff feel they are making positive gains, and therefore are stimulated to persist). They also help to structure the situation and ensure consistent rewards. Paul and Lentz (1977) found the chronic mental patients with TE did as well as those in a therapeutic community in terms of full release or reduction of medication, and they did considerably better than those in a hospital setting.

> Mental institutions are therapeutic communities, but other groups of people living together can also be described as a 'therapeutic community' if the whole social environment is designed to have a beneficial and therapeutic impact on the residents.

Evaluation of the behavioural model

Strengths

- The therapies are **successful for the target range of disorders**, e.g. phobias, obsessive-compulsive and developmental disorders. In fact, for some disorders it is the only viable option – e.g. the brain injured.
- The firm scientific basis and operationalised procedures make the theory and therapies **easy to research.**

Weaknesses

- There are **ethical** questions about manipulating behaviour.
- Treatment is of **symptoms not underlying causes**, which may remain – but behaviourists argue that the symptoms are all that matters.
- The success of behavioural therapies may be quite **unrelated to learning theory**, for example it may be a matter of receiving increased attention.

Psychological models of abnormality: The cognitive model

Assumptions of the cognitive model

The cognitive model emphasises the role of thoughts, expectations and attitudes (i.e. cognitions) in mental illness, either as causes or mediating factors.

- It is the way you think about a situation which is maladaptive, which is different to maladaptive behaviour (as suggested by the behavioural model).

The cognitive (or cognitive-behavioural) model grew out of the behavioural model because the latter was seen as inadequate in its focus on external behaviour only.

- 'Cure' can be achieved by **restructuring** a patient's thinking and enabling them to change their self-beliefs and motivations.
- The psychotherapy is **client-centred** – only the client knows their own cognitions.

Implications of the cognitive model for treatment

This model assumes that disturbance lies in the way one thinks about things and therefore treatment should focus on training an individual's ways of thinking. Examples include the following.

Rational-emotional therapy (RET)

Ellis (1962) suggested that patients develop a set of irrational beliefs which lead them react to situations with undesirable emotions (ABC – **A**ctivating event – **B**eliefs about the activating event – **C**onsequences). For example, a person might believe that he must be competent in everything he does in order to be worth – while. When he fails at something, he is plunged into despair. The therapist is directive and aggressive and challenges beliefs, e.g. 'who says you must be perfect?', leading the patient to ask the same questions. Bradsma *et al.* (1978) reported that RET is effective with certain types of patient (those who are perfectionist and capable of rational thought).

Cognitive restructuring therapy

Beck (1976) developed a therapy for depression. The therapist identifies the patient's self-defeating assumptions and substitutes more adaptive ones. This should disprove the patient's negative self-image. The therapy may be effective with eating disorders and even schizophrenia. Hollon *et al.* (1988) gave 64 adults suffering from major depression either drug or cognitive therapy, or both for 12 weeks. Each treatment led to improvements. In the 'drug only' group there were no changes in 'explanatory style' but there were considerable changes in the other groups. There was some evidence of relapse in the 'drug only' group over the next two years but not in the other patients.

Stress inoculation therapy

Meichenbaum (1975), see p.102.

Evaluation of the cognitive model

Strengths

- In general these therapies are **quick**, and are becoming **increasingly popular**.
- They are **successful** for a **target range** of **disorders** (depression, anxiety and eating disorders, and sexual problems).
- It is an **objective approach** that lends itself to research.

Weaknesses

Like the behavioural model, this approach does not investigate causes but just treats behaviours – which appeals to some patients who prefer not to search for deep meanings.

Progress check

1 What is the behaviourist view on thoughts and feelings?
2 What is one limitation to the behavioural approach?
3 Which therapy involves patient insight?

3 Psychoanalysis.

2 E.g. doesn't treat underlying problems, unethical to manipulate behaviour.

1 They are not relevant to understanding behaviour.

5.5 Critical issue: Eating disorders

After studying this topic you should be able to:

- *describe the clinical characteristics of both anorexia nervosa and bulimia nervosa*
- *outline and evaluate biological explanations for eating disorders*
- *discuss psychological, (psychodynamic, behavioural and cognitive explanations) for eating disorders*

LEARNING SUMMARY

The clinical characteristics of eating disorders

 U2

The DSM-IV lists four criteria for the diagnosis of anorexia: weight, anxiety, body-image distortion and amenorrhoea.

Key Term **Eating disorders** are one category of mental disorder. Individuals with eating disorders have some problem with food, for example they may overeat (e.g. obesity), undereat (e.g. anorexia), or vomit repeatedly (ruminative disorder). There is evidence that such disorders may have a genetic basis but are also triggered by environmental stressors.

Anorexia nervosa

Key Term **Anorexia nervosa** is literally a 'nervous lack of appetite'. The main characteristics are as follows.

- There is a deliberate and prolonged **restriction of calorie intake** and considerable weight loss (weight falling to less than 85% of normal weight).
- They have an intense **fear of gaining weight**, but anorexics are often very hungry and preoccupied with food.
- Anorexics have a **disturbed body image** – they usually continue to see themselves as overweight despite large weight loss.
- It is accompanied by **amenorrhoea** (no menstrual cycle).
- It is largely a problem of **middle-class, adolescent girls** (although the percentage of males is increasing).
- It is sometimes seen as a **modern problem**, however Tolstrup (1990) documents cases prior to 1600, when the condition was described in connection with religious life.
- Two types of anorexia have been identified: the **restricting type** (constant fasting) and the **binge eating/purge type** (those who periodically binge and purge). The 'restricting type' tend to be more introverted, younger, and deny their distress.

One difference between anorexia and bulimia is that anorexics are characteristically concerned with perfection, whereas bulimics suffer from a constant craving for food/attention.

Bulimia nervosa

The DSM-IV lists five key characteristics of bulimia: binge, purge, frequency, body-image and that it occurs independently of anorexia.

Key Term **Bulimia nervosa** is a more common problem than anorexia and probably more related to dieting. The main characteristics are as follows.

- It is characterised by periods of **compulsive bingeing** followed by forced vomiting or the use of laxatives or other means (**purge**).
- Binge-purge eating is reasonably common among dieters, i.e. some dieters eat a lot and then make themselves sick. However, when it occurs **more than 2 times a week** for over 3 months it is abnormal. The abnormal behaviour also involves eating enormous amounts of **high-calorie food** and then purging.
- Bulimics are **obsessed about their weight**, though it is usually nearer normal than anorexics. Most of them are within 10% of their correct body weight.

Explanations of anorexia nervosa

Biological (medical) explanations

Genetic transmission

Twin studies illustrate this. Holland *et al.* (1984) found a 55% concordance rate for identical (MZ) twins compared with only 7% for non-identical (DZ). See also Holland *et al.* (1988) below.

Evaluation

The fact that not all MZ twins develop the disorder means that genetic transmission cannot be the sole explanation.

Biochemical abnormalities

Disordered hormones may be a cause. Amenorrhoea may occur before weight loss, which suggests a disorder of the endocrine system. Fava *et al.* (1989) found changes in the levels of serotonin and also noradrenaline in anorexics.

Neuroanatomy

Damage to the hypothalamus may result in a loss of appetite, as well as disturbances to menstruation.

Evaluation of biological explanations

Strengths

- Biological models can explain why anorexia is related to adolescence – because it is a **time of hormonal change**.
- The diathesis-stress model proposes that **genetic vulnerability** must be part of the explanation, though there also needs to be some trigger ('stress').

Weaknesses

- Biological explanations can't explain the **recent increase** in cases of anorexia.
- It isn't always possible to distinguish **cause and effect**.

AQA (A) Key study: Biological explanation of anorexia nervosa

Holland *et al.* (1988) Evidence for a genetic basis

Aims This study aimed to find out whether anorexia nervosa is related to genetic factors. One way to investigate this is to look at twins who develop the disorder. If anorexia is genetic then we would expect more MZ twin pairs to develop anorexia than DZ twin pairs because they have identical genes (whereas DZ twins share 50% of their genes). Both kinds of twins are assumed to share the same environment during development.

Procedures Twin studies are natural experiments. The participants in this study were 34 pairs of twins (males and females) and one set of triplets. Participants were selected because they were a twin and one member of the pair (or triplet) had been diagnosed with anorexia nervosa at a London hospital. Genetic relatedness (i.e. whether they were MZ or DZ) was established by blood group analysis or by use of a physical resemblance questionnaire. Both twins were interviewed to establish presence or absence of an eating disorder, and this data was used to confirm or diagnose anorexia.

Findings Far more MZ twins (56%) were concordant for anorexia nervosa than DZ pairs (7%). Concordant means that both members of the pair had the disorder.

In three cases the partner twin was found to have had other psychiatric illnesses, and two others had minor eating disorders.

Conclusions	These findings suggest that anorexia has a strong genetic basis because it occurred more when individuals shared the same genes than when they were simply related. However, concordance was not 100% which suggests that genes simply predispose individuals to develop an eating disorder (or other disorder). Only in certain circumstances (environmental triggers) does anorexia develop.
Criticisms	Since the twins were reared together they also shared environmental influences and this may be greater for MZ twins who look and behave more similarly than DZ twins, and therefore are treated more the same.
	It could be that one twin imitates the twin who developed the disorder first. However, some of the twins developed the disorder when living in separate countries. This would also not explain the difference between MZ and DZ twins.

Progress check

1 Suggest one limitation with the biological explanation for anorexia.
2 Suggest one strength of the biological explanation.

2 E.g. supported by twin research.
1 E.g. can't account for recent increases.

Psychological models: Psychodynamic explanations

Family systems theory

> In early childhood the child first establishes his or her identity. This is the first period of 'individuation'. During adolescence this process starts again.

Minuchin *et al.* (1978) suggested that anorexic's families are **enmeshed**. The members don't have a clear identity and the family finds it hard to resolve conflicts. This leads to anxiety which may be projected onto the 'ill' child, i.e. the eating disorder arises as a means of dealing with family conflict. Humphrey *et al.* (1986) did find that such families have more negative and fewer positive interactions than families with a normal adolescent.

Autonomy

Anorexics tend to be somewhat obsessive personalities, with low self-esteem and a fear of their own autonomy. Bruch (1987) suggested that certain mothers wish their daughters to remain dependent and therefore encourage anorexia. Anorexia develops as a means of asserting autonomy by exerting control over their body. The fact that most anorexics come from middle-class families where there are high expectations supports this.

Evaluation of psychodynamic explanations

Strength

The role of autonomy could explain why anorexia is **common during adolescence**. Blos (1967), a psychodynamic theorist, proposed that adolescence is a time of reindividuation.

Weaknesses

- Psychodynamic theories can't explain the **recent increase** in anorexia.
- Parental conflict may be an **effect rather than a cause** of anorexia.
- The accounts are difficult to prove wrong (**falsify**).

Adolescence may be a prime time for anorexia because it is then that girls especially are aware of making themselves attractive. They also often put on weight with puberty and this triggers off slimming.

Psychological models: Behavioural explanations

Classical conditioning

Leitenberg *et al.* (1968) suggested that anorexics have learned that eating is associated with anxiety, because eating too much makes people overweight.

Operant conditioning

Weight loss is reinforcing because people praise it (positive reinforcement) and the individual has escaped from an aversive stimulus (negative reinforcement).

Social learning theory

Feminine stereotypes in the media and the current emphasis on dieting promote a desire to be thin which is exaggerated in vulnerable individuals. This explanation is supported by cross-cultural studies, see the key study by Lee *et al.* (1992) on p.126.

Evaluation of behavioural explanations

Strengths

• Social learning theory can account for **increased incidence** of anorexia.
• Conditioning theory can explain how the disorder is **maintained**.
• **Behavioural therapies have been successful** in treating anorexia.

Weakness

• **Social factors alone** can't explain anorexia because otherwise more people would suffer from it.

Psychological models: Cognitive explanations

Distortion of body image

Garfinkel and Garner (1982) found that anorexic patients typically overestimate their body size compared with 'normal' controls. This distorted thinking may explain why they lose more weight than normal individuals.

Evaluation of cognitive explanations

The disordered thinking may be an *effect* rather than a cause of anorexia.

AQA (A) Key study: Psychological explanation of Anorexia nervosa

Hennighausen *et al.* (1998) Distorted perception of body shape

Aims Previous research has not consistently found that anorexic patients overestimate the size of their body or body parts in comparison with controls. Some studies have found no difference and others have found large inaccuracy. These inconsistent findings have led to a suggestion that the body-shape criteria be dropped from the DSM. This study aimed to investigate the importance of body shape.

Procedures The participants were all female, 36 anorexic patients and a matched control group of 18 patients who had diagnosed mental disorders but not any that might produce perceptual distortions (e.g. schizophrenia).

Participants were asked to record (1) their real body image (RBI) and (2) their ideal body image (IBI). This was done using a computer representation of each patient in a swimsuit which could be altered on screen to change the measurements.

Participants were also given an eating disorder questionnaire to complete.

Findings There was no significant difference between the anorexic patients and the control group for RBI but there was a significant difference for IBI.

Many anorexic patients correctly estimated their real body size, as did the control patients. However, some anorexic patients over- or under-estimated their real body size considerably.

Both anorexic and control preferred a slimmer ideal body shape than they actually were. Despite this, the controls expressed lower body dissatisfaction on the eating disorder questionnaire.

Conclusions The findings show that anorexic patients do not systematically overestimate their body size, which challenges this criteria in the DSM. However, the individual differences in anorexic patients may be significant. It may be that some anorexic patients have some form of perceptual disturbance.

The findings also indicate that all women have a desire for thinness but controls are not as dissatisfied about this. The key factor in anorexic patients may be the willingness to do something about this desire whereas the control patients accepted the discrepancy between actual and ideal body shape.

Criticisms The control group were also patients and therefore the findings cannot be generalised to normal individuals (low population validity). Mental patients may have disturbed body images because of low self-esteem.

This is a natural experiment as the independent variable (anorexic or not) varies naturally. This means that we cannot draw conclusions about cause-and-effect, i.e. that anorexia is the cause of disturbed perceptions.

Progress check

1 Name one psychodynamic explanation for anorexia.
2 How can operant conditioning explain anorexia?

2 Individuals are rewarded for weight loss and therefore continue to lose weight.

1 E.g. family systems theory.

Explanations of bulimia nervosa

There is a considerable degree of overlap in the explanations offered for anorexia nervosa and bulimia nervosa, so the following account will be less comprehensive.

Biological explanations

Genetic transmission

Kendler *et al.* (1991) found a 23% concordance rate for bulimia in identical twins compared with about 9% in non-identical twins (see detailed report below).

Biochemical abnormalities

Decreased serotonin activity may be responsible for bulimia. People with bulimia suffer specifically from carbohydrate craving (Turner *et al.*, 1991) and increased consumption of carbohydrates increases production of serotonin. This has led to the use of selective serotonin reuptake inhibitors (SSRIs) in the treatment of bulimia. Blouin *et al.* (1992) suggested that there is seasonal variation in bulimics similar to seasonal affective disorder, i.e. in the darker months they become depressed/more prone to binge/purge. This could be related to increased levels of serotonin.

Psychological explanations

Psychodynamic explanations

Family conflicts have also been identified in families with bulimics.

Behavioural explanations

- **Conditioning.** Rosen and Leitenberg (1985) suggest that bingeing causes anxiety; purging reduces that anxiety: a cycle which is reinforcing.
- **Social learning theory explains cultural differences.** For example, Nasser (1986) found that 12% of Egyptian women who were studying in London developed bulimia compared with no cases in Cairo.

Cognitive explanations

- **Disinhibition hypothesis:** Ruderman (1986) suggested that when a dieter has a rigid cognitive style they respond to situations of overeating by going over the top (becoming disinhibited). Once they have overeaten they purge to rectify their mistake.
- **Distorted body image:** Cooper and Taylor (1988) reported that bulimics usually show a substantial discrepancy between their estimation of their true body size and the size they would ideally like to be. This distorted thinking would encourage the desire to lose weight.
- **Coping style.** Vanderlinden *et al.* (1992) suggested that bulimics have a tendency to perceive events as more stressful than most people do, and use binge/purge as a means of coping with the stress or gaining a sense of control.

Progress check

1 What is the 'disinhibition hypothesis'?
2 Name one other explanation for bulimia.

2 E.g. genetic, socio-cultural factors (social learning).
1 Overeating results in a disinhibition of normal rigid self-control.

AQA (A) Key study: Biological explanation of bulimia nervosa

Kendler *et al.* (1991) Evidence for a genetic basis

Aims Kendler *et al.* sought to see whether bulimia (like anorexia) had a genetic basis. Evidence from the study of MZ and DZ twins was again used.

Procedures This was a natural experiment. Over 2,000 female twins were found using a register of American twins where one member of the twin pair had been diagnosed with bulimia. The other twin was interviewed and a diagnosis determined using standard criteria.

Findings In MZ twins there was 26% concordance between twin pairs and 16% for DZ twins. Of the sample interviewed, there were 123 cases of bulimia. Most of these participants also reported other mental disorders at some time in their lives including anorexia (10% of them), depression (51%), phobia (42%) and anxiety disorder (11%).

Conclusions This suggests that bulimia has a strong genetic component, though it is not as strong as found for anorexia. About half of the variation in bulimia is due to genetic factors and half to environmental factors.

The data also suggests that there is a link between all mental disorders. An individual may inherit a risk for mental disorder rather than just for bulimia, and life events act as triggers for specific disorders.

Criticisms Twins may not be representative. Klump *et al.* (1999) studied individuals with eating disorders who were MZ, DZ or non-twin and found differences between the groups in terms of the symptoms. This suggests that twins may not be representative of the general population for eating disordered behaviour.

A more recent study by Bulik *et al.* (2000) concluded that bulimia is 83% genetically influenced and anorexia nervosa is 58% genetic, which both supports and contradicts Kendler *et al.*'s findings. It is supportive because it is further evidence of a genetic cause. It is contradictory because it suggests a greater genetic component.

AQA (A) Key study: Psychological explanation of bulimia nervosa

Lee *et al.* (1992) Bulimia in hong Kong chinese patients

Aims Lee *et al.* note that bulimia is rare among the Chinese living in Hong Kong. If it is a genetic disorder then we would expect the incidence to be the same in any country. This study aimed to consider the explanations for the low incidence.

Procedures This research study involves no direct investigation but is a review of other research and a consideration of possible explanations. Thus it is not empirical research but research through reasoning. It is a form of observation and qualitative research.

Findings
- Clinical psychologists in Hong Kong are unfamiliar with the disease and are not making the diagnosis.
- Obesity is rare among the Chinese and dieting is uncommon. Chinese girls do not have a fear of fatness (leading to anxiety) and fatness is even valued.
- The Chinese diet is generally low in fat whereas in the West fatty foods are desirable, but also associated with shame and guilt.
- There is less role-conflict among Chinese women because in their society success is more related to 'family' values than to a good personal appearance or career accomplishment.
- Less exposure to role models. Chinese women are not aware that self-induced vomiting is an effective method of weight control.

Conclusions The conclusion that can be drawn from these observations is that the rarity of bulimia nervosa in Hong Kong is related mainly to the absence of the relevant sociocultural factors. This, in turn, suggests that when bulimia is common it is due to sociocultural factors – factors in the society that enable the disorder to develop, such as fear of fatness, association between eating and guilt, role conflict for women and exposure to role models

Criticisms It is possible that cultural differences are due in part to genetic differences in predisposition to the disease. Biological (genetic) differences can be seen in the fact that the Chinese do tend to be slimmer than Westerners. Biological differences might make them less genetically predisposed to weight problems.

As this study is not an experiment we cannot claim that sociocultural factors cause bulimia. We can only consider the value of the arguments and look for supporting empirical evidence from other studies to confirm the findings.

Sample question and student answer

1

(a) Outline **two** attempts to define abnormality. [3 + 3]

(b) For **one** of the definitions in part (a) suggest **two** limitations to this definition. [3 + 3]

(c) 'Eating disorders, such as anorexia nervosa and bulimia nervosa, are becoming a major problem throughout the world'. To what extent can psychological theories of eating disorders account for the facts. [18]

The question requires an outline of two definitions and the candidate has fulfilled this requirement. Both definitions are clearly outlined and accurate. (3 marks + 3 marks)

The candidate has identified two (possibly three) limitations. There would not be an <u>extra</u> credit for a third limitation but it adds to the detail provided for the first limitation described. The second limitation is adequate but an actual example of a behaviour (such as hearing voices) would have extended this answer. (3 marks + 2 marks).

Social learning theory is described in the first paragraph and used to explain eating disorders. This is all credited as description (AO1). The remainder of the answer evaluates (AO2) this explanation. This means there is about the right ratio of AO1:AO2 (1:3). The commentary is reasonably informed though no actual studies are cited, the candidate nevertheless displays a reasonable psychological knowledge and the structure indicates good skills of analysis (AO2=10 marks). The description is accurate but key details about social learning theory are omitted, such as reference to vicarious reinforcement (AO1=5).

(a) One way to define abnormality is in terms of statistical norms. The standard for what is normal is set in terms of what most people in any population are like. Any behaviour that is statistically infrequent is then regarded as abnormal. A second way to define abnormality is in terms of mental health. This means that we say what kind of psychological behaviours are signs of good mental health, such as a lack of depression or a lack of distress. If these are lacking in an individual then they are psychologically abnormal.

(b) I will consider the statistical infrequency model. One limitation is that it overlooks the fact that many statistically infrequent behaviours are quite desirable, such as genius. At the same time some statistically frequent behaviours would be regarded as undesirable (such as overeating) and therefore should really be abnormal. A second limitation is that this definition is related to the culture that sets the norm. Behaviours that are statistically infrequent in one country (and therefore regarded as abnormal) might not be infrequent in another culture.

(c) Cultural differences can be best explained with reference to social learning theory. People learn behaviour by imitating other people. If the other person is reinforced for doing something then the observer will be more likely to imitate the behaviour. If the other person is seen as highly desirable then it will also be more likely that they will be imitated. In our culture the ideal woman is portrayed by fashion models, rock stars and TV personalities who are very slim. Therefore, young girls want to imitate this in order to be desirable. In other cultures girls are not exposed to the same models and this would explain why there is less anorexia and bulimia – though the rates are increasing, which would be reasonable as other countries are more exposed to things like Barbie dolls and the Spice Girls.

However, this cannot be the whole explanation for eating disorders because then all girls would develop the disorder because we are all exposed to these role models. The diathesis–stress model suggests that mental disorders arise first of all because an individual has a genetic predisposition for the disorder (and studies show that MZ twins are more likely to develop anorexia than DZ twins). Second because of some environmental stressor(s). Therefore, in the Western world it is only those individuals who have both the vulnerability and the stress who will then be susceptible to the effects of role models. Perhaps in other cultures, other mental disorders develop.

The social learning account of eating disorders also can't really explain why it is <u>adolescent</u> girls who are especially effected, though it could be that they are at a time of their life when their self-image is most vulnerable and their increasing self-awareness means that they want to

Sample question and student answer (continued)

be slim. On the other hand, psychodynamic theories suggest that anorexia comes from a desire to be independent and do this by controlling one's body.

The social learning explanation can explain why girls more than boys are affected because there are fewer slim role models for boys – though this too may be increasing.

TOTAL: 26 out of 30 marks

Practice examination questions

(a) Give **two** limitations of the 'statistical infrequency' definition of psychological abnormality.   [3 + 3]

(b) Outline **two** assumptions of the psychodynamic model in relation to the causes of abnormality.   [3 + 3]

(c) Outline **one** psychological model of abnormality and consider its strengths and limitations.   [18 marks]

AQA A style question

Chapter 6

Social psychology

The following topics are covered in this chapter:

- *The social approach*
- *Attitudes and prejudice*
- *Social influence: Conformity and minority influence*

- *Social influence: Obedience to authority*
- *Critical issue: Ethical issues in psychological research*

6.1 The social approach

After studying this topic you should be able to:

- *describe the key assumptions of the social approach in psychology*
- *evaluate the social approach in terms of its advantages and limitations*
- *discuss some of the methods used by the social approach*

LEARNING SUMMARY

Key assumptions of the social approach

AQA A	U3
AQA B	U2
EDEXCEL	U1
OCR	U1, U2

The **social approach** is a contrast to the **physiological approach**, which focuses on internal bodily processes. The **cognitive approach** also focuses on internal processes but there is a '**social cognitive' approach** in psychology which seeks to explain the influence of others in terms of how social factors affect our thinking.

A **sub-culture** is a group of individuals living in one culture who share a distinct set of rules, morals, etc.

'Social' refers to any situation involving two or more members of the same species. The assumptions of the social approach are that:

- An individual's behaviour can be explained in terms of the way that other **conspecifics** (members of your species) affect you.
- Other **individuals** may influence you. For example, you may imitate what others do (social learning theory) or obey someone else (see 'Obedience' on p.148).
- **Groups** of people may influence you. For example, people conform to group norms (see 'Conformity' on p.141).
- **Society** (culture) in general may influence your behaviour, e.g. methods of child rearing tend to be cultural or sub-cultural.

Social psychology is distinct from **sociology**, which is less concerned with the individual as a separate entity and more with the structure and functioning of reference groups such as the family and social classes.

Evaluation of the social approach

Weaknesses of this approach

- There is always a danger in relying on **one kind of explanation alone**. Social explanations, like all others in psychology, are unlikely to be the whole story. In a sense 'social' is equivalent to 'nurture', and we always need to consider the 'nature' (biological/physiological) explanations as well.
- In addition, the social approach **overemphasises the group** at the expense of individual psychology. For example, **social constructionists** aim to explain behaviour in the way that groups of people construct reality. The shared meanings held by groups influence behaviour. This approach overlooks the individual's role by focusing on group/cultural influences.

Strengths of this approach

- The social approach is a **major contribution** to psychology in that it involves the human element of the environment. There are social explanations within many other approaches, e.g. developmental social psychology.

Methods used in the social approach

Field experiments

Social psychology utilises field experiments to make conditions more naturalistic. The key feature of a field experiment is that participants do not know they are taking part in an experiment. There is still control of the IV, but extraneous variables are not as closely controlled. An example of a field experiment in social psychology (Piliavin *et al.*, 1969) is in the OCR core study on p.133.

Evaluation

The advantages and disadvantages of field experiments are discussed on p.161. It is important to recognise that such experiments overcome the problem of the psychology experiment as a social situation: issues such as **participant reactivity**, **demand characteristics** and **evaluation apprehension** are all social behaviours inherent in laboratory experiments.

Participant reactivity, demand characteristics and **evaluation apprehension** all concern the active involvement of the participant in research. They are discussed on p.171.

Surveys

Surveys (interviews and questionnaires) are also discussed later in this book (see p.161–163). Social psychologists often investigate people's attitudes and use attitude scales, a kind of survey (see p.132–133).

Evaluation

In brief, they enable large amounts of data to be collected but suffer from problems such as **social desirability bias** (the tendency to provide answers that make the interviewee appear nicer or better).

Discourse analysis

This methodology is related to social constructionism. The aim is to analyse discourses, i.e. the things people say or write (including music). Through such an analysis we can identify shared meanings and the things that influence behaviour. For example, one might analyse the lines of a popular song such as a lyric from a Beatles record of the 1960s to discover what the lyrics tell us about youth culture of that period.

Evaluation

This methodology is a contrast to the traditional experimental approach in psychology which aims to be objective. Discourse analysis recognises that objectivity is never actually obtainable and that intense scrutiny made of each discourse produces data that is as biased (or unbiased) as any other form of research.

Progress check

1 What is the main assumption of the social approach?
2 Suggest one drawback to the social approach.

2 E.g. the tendency to overlook biological or individual factors.

1 That behaviour can be explained in terms of the influence of two or more conspecifics (members of the same species).

6.2 Attitudes and prejudice

After studying this topic you should be able to:

- outline the structure and function of attitudes, and the links between attitudes and behaviour
- describe and evaluate research into attitude change and persuasion
- explain the concept of stereotypes and the different kinds of prejudice that exist
- describe and evaluate research into the causes of prejudice and discrimination

Attitudes

AQA B — U2

The word 'attitudes', refers to relatively permanent feelings and can be used to explain why people behave in certain ways.

Structure and function of attitudes

The structural approach

> If we put all three components together we have a definition for attitudes: 'A liking or disliking of an object based on cognitions about the object that leads to a readiness to behave in a certain way.'

Attitudes have three components:

- **affective** – the extent to which you like or dislike a thing
- the readiness to **behave** in a certain way
- beliefs (**cognitions**) about the thing.

The functional approach

Attitudes serve the following four functions.

- **Adaptive** – Attitudes help us to avoid unpleasant things and seek out favourable ones, e.g. feeling wary of dangerous sports might enhance your survival.
- **Knowledge** – Attitudes are part of our knowledge about the social world, and an integral part of stereotypes that help us simplify our social perceptions. (We look at stereotypes in a later section of this chapter.)
- **Self-expressive** – Attitudes are a means of expressing our emotions, we use them to show like or dislike.
- **Ego-defensive** (see 'The psychodynamic model on p.116) – Attitudes protect the ego by: (1) promoting a positive self-image through positive self-attitudes. For example, as a woman I make myself feel better by feeling good about women generally. (2) projecting feelings of threat or conflict onto others, (as in the case of prejudice).

Measuring attitudes

The Likert scale (Likert, 1932)

Probably the most widely used method, this involves, typically, about 30 statements being prepared on a topic, representing both pro- and anti- views. The respondent then rates each statement on a 5-point or 7-point scale.

A score is calculated by reversing the numerical value for anti-statements, and then adding the values up.

Semantic differential technique (Osgood *et al.*, 1957)

It is possible to measure the affective component of an attitude using bipolar adjectives. Respondents are asked to rate an attitude object, such as a person, thing or word.

This means that an attitude can be evaluated on a number of different dimensions, whereas the Likert scale only represents one dimension of an attitude (agreement or disagreement).

Projective techniques

Respondents are shown a picture and asked to give their interpretation. Their attitudes are projected on the picture and revealed in their descriptions.

- **The Rorschach test:** Respondents are asked to describe a set of standardised ink blots. Their responses are interpreted in terms of, for example, whether they have used the whole plot in their response, whether they have included unusual detail or whether they describe something animate or inanimate.
- **The Thematic Apperception test:** A series of pictures are presented and respondents are asked to make them into a story. The individual's story reflects their attitudes because the pictures are vague and open to all sorts of subjective interpretation.

Progress check

1 Name the three components of an attitude.
2 Which method of measuring attitude change represents one dimension only?

2 The Likert scale.
1 Affect, behaviour, cognition.

Attitudes and behaviour

Allport (1935) said 'Without guiding attitudes the individual is confused and baffled' – in other words, attitudes serve to organise behaviour. However, there is evidence that behaviour cannot be so simply predicted from attitudes.

Empirical studies

- LaPiere (1934) produced evidence that attitudes and behaviour are not consistent. He travelled around the USA for two years with a Chinese couple and noted that only once were they refused service by hoteliers. However, 92% of the same hoteliers claimed in response to a postal questionnaire that they did not serve Chinese. Critics have suggested that the fact that LaPiere was white and the Chinese couple were 'Americanised' may have affected the hoteliers' reactions.
- DeFleur and Westie (1958) asked white students to be photographed with black colleagues. Thirty per cent of the students behaved differently from their previously expressed views (either they were prejudiced and agreed to be photographed or were unprejudiced but refused to be photographed).
- On the other hand, Bagozzi (1981) questioned people about their attitudes, intentions and behaviour with respect to donating blood. He later checked to see which of his participants did actually give blood and found that, as expected, attitudes did affect intentions and ultimately behaviour.

So, what factors might lead to a discrepancy between attitudes and behaviour?

Availability

At any time your behaviour is a selection between possible courses of actions, and one attitude may take precedence over another. For example, a person may favour nuclear power but object to a nuclear power station being cited within view of their house.

Relevance

Our image of a prejudiced group may be different from the reality. In LaPiere's study, the Chinese couple spoke and dressed like Americans and were with an American, therefore they may not have been perceived as Chinese. Fishbein and Ajzen (1975) call this **correspondence**, the degree to which an attitude and action focus on identical objects in the same context at the same time.

OCR core study: Subway samaritan

Piliavin *et al.* (1969) Good Samaritanism: An underground phenomenon?

Aims In 1964, a young woman, Kitty Genovese, was murdered on her way home despite the fact that there were 38 witnesses. Why did no one help? It might be because there was a **diffusion of responsibility**. No one helps because everyone thinks someone else will do it. Latané and Darley (1968) conducted a laboratory experiment and found that as group size increased, helping behaviour decreased. This is called the **bystander effect**. Piliavin *et al.* wondered whether behaviour would be the same in a more naturalistic setting.

Procedures This was a field experiment: nearly 4,500 male and female passengers on a New York subway were observed on weekdays between 11 a.m. and 3 p.m. On average there were 43 people in a compartment on any one trial. Each trial lasted $7\frac{1}{2}$ minutes. On each trial, a team of 4 students boarded the train separately. Two females acted as observers, one male was a confederate and the other acted as a victim. There were four different teams, with a Black 'victim' in one of the teams.

> This study used an **opportunity sample** – a sample which is representative of a particular group of people. Can we make generalisations about all people from this data?

There were two experimental conditions used to test the hypothesis that 'People who are responsible for their own plight receive less help'.

- *'Drunk' condition:* The victim smells of alcohol and carries a bottle wrapped in a brown paper bag.
- *Cane condition:* The victim appears sober and carries a cane.

Seventy seconds after the train pulls out of the station, the male victim staggers and collapses. If no help is offered the confederate steps in to help after 70 seconds. The observers recorded how long it took for help to be forthcoming, as well as information about race and gender.

Findings The cane victim received spontaneous help 95% of the time whereas the drunk victim was spontaneously helped 50% of the time.

The cane victim was helped on average within 5 seconds whereas the drunk victim was helped after 109 seconds.

Black victims received less help less quickly, especially in the drunk condition.

The more passengers who were in the immediate vicinity of the victim, the more likely help was to be given. This is the reverse of the 'diffusion of responsibility' effect.

In terms of gender, 80% of the first helpers were males.

Conclusions Piliavin *et al.* proposed a **arousal-cost-reward model** to explain why people sometimes help, despite the presence of other bystanders.

- An emergency situation creates a sense of arousal in a bystander.
- The arousal can be reduced by helping (directly or indirectly).
- Help will not be forthcoming if the costs are too great, e.g. effort, embarrassment, disgusting experience, possible physical harm.

In the subway situation the **costs of not helping** (perceived censure from others) meant that people did help, whereas in the Kitty Genovese case the bystanders couldn't see each other and, in this case, the costs were too high and therefore help was not forthcoming.

OCR Revision question a) The subway Samaritan study was a field study. Describe **one** advantage and **one** disadvantage of conducting field studies and relate them to this study. [4] (January 2002, Core Studies 1, question 7)

Situation

If our personal attitudes run contrary to prevalent social norms we may well follow the crowd. Minard (1952) studied prejudiced whites in a West Virginian mining town. In a general survey only 20% admitted to having black friends. However, down the mines, where black and white worked together, 80% expressed friendship towards blacks. This can also be taken as an example of relevance.

Personality variables

Some people may be more or less consistent than others. Snyder (1979) found that low self-monitors behaved in consistent ways while high self-monitors are more influenced by the situation, and behaved in ways appropriate to the situation rather than their attitudes.

A 'self-monitor' is someone who is very conscious of his or her behaviour.

Theory of reasoned action (Ajzen and Fishbein, 1975)

This model was developed in relation to attitudes towards health behaviour and subsequent behaviour, but applies generally. An individual's behaviour (or rather their 'intention' to behave in a particular way) is determined by:

* perceived facts or beliefs about the behaviour, i.e. a person's attitude regarding the behaviour
* social or subjective norms that modify personal beliefs.

For example, smoking behaviour might be determined by 'smoking causes cancer' (a belief about the outcome) and 'my parents smoke' (a social norm) leading to 'I won't be so foolish' (an intention) which finally results in refusing a cigarette.

Evaluation

This model assumes that people behave rationally, whereas this is not always true.

Attitude change

Attitudes are resistant to change, but they do change. Methods of attitude change are of interest commercially (e.g. advertising) and in implementing new social policies (e.g. encouraging parents to have their baby vaccinated against whooping cough).

So, when and how do attitudes change?

Cognitive dissonance (Festinger, 1957)

Dissonance is 'a negative drive state which occurs whenever an individual holds two cognitions (ideas, beliefs, attitudes) which are psychologically inconsistent'. Dissonance leads to attitude change in order to restore a state of balance. Situations leading to dissonance include the following.

* Forced-compliance or counter-attitudinal behaviour – The classic cognitive dissonance experiment, conducted by Festinger and Carlsmith (1959), involved students performing a very boring task (turning pegs in a board). They were then asked to tell another participant who was waiting to do the task that the task was very interesting. Some of the participants were paid $20 others $1. When finally asked to rate the task, the more highly paid participants rated the task as boring whereas the low paid said it was enjoyable. The high paid have a reason for lying so they experience no dissonance, whereas the low paid have to overcome their dissonance by adjusting their assessment of the task.
* Post-decisional dissonance – These are the feelings of unease that arise after a person has made a decision. Such dissonance is reduced by enhancing the attractiveness of the elected choice. Brehm (1956) asked women to rate various household items in terms of their preferability, and then gave them one of their top two. When the women were asked to rate the items again, the rating for the one they now owned went up and the other went down.

Evaluation

- Dissonance produces novel and counter-intuitive predictions, and a great deal of interesting research.
- However, dissonance can't be measured, and it is difficult to identify the existence of a psychological state of tension as suggested by dissonance.
- The empirical findings can be explained in terms other than dissonance, e.g. Bem's (1972), self-perception theory. According to this theory, we acquire our attitudes by observing our behaviour in certain situations and thus we may also change our attitudes because we observe a change in behaviour. Attitude change occurs as a result of self-attributions not dissonance.

Persuasive communication

Persuasive communications aim to induce a person to adopt a particular set of values. Hovland *et al.* (1953) identified four basic variables called the 'Yale model'.

- **Source (who)** – e.g. power, expertise, credibility, motives, similarity, likeability and other personal attributes such as race and religion.
- **Message (what)** – Rhetorical questions, such as 'Isn't it clear that Daz is better than powder B?' are more persuasive. Where threats are made such as, 'smoking can kill', this may arouse a defensive response unless the viewer is given an effective means of avoiding the consequences. On the other hand, techniques using shock tactics, as in some of the drink-drive advertisements, have been successful.
- **Receiver (to whom)** – The more intelligent receiver is better able to remember the message, but also more likely to be more confident about already held attitudes and therefore more resistant to change. Sherif and Hovland's (1961) proposed a 'latitude of acceptance or rejection': where the view presented differs too much from the listener's initial stance, it is unlikely to be successful.
- **Context (where)** – whether the message is written, visual, spoken, audio-visual or face-to-face. It appears that more complex messages are best when written.

Evaluation

- Some of the original findings may be oversimplifications.
- Explains when and how people may change their attitudes but not *why*.
- People have a considerable ability to resist persuasion. One element in this is reactance: attempts to restrict or control personal decisions may lead to a move in the opposite direction.

Dual-process model of persuasion

Moscovici (1980) used the ideas of majority and minority conformity (described on p.146) to explain when attitude change is likely to occur. Moscovici claims that the two processes (majority and minority influence) are different in that:

- **Majority influence** is likely to result in a public change of behaviour but no private realignment as a result of normative and/or informational influences. This is because majority views are accepted passively.
- **Minority influence** produces conversion, i.e. a change of private opinion. This is because deviant ideas produce cognitive conflict and a structuring of thought. In a sense, obedience is a form of minority influence (see p.148)

Progress check

1 What is cognitive dissonance?
2 What two processes underlie the dual-process model?

2 Minority and majority influence.
1 The state of disequilibrium experienced when two conflicting attitudes are held.

Prejudice and discrimination

AQA B	U2
EDEXCEL	U1
OCR	U1, U2

The study of attitudes and prejudice comes within the area of **social cognition**, a branch of social psychology that joins cognitive psychology (how people think) with social psychology (the study of the interactions between people).

Clearly, this section on prejudice is related to the previous one on attitudes because prejudice is an attitude.

What is your stereotype of a bus driver? Do most people have similar stereotypes of a bus driver? How might you explain this?

A **prejudice** is a **biased attitude** towards others based mainly on group membership. Prejudice is literally the act of pre-judgement, an attitude held prior to direct experience about a group of people.

Discrimination is the behaviour arising from a prejudice, i.e. the manifestation of prejudice. Discrimination literally means to 'distinguish between', and prejudice leads you to distinguish between groups of people and favour one or the other group.

Stereotypes

Prejudices are often based on stereotypes. A stereotype is a social perception of an individual in terms of group membership or physical attributes rather than actual personal attributes. A stereotype is a fixed and often simplistic view of a group of people. Stereotypes are a kind of **schema**, organised packets of information.

Why do we have stereotypes?

They are an example of human cognitive processes: categorising, making generalisations and generating expectations.

How do stereotypes develop?

- **Social representations** – we learn them indirectly through exposure to cultural stereotypes in the media.
- **Conditioning** – we learn them directly through classical conditioning. Staats and Staats (1958) told participants to learn word pairs: a nationality name paired with another word. In one group, Dutch was always paired with a favourable word, and Swedish with an unfavourable word. This was reversed with the other group. When participants were asked to rate national groups this was correlated with the learned pairings.

Evaluation of stereotypes

- Their advantage is that they summarise large amounts of information and provide an **instant picture** from meagre data. We are 'cognitive misers' and stereotypes allow us to conserve cognitive energy.
- Their disadvantage is that they are, at least partly, **inaccurate** because they do not allow for exceptions and are based on superficial characteristics. They tend to be irrational, resistant to change and to lead to prejudice and discrimination.

Causes of prejudice

There are many explanations of how prejudice develops. We will consider three here.

Social identity theory (SIT)

A person's self-image has two components: personal identity and social identity. Social identity is determined by the various social groups to which you belong, such as your football club or your gender. There are three causal processes involved in the determination of social identity:

- Categorisation: we group people into social categories, which leads to the formation of in- and outgroups. This categorisation process simplifies interpersonal perception.
- Social comparison: comparisons are made between groups in order to increase **self-esteem**. **Ingroup favouritism** and **outgroup negative bias**

enhance social and personal esteem, and lead to biased perceptions of in- and outgroup members. Tajfel (1982) demonstrated this in his study of the minimal group (see OCR core study on p.139).

- **Social beliefs:** our beliefs/attitudes generate different social behaviours.

Empirical support

SIT generates various predictions that can be tested.

- **Illusion of outgroup homogeneity:** members of an outgroup are perceived as less diverse than members of the ingroup, thus confirming existing stereotypes. Linville *et al.* (1989) asked elderly people and college students to rate their own group and the other group in terms of traits such as friendliness. Both tended to perceive the ingroup as more differentiated (e.g. there were both friendly and unfriendly group members) and the outgroup as more homogeneous (all group members were much the same).
- **Reaction of group members to threat:** SIT would predict that individuals would enhance the perceived group differences as a means of coping with threat in order to maintain a positive social identity. Breakwell (1978) compared adolescent football fans who were classed as being fanatics or not. Those who were not fanatics might feel threatened when quizzed about being a fan because they might feel they weren't very good fans and therefore would be more likely to respond by emphasising their support – which was what the study found.

Evaluation of SIT

- It offers a **good explanation** of why members of an ingroup favour themselves over an outgroup, and that this might lead to prejudice.
- It generates a number of **testable propositions**.
- It can account for prejudice in situations of **minimal information**.
- It doesn't fully explain the **violence** associated with some prejudices.

Realistic conflict theory

Prejudice stems from direct competition between social groups over scarce and valued resources, such as unequal distribution of wealth, unemployment or disputes over territory. In- and outgroup attitudes are turned into hostility because the outgroup becomes the scapegoat for economic problems.

Empirical evidence

- **Robbers Cave Experiment** (Sherif *et al.*, 1961) is the classic study of how prejudice forms through the effects of in- and outgroup behaviour. Twenty-two White, well-adjusted, 11-year-old boys were selected to go on a summer camp for three weeks.
  - In Stage 1 the ingroup was developed. The boys were divided into two groups, they were given lots of co-operative activities and a sense of group identity (a name, hats and t-shirts).
  - In Stage 2 the groups became aware of each other and a tournament was organised (competition). There was aggression and fights after every match.
  - In Stage 3 the researchers resolved the conflict through co-operative activity involving superordinate goals, such as repairing a failed water supply.

  Three factors led to the prejudiced behaviour: ethnocentrism (in- and outgroups), competition and stereotypes.
- However, a similar study by Tyerman and Spencer (1983) observing an annual scout camp with conditions fairly similar to the Sherif study, concluded that the presence of competition did not lead to intergroup conflict and hostility.
- Hovland and Sears (1940) found a negative correlation between the number of lynchings (mainly Blacks) in the southern USA in the years 1882 to 1930 and the economic indices of the time. High aggression (measured by lynchings)

towards Blacks may be one consequence of prejudice. The economic index is an indication of frustration: when the price of cotton is low there will be fewer jobs and greater hardship.

Evaluation

- Prejudice is likely to exist prior to conflict, but **conflict is the trigger** to hostile behaviour.
- The theory **can be applied** to reducing prejudice by creating superordinate goals. Aronson *et al.* (1978) developed the jigsaw method to foster mutual interdependence. Schoolchildren worked in groups where each member had a piece of work to prepare and teach to other group members for an end-of-project test. This lead to moderate attitude change.

The authoritarian personality

An authoritarian parenting style is one which relies on having a clear social hierarchy and expects obedience to those in authority.

Adorno *et al.* (1950) proposed that some individuals may be more prejudiced, conformist and obedient personalities. This hypothesis grew out of a desire to understand the anti-Semitism of the 1930s, believing that such prejudiced behaviour might be explained in terms of having an authoritarian upbringing and cognitive style. In order to test this, Adorno *et al.* developed a set of scales for testing authoritarianism, such as the potentiality for Fascism (F) scale. They tested about 2,000 White, middle-class Americans, finding that the authoritarian personality has the following characteristics:

- **Positive self-concept** of themselves, and of their parents.
- **A cognitive style** that tended to be rigid.
- **Values** that favoured law and order, and were more concerned with status, success, and traditional customs.
- **A personal style** that avoided psychological interpretations and tended to repress feelings.
- **An experience of child rearing** in which their parents tended to give conditional love, used strict discipline, expected unquestioning loyalty and were insensitive to the child's needs. Such experiences would create an insecure adult who respects authority and power, conforms more readily to group norms, and who may increase their self-esteem through ingroup favouritism (social identity). A person with repressed feelings will project these onto scapegoats (realistic conflict).

Evaluation

- This accounts for both the existence of **prejudices and the hostility element** which is often present in people who are highly prejudiced.
- There were a number of criticisms of the **data collected**, e.g. that the sample was biased, and some data was retrospective.
- There were also criticisms of the **questionnaires**, e.g. there may have been a response set on the F-scale (agreement leads to authoritarian-type answers), and authoritarianism of the left was overlooked.
- The study was **correlational** so we cannot say that parenting style *caused* the prejudiced personality.

Categories of prejudice

Racial prejudice

Moghaddam *et al.* (1994) note that some apparent racism may be in part explained by self-attitudes. They found that Haitians living in Canada overestimated the extent that they were outsiders and may expect to be rejected, and this led to a self-fulfilling prophecy.

Gender prejudice

Condry and Condry (1976) showed films of a baby, labelled alternatively as a boy or girl, and asked participants to rate emotional responses. They found that assumed gender led to different interpretations of the same behaviour. Fidell (1970) sent personnel profiles about a man or woman (e.g. Patrick or Patricia Clavel) to over 200 psychology professors – people who might have been expected to know better. The professors were asked to rate the applicants in terms of potential job prospects. They rated the man more highly. Mischel (1974) used the essay-assessment technique to show how gender affected rating of academic abilities, again favouring men (John was better than Joan) but only if the essay was on masculine topics such as law or city planning; women did better on essays related to dietetics or primary education.

Age prejudice

People hold negative stereotypes of the young, the old, the middle-aged – in fact, about all age groups. Such stereotypes may be held by people of all ages, including peers.

Progress check

1 What is 'ingroup favouritism'?
2 Which explanation of prejudice can account for the hostility sometimes associated with prejudice?

2 Realistic conflict theory or authoritarian personality.
1 The perception of your own social group as being more desirable/capable/successful.

OCR core study: Ethnocentrism

Tajfel (1970) Experiments in intergroup discrimination

Aims Is it possible to create discrimination (ingroup favouritism and outgroup negative bias) even where no prejudice exists? This would demonstrate social identity theory.

Experiment 1

Procedures A laboratory experiment with eight groups of boys, aged 14 to 15, from a school in Bristol.

1 **Establishing the ingroup:** The boys were told that the purpose of the experiment was to investigate visual judgements. They were shown slides of dots and for each slide asked to estimate the number of dots. They were then told whether they were over- or under-estimators (arbitrarily).

2 **The matrix game:** Each boy went to another room on their own, and was given a booklet containing 18 pages. On each page there was a matrix such as the one in the table below. Each boy had to tick one column in the matrix. For example, in the matrix below, the arrow indicates a choice of the column holding the numbers 4 and –9 (so member 74 would gain 4 points and member 36 would lose 9 points). This column choice would then determine the number of points awarded to members named on the left of the matrix (in our example, members 74 and 36). At the end each boy would receive their total number of points in real money.

					↓								
Member no. 74 overestimator	12	10	8	6	4	2	0	–1	–5	–9	–13	–17	–21	–25
Member no. 36 underestimator	–25	–21	–17	–13	–9	–5	–1	0	2	4	6	8	10	12

Matrix used in Tajfel study (1970)

OCR core study *(continued)*

Findings When the matrix involved making an *inter*group choice, the boys tended to give more money to members of their own group.

When the boys had an entirely ingroup (or outgroup) choice to make, they tended towards the point of maximum fairness (this would be 0 and −1 in the example above).

Conclusions Boys awarded points on the basis of ingroup favouritism alone.

Experiment 2

Participants 48 boys in three groups of 16.

Procedures This time the groups were ostensibly divided on the basis of aesthetic preference (liking for art) of paintings by Paul Klee and Wassily Kandinsky. Different matrices were used in this second experiment because this time Tajfel did not want to look at the effect of relative weight in pulling decisions one way or the other. Instead, he wanted to assess three things:

- **Maximum joint profit (MJP):** the largest possible award for 2 people
- **Maximum ingroup profit (MIP):** largest possible award to ingroup member
- **Maximum difference (MD):** largest possible difference in gain between a member of ingroup and a member of outgroup, in favour of the former.

An example of one of these matrices is shown in the table below.

Member no. 74 of Klee group	19	18	17	16	15	14	13	12	11	10	9	8	7
Member no. 36 of Kandinsky group	1	3	5	7	9	11	13	15	17	19	21	23	25

In this case, if the participant was a member of the Klee group:
- *MJP would be a choice of 7 and 25*
- *MIP would be 19 and 1*
- *MD would be 19 and 1 (favouring the Klee group).*

Findings MJP exerted hardly any effect at all. In other words, boys did not make their choices on the basis of trying to give both parties their best joint deal.

MIP and MD exerted a strong effect. Participants always tried to give their ingroup members the best deal at the cost of the outgroup member.

In a situation where the choice was between two outgroup members, participants' choices were not as near the MJP as when choosing between two ingroup members. Participants were simply less fair with outgroup members.

Conclusions The experiments demonstrated the ease with which outgroup discrimination could be triggered, based on only minimal social identity.

Criticisms However, the participants were all adolescent boys (a biased group), they knew each other well, and there was not a great deal at stake.

OCR Revision question
a) From the study by Tajfel on discrimination, what are the key features of ethnocentrism? [2]

b) According to Tajfel, what are the minimum conditions for creating ethnocentrism? [2] (1999 Paper 1, question 10)

6.3 Social influence: Conformity and minority influence

After studying this topic you should be able to:

- *describe and evaluate research studies of conformity*
- *critically consider the problems associated with research into conformity*
- *explain why people conform to majority influence*
- *explain when and why people conform to minority influence*

Research into conformity

AQA A ▶ U3
AQA B ▶ U2

True independence is following one's conscience rather than being non-conformist. For example, Galileo's resistance to ideas of his time was healthy non-conformity (independence) whereas going round a roundabout in an anticlockwise direction is foolish.

Apparent non-conformity occurs when an individual is apparently not conforming to group norms but is, in fact, conforming to a different set of group norms. For example, wearing 'punk' clothes is conforming to another set of norms.

Definitions

Key Term Social influence is the effect that other people have on each other. Psychologists study how these influences affect our behaviour and thoughts.

Key Term Conformity (majority influence) is a change in behaviour as a result of real or imagined group pressure or norms. Kelman (1958) suggested that there are three kinds of conformity:

- **Compliance** – conforming with the majority, in spite of not really agreeing with them; public but not private change of opinions.
- **Identification** – conforming to the demands of a given role because of identification with that role, as in the behaviour of a traffic warden and in Zimbardo's prison study (see Haney *et al.* OCR core study on p.143). This kind of conformity generally extends over several aspects of behaviour. There still may be no change to personal opinion.
- **Internalisation** – personal opinion does change because the new norms are internalised.

Norms are the rules established by a group to regulate the behaviour of its members.

Empirical studies

Informational social influence

In many situations, especially social ones, there is no 'right' answer and therefore we look to others for **information**. This may change private opinion because the individual now regards the majority opinion as the correct answer.

Allport (1924) and Jenness (1932) found that people behaved differently in groups than when they were working alone. Participants shifted their individual judgements (about the pleasantness of odours or number of beans in a bottle respectively) towards group means after having group discussions.

Sherif (1936) used the autokinetic effect (a point of light moves erratically when viewed in total darkness) to demonstrate group influence. He showed the light to individuals and asked them to estimate how far and in which direction it moved. After about 100 trials the individuals had reached a consistent level of judgements. Sherif then asked groups of participants to work together. They were not asked to arrive at a group estimate but nevertheless, after a few exposures, the judgements of the group tended to converge and persisted when the individuals were tested later. The group performance had created a socially determined standard or norm. This convergence towards a norm is useful in ambiguous situations. It helps us know how to behave (i.e. **informational social influence**).

One psychologist asked a group of his students to try the following: go up to a stranger on an underground train and ask for their seat, offering no excuse. They all said they couldn't do it, which reveals the enormous inhibitory anxiety that ordinarily prevents us from breaching social norms (Tavris, 1974).

Normative social influence

People also conform because they want to be liked by the other members of the group, and also want to avoid being rejected. This may have played a part in Sherif's study. Normative influence is not likely to change private opinion. It may occur in various situations:

- In an **unambiguous** situation: see Asch's study, in the key study below.
- When conforming to **social roles**: see Haney *et al.*'s core study on p.143.
- Under **anonymous conditions** (public opinion not expressed). Crutchfield (1955) used a more efficient method than Asch, testing 600 participants using the **Crutchfield apparatus** (a cubicle with switches and lights). Participants are given a question, they can see the selection made by other (non-existent) participants, and are asked to register their own choice. When the question was clear-cut, 30% conformed. If the question was an insoluble mathematical one (therefore ambiguous), conformity was 80%. If the question asked for agreement or disagreement with a statement of opinion, 58% conformed. This demonstrates both informational and normative conformity.

Progress check

1 Define conformity.
2 What kind of conformity results in a change of personal opinion?.

1 Change in behaviour as a result of real or imagined group pressure or norms.
2 Identification.

AQA (A) Key study: Conformity (majority influence)

Asch (1952) Opinions and social pressure

Aims   Asch suggested that Sherif's results were due to the fact that the stimulus was ambiguous. What would happen if there was no ambiguity? Would people still conform to majority opinion even if the answer required of them was clearly wrong? What would be the effect of social pressure?

Procedures   This was a laboratory experiment that involved deception. The participants were 123 male college students, each paid $3. They were asked to take part in a study of visual perception. They were tested in groups of 7–9 participants. Each group was shown 2 pieces of card. One had a 'standard' line on it, the other had 3 lines of varying length. Each member of the group was asked to say out loud which line they thought was the same length as the standard.

In fact, all the members of the group except one were confederates. The true participant was the last but one to answer. On each trial the answer was clear. On the third trial, and several later ones, the confederates unanimously gave the wrong answer. There were 12 trials in all, half of which were 'critical' (the confederates gave wrong answers).

Participants were shown the line on the left and asked to state which of the three lines on the right was the same length.

 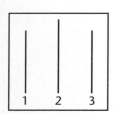

Findings   Approximately 75% of the participants conformed at least once, 5% conformed all of the time, 24% never conformed. The average rate was 37%.

Participants were interviewed afterwards and gave one of three reasons for why they did conform: (1) **distortion of perception** – they really did think their wrong answers were right, (2) **distortion of judgment** – they felt doubt about the accuracy of their judgment and therefore yielded to the majority view, (3) **distortion of action** – they didn't want to be ridiculed and therefore went along with the majority.

Conclusions This was astonishing evidence that some people are extremely willing to conform with group norms even when the answer is clearly wrong. However, it should be remembered that on two-thirds of the trials the participants remained independent, which is also clear evidence that people resist the pressure to conform at least in situations of certainty.

Criticisms This was a highly artificial situation. The consequences of complying were not harmful and the pressure to comply was great. In some real-life situations this would not be true. Venkatesan (1966) found that in some situations reactance is displayed – a reaction against a group norm (see page 146). In this study, groups of students were asked to select one of three identical suits. The true participant (last to register an opinion) conformed to majority opinion except when most of the confederates made statements strongly favouring one suit. When individuals feel forced to conform they may react by asserting their independence.

The participants' behaviour was due to normative social influence which is strong in a group of strangers, where the need to establish social contact is greater than the need to be correct. The same might not be true for established groups, though there may be other pressures to conform. However, Williams and Sogon (1984) found that conformity was even higher when they tested participants who all belonged to the same sports club.

Later variations

Asch conducted a number of subsequent variations and found the following.

- A group of three was sufficient to create the effect; larger numbers did not increase conformity.

- The presence of one dissenter cut conformity rates by 25%, even when the dissenter disagreed with the participant as well as the group. This is an example of minority influence (see below).

- Conformity increased if the group members were regarded as of high status.

- Conformity decreased if the participants were not face-to-face (see also Crutchfield, above).

OCR core study: Prison simulation

Haney, Banks and Zimbardo (1973) Stanford study of prisoners and guards

Aims Zimbardo questioned whether prison guards' behaviour was caused by the situation, or by the personality of the guards (a situational or dispositional explanation respectively).

Procedures This study involved role play and observation. A college newspaper advertisement sought male volunteers for a psychological study of 'prison life', to be paid $15 a day. There were 75 respondents who were given a series of psychological tests and interviews. The 24 most stable men were selected and randomly assigned to being a prisoner or a guard. There were 2 reserves and 1

OCR core study *(continued)*

dropped out, finally leaving 10 prisoners and 11 guards. They were all students, and largely middle-class.

The 'prisoners' were unexpectedly 'arrested' at home. On entry to 'prison' they were put through a delousing procedure, searched, given a prison uniform with ID number, nylon stocking caps, and an ankle chain. They were told to refer to each other only by number. They were in prison 24 hours a day.

The guards only referred to the prisoners by number. The prisoners were allowed certain 'rights': three meals a day, 3 supervised toilet trips, 2 hours for reading or letter-writing, and 2 visiting periods and movies per week. They had to line up 3 times a day to be counted and tested on the prison rules.

The guards had uniforms, clubs, whistles, handcuffs and reflective sunglasses (to prevent eye contact).

Findings Both guards and prisoners took, alarmingly, to their roles. For example:

- The guards grew increasingly tyrannical. They woke prisoners in the night, locked them in a closet and got them to clean the toilet with their bare hands.
  Even when participants were unaware of being watched they played their roles – for example, prisoners talked among themselves as if they were prisoners.

Zimbardo's study is sometimes
used when discussing
obedience. The guards and
prisoners were **conforming** to
roles but the prisoners were
also **obeying** the guards.

- Five prisoners had to be released early because of extreme depression (crying, rage and acute anxiety). In fact the whole experiment was ended after 6 days, despite the intention to continue for 2 weeks.

Haney *et al.* tested the participants' personality and found no differences between the prisoners and guards. They did find that the participants who left early tended to have less conforming personalities.

Conclusions This was a remarkable demonstration of the strength of social norms and people's reluctance to 'disobey' them. Participants' behaviour was the result of normative social influence and identification rather than internalisation. It is most accurate to say that the participants complied rather than showed 'true' conformity (internalisation) since they probably did not change their personal beliefs.

The concept of
deindividuation refers to
losing one's sense of
personal identity in certain
situations, such as being in a
crowd or when wearing a
uniform or mask.

Haney *et al.* suggested that three processes can explain the prisoners final 'submission':

- *deindividuation*: the prisoners lost their sense of individuality. They even referred to themselves by number.
- *learned helplessness:* the unpredictable decisions of the guards led the prisoners to *give up responding*.

Learned helplessness is a
condition where an individual
learns to stop responding
because, in the past their
responses were ineffective.
Therefore they learn that
there is no point trying.

- *dependency*: the fact that the prisoners depended on the guards for everything emasculated the men and increased their sense of helplessness.

Criticisms *Ethics:* Participation in this study must have caused all participants emotional distress. One defence of this is that the extremes of behaviour could not have been anticipated at the outset.

Artificiality: It is possible that participants took on very specific role behaviours because that is what they were asked to do (**demand characteristic**). In real life a person might adapt a role to suit their personal beliefs and the requirements of the situation.

OCR Revision question In the prison simulation study by Haney, Banks and Zimbardo, features of the procedure led to the prisoners becoming dependent on the guards.

a) Identify **two** behaviours for which the prisoners were dependent on the guards. [2]

b) Describe **one** psychological effect this dependency had on the prisoners. [2]
(January 2001, Core Studies 2, question 3)

Evaluation of research into conformity

Experimental artefacts

This refers to features of the experiment which are artificial, for example:

- **Demand characteristics.** Participants behave in certain ways because features of the experiment 'demand' a typical response.
- **Desire to please the experimenter.** In Crutchfield's (1955) conformity experiment many participants said afterwards that they hadn't wanted to spoil the results so they had gone along with the others.
- **Experiments are social situations.** In Asch's (1955) study the participants expressed how much of an outsider they felt by dissenting. Belonging to the group is more important than correctness.

Ecological validity

To what extent do the results generalise to other situations and real life?

- **In real life** people sometimes have the option to simply do nothing, which may not be possible in an experiment.
- All of the experiments involved **strangers.** We may behave differently with individuals or groups who know us and we know them.

Child of the times

Social norms are always changing.

- Perrin and Spencer (1980) replicated Asch's study using British students but did not obtain evidence of conformity – concluding that today people may have learned to be more self-reliant.
- Doms and Avermaet (1981) did reproduce the same results as Asch and suggest that Perrin and Spencer's use of science and engineering students could have biased their results. It is also possible that Asch's findings became generally known (i.e. people have become aware of the tendency to be over-conformist in certain situations) and this new general knowledge has influenced the behaviour of participants in the more recent studies.

Ethical issues

These are discussed in the next topic section on p.154.

Why do people yield to majority influence?

The term 'majority' refers to the greater number. Norms can be determined by a majority or a minority. Minority influence is considered later.

Informational social influence

People like to be right and assume that if most people share a particular view, it must be right. The majority are assumed to supply correct information. Informational social influence operates especially in situations of ambiguity and may lead to internalisation.

Normative social influence

People want to be accepted by social groups and therefore seek to conform to the norms for that group. Normative social influence operates most when with groups of strangers and is likely to lead to compliance rather than internalization.

Individual differences

Some people are more likely to be conformist. There is evidence that women tend to be more conformist – for example, Eagly and Carli (1981) claim that women are more easily influenced than men but Eagly (1978) suggests that women may be more oriented towards interpersonal goals and thus *appear* more conformist.

1 What is 'majority' influence?
2 Name two factors which might increase your willingness to conform to a majority opinion.

2 E.g. to be liked by others, because you are uncertain of the right answer.

1 When more than half of the people in a group share an opinion and this influences other individuals.

Minority influence

AQA A   U3
AQA B   U2

Key Term **Minority influence** occurs when a minority of people within a group hold an opinion different to the majority. Through the use of consistent yet flexible arguments a minority may change the views of the majority.

Moscovici (1980) claims that the two processes of majority and minority influence are different.

- **Majority influence** is likely to result in a public change of behaviour but no private realignment.
- **Minority influence** produces conversion, i.e. a change of private opinion. This is because deviant ideas produce cognitive conflict and a structuring of thought. Innovation of ideas must occur through minority influence and therefore this may be the more important kind of social influence.

Empirical studies

Moscovici *et al.* (1969) demonstrated minority influence in a classic study described on p. 147. This showed that consistency was important and that private rather than public opinion was more likely to change.

Flexibility is also important. Nemeth and Brilmayer (1987) arranged for a group to role play a jury considering the amount of damages to be awarded for a ski accident. When a lone minority refused to change his position, he had no effect on the opinion of others whereas a person who was prepared to shift in the direction of the majority exerted more influence.

Situational factors have also been found to be important. Moscovici and Nemeth (1974) found that a person who expresses a minority opinion is more likely to be influential if seated at the head of the table.

Why do people yield to minority influence?

1 Consistency

The minority must be consistent in their opposition to majority opinion.

2 Flexibility

The minority must not appear to be rigid and dogmatic. If they show some flexibility they will be more effective.

3 Conversion rather than compliance

A committed minority will lead people to rethink their position. Majority influence involves the reverse: compliance but not conversion.

In fact, minority influence is probably of more importance than majority influence in terms of social change.

4 Relevance

The minority will be more successful if their views are in line with social trends (called the '*zeitgeist*').

AQA A Key study: Minority influence

Moscovici *et al.* (1969) Calling a blue slide green

Aims Research has tended to focus on the importance of majority influence yet such influence doesn't actually explain how change in opinion (innovation) comes about. Majority influence maintains the status quo, yet opinions and social trends do change. To what extent do people respond to minority influence?

Procedures This was a laboratory experiment involving deception. There were 32 groups of 6 people with good eyesight. Females were preferred because of their 'greater involvement in evaluating the colour of an object'. Two members of each group were confederates. Each group was shown 36 blue-coloured slides. They were told that the experiment was about colour perception and that they would be asked to report the colour aloud.

- Experiment 1: Two confederates in the group (the minority) consistently said that the slides were green. The confederates either answered first and second, or first and fourth.
- Experiment 2: A further 10 groups followed the same procedure as in experiment 1 and then afterwards were asked to do a similar task individually, writing down their answers. Moscovici *et al.* proposed that some individuals might conform to the majority publicly but privately might show a change of opinion.
- Experiment 3: The confederates answered 'green' 24 times and 'blue' 12 times, i.e. they were not consistent.
- Control group: In each experiment there were also control groups with no confederates.

Why is it necessary to have a control group?

Findings The participants agreed with the minority view on 8.42% of the trials (i.e. they said the slides were coloured green). 32% agreed at least once (which, of course, means that 68% never agreed). There was no significant difference in relation to the position of the confederates. In groups where very few members gave the response 'green' in public, there was a greater number of 'green' judgements privately. When the confederates were inconsistent, agreement was reduced to 1.25%.

Compare the rate of conformity in this experiment with Asch's study. In which study did participants show greater conformity?

Conclusions This shows that minorities can influence majority opinion. Consistent minority opinion had a greater effect than inconsistent opinion. The minority influence was stronger on private opinion than publicly expressed opinion, which is the reverse of majority influence.

Criticisms Moscovici claimed that consistency was sufficient for minority influence but that may not be so. Nemeth *et al.* (1974) replicated the above study but varied consistency by changing the confederates' responses on different trials. In other words, they didn't always say 'green' – on some trials they said 'green' and on others they said 'green-blue'. The minority had no influence at all under these conditions whereas when the confederates said 'green' to every slide there was 21% conformity.

This again was an artificial task and thus lacks ecological validity. The findings may not apply to real-life settings where there may be many other factors at work.

Progress check

1 What is a 'demand characteristic'?
2 Name one factor which can explain minority influence.

2 E.g. consistency, or flexibility.
1 A feature of the experimental situation which invites participants to behave in a particular way.

6.4 Social influence: Obedience to authority

After studying this topic you should be able to:

- *describe and evaluate research studies of obedience to authority, including Milgram's work*
- *discuss issues of ethics and validity in the context of obedience research*
- *explain the psychological processes involved in obedience*
- *explain why people may resist obedience (independent behaviour)*

LEARNING SUMMARY

Research into obedience to authority

AQA A	U3
AQA B	U2
EDEXCEL	U1
OCR	U1, U2

> Conformity and obedience both involve changing behaviour in response to social influence. Conformity is a response to group pressure (whether majority or minority). Obedience is to a single individual or law.

Obedience

Key Term **Obedience** to authority is behaving as instructed but not necessarily changing your opinions. Usually it is in response to individual rather than group pressure, though you might obey group norms. Obedience happens when you are told to do something, whereas conformity is affected by example.

Research studies

Milgram's laboratory research

Milgram's first study (1963, see OCR core study on p.150) showed surprisingly high levels of obedience: 65% obeyed every order even when it threatened the life of the 'victim'. Milgram (and others) conducted a number of subsequent variations, each of which inform us about the conditions under which obedience is likely to take place.

- **Proximity of 'learner':** If the 'teacher' was placed in the same room as the 'learner' and had to press the learner's hand on the shock plate, obedience fell to 30%.
- **Proximity of experimenter:** When instructions were given over the phone the 'teacher' often said they were giving the shocks when they weren't. Overall, 21% of 'teachers' continued to obey.
- **Perceived authority:** When the experiment was conducted in a run-down building rather than a prestigious university setting, obedience fell to 47.5%.
- **Individual differences:** The experiment was repeated with over 1,000 participants from all walks of life. It was found that educated participants were less obedient, and military participants were more obedient.
- **Social support:** If the 'teacher' was paired with two other 'teachers' who dissented, then only 10% of the real participants continued to 450 volts.
- **Deindividuation:** Zimbardo (1969) arranged for the learner to be introduced to the participant and to wear a name tag, or to wear a lab coat and hood. The latter condition led to more electric shocks.
- **Cultural differences:** Milgram (1961) repeated his research with French and Norwegian participants and found differences. Smith and Bond (1993) report a number of cross-cultural replications with different rates of obedience, for example 85% in Germany and 40% for male Australians. It is likely that such studies did not exactly replicate Milgram's study.
- **Gender differences:** Milgram found that female participants were equally obedient but Kilham and Mann (1974) found much lower conformity rates in Australian women (12% compared to males at 40%).

> People often express surprise at the unexpected results of these studies because people appear to be much more obedient than we expect. This is the result that is often overlooked: the surprise is that we are surprised by human behaviour! This is the value of psychological research compared with reasoned argument – we may produce counter-intuitive findings.

Field studies

- **Nurses:** Hofling *et al.* (1966) conducted a more real-life experiment where nurses were told to administer a drug to a patient. The instruction they received was contrary to their rules: nurses were not permitted to accept instructions over the telephone, nor from an unknown doctor, nor for a dose in excess of the safe amount. Nevertheless, 21 out of 22 nurses obeyed the order (95%). Nurses defended themselves by saying it often happens, a doctor would be annoyed if they refused. However, their behaviour might be interpreted as conforming to expected role behaviour rather than being obedient.

- **Obedience to a uniform:** Bickman (1974) arranged for experimenters to be dressed casually, or in a milkman's uniform, or a guard's uniform which made them look like a police officer and to issue orders to order New York pedestrians (e.g. 'Pick up this bag for me', 'This fellow is overparked at the meter but doesn't have any change. Give him a dime'). Participants were most likely to obey the experimenter dressed as a guard, which supports the finding that obedience can be related to the amount of perceived authority.

Role play

Meeus and Raajmakers (1995) told participants that they were investigating how interviewers handle stress. The participants were the interviewers and were given statements that aimed to humiliate the interviewees (confederates) such as 'This job is too difficult for you'. The confederates were instructed to appear progressively more distressed, finally pleading for the interview to stop and refusing to answer any more questions. Nevertheless, twenty-two out of the total of twenty-four participants delivered all 15 'stress remarks'.

Evaluation of obedience research

Milgram's study has been criticised because it lacked internal and external validity, and ignored ethical considerations.

Experimental validity

Key Term Experimental validity is the extent to which the experimental set-up is believable. Experimental validity includes both internal and external validity. 'Internal' refers to what goes on inside the experiment and 'external' refers to what goes on outside the experiment. If experimental validity is low then the findings of a study are meaningless.

Internal validity

- Orne and Holland (1968) claimed Milgram's participants must have been aware that **something didn't add up**. Why wasn't the experimenter giving the shocks himself? However, in a replication of Milgram's experiment by Rosenhan (1969), nearly 70% of participants reported that they believed the whole arrangement – i.e. that this was a genuine learning experiment.
- Orne and Holland also suggested that obedience was a **demand characteristic** of Milgram's experiment. Participants obeyed because they entered into a social contract, and also because obedience is a natural feature of the experimenter–participant role.
- **Mundane or experimental realism.** The artificiality of an experiment means that it lacks mundane realism (it doesn't seem real). However, this can be overcome if it has experimental realism, i.e. the experiment is so engaging that participants are fooled into thinking the arrangement is real rather than artificial. Milgram argued that his study had both. Obedience to authority is the same whether the setting is artificial or occurring more naturally outside the laboratory, therefore the experimental design does have mundane realism. The experiment must have been highly engaging in order for the participants to behave in the way that they did, therefore there is also experimental realism.

A demand characteristic is a feature of an experiment that invites participants to behave in certain, predictable ways. Participants are susceptible to such cues because they want to know how they are expected to behave.

External validity

Any aspect of a study which means we cannot generalise from the study to other settings, or other people, or to other periods of history threatens the usefulness or validity of the findings.

Key Term Ecological validity is the extent to which the experimental findings can be generalised to real life and other settings. Milgram's study has been said to lack ecological validity because it was conducted in a laboratory environment which lacks realism. However, the findings have been replicated in many other settings, which is not true of the study by Hofling et al. This latter study may apply only to the particular doctor–nurse relationship and thus lacks ecological validity whereas Milgram's study may apply to obedience relationships much more generally, and thus is higher in ecological validity.

Population validity is the extent to which experimental findings can be generalised to other people. Milgram's study lacked population validity because it concerned US men.

Ethical considerations

These are discussed in full in the next topic section on p.154. Using role play is an alternative to conducting an experiment. However, even though participants are playing a role, as in Meeus and Raajmaker's study (see above) and Zimbardo's study (see p.143–144), this did not overcome problems of deception or distress because participants experienced both. It is also difficult to know whether individuals don't actually *exaggerate* their behaviour in such situations and therefore the study would be low in ecological validity.

> Some people feel that field studies such as Hofling et al. have greater ecological validity than Milgram. However, this study only shows that *nurses* are obedient to *doctors* not that people in general are obedient to authority. In addition, attempts to replicate Hofling et al.'s study have not been successful (e.g. Rank and Jacobsen, 1977) and this suggests that the results cannot be generalised.

Progress check

1 Name one researcher who has investigated obedience, besides Milgram.
2 What is internal validity?

2 The extent to which an experimental arrangement/design is believable.

1 E.g. Hofling *et al.*, Zimbardo, Langer *et al.*

OCR core study and AQA (A) Key study: Obedience to authority

Milgram (1963) Behavioural study of obedience

Aims Obedience is generally reasonable except when it is to unjust authority. Will people inflict great harm simply because they are ordered to do so? History provides much evidence to suggest that they will, most infamously the behaviour of some Germans in response to their Nazi leaders. Would ordinary Americans behave in the same way, or are Germans different?

Procedures This was a controlled observation. Forty males, aged between 20 and 50, whose jobs ranged from unskilled to professional. They were all volunteers, recruited through newspaper advertisements or flyers through the post. When they arrived for the supposed memory experiment they were paid $4.50 at the onset and introduced to another participant, who was in fact a confederate of the experimenter. They drew lots for their roles, though the confederate always ended up as the 'learner' while the true participant was the 'teacher'. There was also an 'experimenter' dressed in a lab coat, played by an actor.

The 'learner' was strapped in a chair in another room and wired with electrodes. After he has learned his list of word pairs given him to learn, the 'teacher' tests

> This experiment is one of the most well known in psychology, probably for two reasons: first of all because of the 'shocking' findings and, second, because of the subsequent ethical objections to it.

him by naming a word and asking the 'learner' to recall its partner from a choice of four possible answers. The 'teacher' was told to administer an electric shock every time the 'learner' made a mistake, increasing the level of shock each time. There were 30 switches on the shock generator marked from 15 volts (slight shock) to 450 volts (danger – severe shock).

The learner gave mainly wrong answers and for each of these the teacher gave him an electric shock which was received in silence until they got to shock level 300. At this point the learner pounded on the wall and then gave no response to the next question. When the 'teacher' turned to the experimenter for guidance, he was given the standard instruction, 'an absence of response should be treated as a wrong answer'. After the 315-volt shock the learner pounded on the wall again but after that there was no further response from the learner – no answers and no pounding on the wall. If the teacher felt unsure about continuing, the experimenter used a sequence of 4 standard 'prods', which were repeated if necessary:

- Prod 1: Please continue.
- Prod 2: The experiment requires that you continue.
- Prod 3: It is absolutely essential that you continue.
- Prod 4: You have no other choice, you must go on.

If the teacher asked whether the learner might suffer permanent physical injury, the experimenter said: "Although the shocks may be painful, there is no permanent tissue damage, so please go on."

If the teacher said that the learner clearly wanted to stop, the experimenter said: "Whether the learner likes it or not, you must go on until he has learned all the word pairs correctly. So please go on."

> It is questionable as to whether this study is an experiment. Can you identify an independent and dependent variable? An independent variable is one manipulated by the experimenter in order to observe its effect on some dependent variable.

Findings No one stopped below the level of intense shock. 22.5% stopped at 315 volts (extremely intense shock). 65% of the 'teachers' continued to the highest level of 450 volts.

Prior to the experiment Milgram asked 14 psychology students to predict the naïve participants' behaviour. The students estimated that no more than 3% of the participants would continue to 450 volts.

> Would you have obeyed? The survey prior to the experiment suggests that people think participants wouldn't obey, yet, in reality, people do.

The participants showed signs of extreme tension: most of them were seen to 'sweat, tremble, stutter, bite their lips, groan and dig their finger-nails into their hands'. Three even had 'full-blown uncontrollable seizures'.

All participants were debriefed, and assured that their behaviour was entirely normal. They were also sent a follow-up questionnaire. 84% reported that they felt glad to have participated, and 74% felt they had learned something of personal importance.

Conclusions Participants showed obedience to unjust authority beyond what anyone expected. The sheer strength of obedience and the tension created by the social pressure to obey were surprising.

Criticisms Milgram suggested various reasons why obedience was so high, such as the prestigious environment (Yale University), and that the participant believed the experimenter is earnest in pursuit of knowledge and therefore obedience is important. In short, features of the experimental set up enhanced the tendency to obey (demand characteristics).

Later variations Further experimental variations (Milgram conducted 21 in all) and a full evaluation of the study are reported in the text. (See p. 148)

OCR Revision question In this study of obedience, Milgram encouraged the participants to continue with the electric shocks.

a) Outline **one** way in which Milgram encouraged his participants to continue. [2]

b) Describe **one** way in which the findings of the Milgram study can be applied to social control in everyday life. [2] (January 2002 Core Studies 2, question 2)

Why do people obey?

AQA A	U3
AQA B	U2
EDEXCEL	U1
OCR	U1, U2

Obedience to authority does depend on what you are being asked to do. It is obedience to *unjust* authority which especially needs to be explained. In many situations obedience and conformity are healthy and appropriate responses.

Situational explanations

A socially obedient environment

In some environments it is the norm to obey authority, whereas in others it is not. Individuals have past experience of being rewarded for obedience, so we obey because that is what we have learned to do. There are roles that require obedience, such as being a nurse or being an experimental participant.

Graduated commitment

A person may be unaware of obedience before it's too late. In Milgram's study the shocks increased by only 15 volts each time, what does one more step matter? Having obeyed initially, to a small request, **binding factors** ensure continued obedience.

The agentic state

Milgram (1974) proposed that the participant becomes an 'agent' of the person in authority. When an individual is in an agentic state they cease to act according to their own conscience and lack a sense of responsibility for their actions. The opposite is true of an **autonomous state**.

Uncertainty

In some situations, such as the psychology experiment or many occasions in real life, we are not sure how to behave and therefore we respond to social cues (**demand characteristics**).

Dispositional explanations

The authoritarian personality

Adorno *et al.* (1950) proposed that some individuals are more likely to be obedient (and conformist) because of the way they were brought up – see p.138.

Need for social approval

Crowne and Marlowe (1964) used the Marlowe-Crowne Social Desirability Scale and found that those low in need for social approval were less likely to conform in an Asch-type experiment.

Resistance to obedience

AQA A U3

There are some situations and individuals who do not obey. In Milgram's study 35% disobeyed. What factors explain independent behaviour?

Empirical studies

Gamson *et al.* (1982) showed that individuals will rebel against authority when there is the possibility of collective action. In this study, volunteers were placed in groups of 9 and each group asked to listen to evidence against Mr C. The participants were ostensibly employed by a (fictitious) public relations firm, MHRC, which was collecting evidence of community opinions to use against Mr C. The groups soon realised that they were being manipulated to produce a tape of false evidence. All of the groups rebelled (stopped producing evidence) but some still signed an affidavit giving MHRC permission to use the video tape in a trial. This shows that, when sufficient numbers take a rebellious stance, the whole group conforms to this. However, in some groups the majority of people did not have anti-authoritarian values. Therefore, despite the fact that some members had expressed rebellion, the whole group signed the affidavit.

Venkatesan (1966) found that in some situations reactance is displayed – a reaction against a group norm. In this study, groups of students were asked to select one of three identical suits. The true participant (last to register an opinion) conformed to majority opinion except when most of the confederates made statements strongly favouring one suit. When individuals feel forced to conform they may react by asserting their independence.

Why do people resist obedience?

The same reasons that can be used to explain obedience can be used to explain resistance – for example, the presence of an authority figure leads to obedience and the lack of sufficient authority leads to resistance. Other explanations include the following.

Rebellion

As in Gamson *et al.*'s study, (p.152) groups may feel more able to resist unjust authority because group members know there is a possibility of collective action.

Increasing one's sense of autonomy (reversing the agentic shift)

Individuals can be reminded that they (not the authority figure) are responsible for their actions. Hamilton (1978) found that under these conditions, agentic shift was reversed and sharp decreases in obedience could be obtained.

Past experience

One of Milgram's participants, Gretchen Brandt, rebelled because she said she had witnessed the ill-effects of obedience growing up in Nazi Germany. Milgram (1974) suggested that the painful memories had taken her out of her agentic state.

Individual differences

Krech *et al.* (1962) suggested that independent people tend also to exhibit the following traits: to be more intelligent, less anxious, have more realistic self-perception, be more self-contained and more original. Crowne and Marlowe (1964) found they had less need for social approval. Burger and Cooper (1979) found that non-conformers had a higher desire for personal control. Stang (1972) found that high self-esteem was related to independence.

Progress check

1   What is the 'agentic' state?
2   Suggest one personality characteristic associated with independent behaviour.

2 E.g. high self-esteem, high desire for personal control.
1 When an individual ceases to act according to their own conscience.

6.5 Critical issue: Ethical issues in psychological research

LEARNING SUMMARY

After studying this topic you should be able to:

- *explain the concepts of deception, informed consent, and the protection of participants from psychological harm*
- *apply these considerations to social psychological research*
- *outline and discuss the ethical guidelines produced by the British Psychological Society*
- *assess the use of ethical guidelines by psychologists*

Ethical issues

AQA A	U3
AQA B	U1
EDEXCEL	U3
OCR	U1, U2, U3

Key Term Ethical issues are dilemmas that arise in psychological research where there are a conflicting set of values concerning the goals, procedures or outcomes of a research study. Examples include deception, lack of informed consent and protection from psychological harm.

Deception

Key Term Deception is dishonesty. Participants should never be deliberately misled without extremely strong scientific or medical justification. It is reasonable to expect to be fully informed when you agree to take part in psychological research. However:

Deception is sometimes relatively harmless

This is the case in some memory experiments, e.g. Mandler (see p.37) did not inform participants that their memory would be tested. Christiansen (1988) reported that participants don't object to deception as long as it isn't extreme.

Deception is sometimes necessary

In the conformity and obedience experiments, knowledge about the purpose of the research would have made the studies pointless.

On occasion deception can be justified

For example, when there are no alternative, deception-free ways of studying an issue.

Debriefing is vital

How would you feel if you had been a participant in Asch's or Milgram's research? Would you feel aggrieved about the deception?

After the study participants should be informed about the deception, and have the opportunity to withdraw their data. In field experiments (such as Bickman's p.149) this is not always possible. Both Milgram and Asch thoroughly debriefed their participants. Milgram's participants reported that they did not regret taking part but Freudian theory might explain this as an ego defence (dealing with anxiety through denial).

Informed consent

Key Term Informed consent should be given wherever possible. Participants should consent to take part and this should be based on having all the information necessary in order to decide whether or not to take part, i.e. being informed about the nature and purpose of the research and their role in it.

Participants can only give informed consent when they know:

- All aspects of the research that might reasonably be expected to influence their willingness to participate.

- Their rights, e.g. to confidentiality, to leave the study, and to withhold their data.

Such consent is not possible when:

- Deception is involved.
- Participants are unable to fully understand, such as is the case with children or participants who have impairments that limit understanding. An alternative is to seek informed consent of, for example, a parent.
- In field experiments or observational studies, when participants are not even aware that they are taking part in a psychological research.

Possible alternatives are:

- Presumptive consent – seeking approval from the general public prior to an experiment, as Milgram did. If others approve, then it is presumed the actual participants would also have agreed.
- Prior general consent – seeking general approval from participants. Gamson *et al.* (see p.152) asked all prospective participants if they would be willing to take part in research on any of the following:
  - brand recognition of commercial products
  - product safety
  - research where you will be misled about the purpose until afterwards
  - research involving group standards.
  When participants agreed to all four they were then informed that only the latter kind of study was in progress. They had agreed to be deceived.
- Role play or questionnaires – participants are asked to behave as if they were in a certain situation (role play) or to state how they would behave in certain situations (questionnaires). However, this is likely to be unreliable. Consider the findings from Milgram's prior survey (people *said* they wouldn't obey).

Compensatory procedures

- The right to withdraw – Milgram did tell participants that they could leave at any time and not forfeit their money. However, in reality, they were ordered to continue by the standardised 'prods'.
- The right to withhold data – during debriefing, participants can decide to withhold their data – in essence asserting their right to informed consent to have participated.

Psychological harm

Key Term Protection of participants from psychological harm includes protecting participants from loss of self-esteem, ridicule, stress and anxiety. The risks should be no greater than in ordinary life.

- Baumrind (1964) criticised Milgram for the stress and emotional conflict experienced by participants. Milgram defended himself by saying that he expected very low levels of obedience; before the experiment he had asked psychiatrists, students and ordinary people how participants would behave. They thought that at most only 3% of the participants might go as far as 450 volts.
- Asch's participants also experienced distress. Evidence for this was obtained by Bogdonoff *et al.* (1961), who found that the participants in an Asch-type study had greatly increased levels of autonomic arousal.

Risks no greater than in ordinary life

This means that participants should not be exposed to risks greater than or additional to those encountered in their normal life styles. A classic study by Watson and Raynor (1920) involved making a loud and unpleasant noise near an infant's head and thus creating a fear response. They argued that the baby (Little Albert) was not exposed to anything more than an ordinary experience. However, Genie's mother (see p.72) objected to the extensive testing her daughter was subjected to, saying that it caused her undue distress.

Aronson (1988) argued that there might have been no ethical objections to Milgram's research if the findings had been less distasteful. In other words, it was the findings rather than the methods which were distasteful.

Progress check

1 When is deception acceptable?
2 What is presumptive consent?

1 When there are no alternative, deception-free ways of studying an issue.
2 Seeking approval from the general public prior to an experiment.

The use of ethical guidelines

AQA A	U3
AQA B	U1
EDEXCEL	U3
OCR	U1, U2, U3

Key Term Ethical guidelines are a set of rules produced by a group of professionals to 'police' themselves and deal with ethical issues. The British Psychological Society (BPS) has a set of ethical guidelines for human and non-human animal research, as well as for clinical practice. The same is true in other countries (e.g. the American Psychological Association). There are also Home Office regulations for the use of non-human animals in research.

The BPS guidelines for research with human participants

This is a summary of the main points.

Introduction

Ethical guidelines are necessary in order to clarify the conditions under which psychological research is acceptable. In all their work psychologists shall conduct themselves in a manner that does not bring psychology into disrepute.

General

The investigation should be considered from the standpoint of all participants. The best judge of whether an investigation will cause offence may be members of the population from which the participants in the research are to be drawn.

Consent

Participants should be informed of the objectives of the investigation and all other aspects of the research which might reasonably be expected to influence their willingness to participate. Special care needs to be taken with children or with participants who have impairments.

Deception

Intentional deception of the participants over the purpose and general nature of the investigation should be avoided wherever possible.

Debriefing

The investigator should provide the participants with any necessary information to complete their understanding of the nature of the research and should discuss their experience in order to monitor any unforeseen negative effects or misconceptions.

Withdrawal from the investigation

Participants should be aware from the outset of their right to withdraw from the research at any time. Participants also have the right to withdraw any consent retrospectively, and to require that their own data be destroyed.

Confidentiality

Subject to the requirements of legislation, information obtained about a participant during an investigation is confidential unless otherwise agreed in advance.

Protection of participants

Investigators have a primary responsibility to protect participants from physical and mental harm, no greater than in ordinary life.

Observational research

Studies based upon observation must respect the privacy and psychological well-being of the individuals studied. Unless those being observed give their consent to being observed, observational research is only acceptable in situations where those observed would expect to be observed by strangers.

Giving advice

During research, an investigator may obtain evidence of psychological or physical problems. An appropriate source of professional help advised.

Colleagues

A psychologist who believes that another psychologist may be infringing ethical guidelines should encourage the investigator to re-evaluate the research.

An evaluation of the use of ethical guidelines

How effective and useful are such guidelines?

Infringements

The severest penalty is disbarment from one's professional organisation.

Universal ethical truths

Ethical guidelines suggest some universal 'truths' yet the guidelines vary in different countries and with respect to changing social attitudes. For example, the French code concentrates on fundamental rights rather than on conducting research.

The cost–benefit analysis

Inevitably, ethical decisions involve weighing costs (e.g. harm to participants, infringement of rights, financial considerations) against benefits (e.g. what the research can tell us about behaviour). Diener and Crandall (1978) have identified the following problems with this.

- It is difficult to predict costs and benefits prior to conducting a study: In Milgram's study there was no expectation that participants would continue, and therefore the potential stress (costs) was not anticipated. Also, the ultimate findings (benefits) were not anticipated.
- It is hard to quantify costs and benefits, even after a study, because such judgements inevitably require subjective judgements (what one person regards as harm differs from another's view).
- Cost–benefit analyses tend to ignore the rights of individuals in favour of practical considerations because one is focusing on issues of, for example, benefits to human kind.
- Baumrind (1975) pointed out that cost–benefit analyses inevitably lead to moral dilemmas, yet the function of ethical guidelines is precisely to avoid such dilemmas.

Sample question and student answer

AQA A style question

(a) Outline **two** reasons why people yield to majority influence. [3 + 3]

(b) Describe the procedures and findings of **one** study that has investigated minority influence. [18]

(c) Outline ethical issues in obedience research and consider whether they have been dealt with effectively. [18]

A brief but accurate answer; the candidate has provided sufficient detail by using the technical language to gain 2+2 marks.

(a) People yield to majority influence because they want to be right. This is called informational social influence. The second reason is that they conform because they want to be liked and fit in. This is called normative social influence.

Many candidates make the mistake of simply writing everything they know about a study rather than focusing on the requirements of the question. In this case the candidate has provided accurate information about the procedures, though it could be more detailed. There is a minimal amount of information about findings (though there is no requirement for procedures and findings to be in balance). The final sentence is irrelevant. This answer would get 4 marks.

(b) Moscovici asked people to describe what colour they thought a picture was. Six people took part and two of them were confederates. The two confederates always described the slides as green whereas they were actually blue. This minority of two affected the responses of the others. 32% conformed at least once. This is less than in Asch's experiment but it is a lot considering they were clearly wrong.

The candidate has structured this response nicely by identifying ethical issues and, at least sometimes, showing where these occurred in obedience research (the paragraph on informed consent is rather minimal). However, the first paragraph is largely a waste of time because they are no links to ethical issues except the last sentence which is little more than a list. This is followed by a number of good points made about deception and whether it was dealt with effectively in the context of three studies. Some further commentary is offered on harm. The final 'issue' is actually a guideline rather than an issue. However, this still leaves three creditworthy issues. Altogether a reasonable though slightly limited response (AO2=9 marks). The description of ethical issues is somewhat lacking in detail (AO1=4 marks)

(c) Milgram found that 65% of his original participants were willing to administer the highest level of shocks to the 'learner'. For all the participants knew, they could have killed the person they were giving shocks to. In Milgram's film, one of them clearly said he thought he'd killed them. The ethical objections to this research include the issues of deception, informed consent, harm, and the right to withdraw.

The participants were deceived because they were not told the true purpose of the research. However, there would be no point conducting the study if they did know the true purpose. The ethical guidelines say that deception is acceptable if there is no alternative. Other studies of obedience have also had to use deception such as Hofling et al. and Bickman. Therefore it would seem inevitable that deception is used in this study.

One way to compensate for deception is to debrief participants afterwards so they do know the true aims of the experiment and they have an opportunity to withhold their data if they want to. Debriefing also provides an opportunity for the researcher to find out if the participant was harmed and to offer any extra support. Milgram did all of this after his experiment. However, in a field study such as Bickman's this was not possible.

One difficulty with this debriefing is that participants may feel even worse when they discover they have been cheated, and upset that they fell for the deception.

The second ethical issue is informed consent. If an experiment involves deception obviously participants can't give their informed consent because they do not know what is actually involved.

In terms of psychological harm, all obedience research involves high levels of anxiety and stress for participants. Just having to decide whether to obey, even though someone else is suffering, imposes great stress on a participant. Just debriefing someone afterwards doesn't remove the stress that they felt. They might say that they feel OK but they may be denying their true feelings. They may feel quite depressed about the way that they behaved. It is true that most of Milgram's participants said that they were glad to have participated and had learned something valuable.

The final ethical issue is the right to withdraw. Milgram told participants that they were free to go, yet the standardised prods made it very difficult for them to leave. In the field experiments such as Hofling's or Bickman's, participants were not aware of this right and couldn't exercise it anyway.

TOTAL: 21 out of 30 marks

Practice examination questions

1

(a) Outline **two** psychological processes that might be involved in obedience. [3 + 3]

(b) Describe how psychologists have dealt with **two** ethical issues that have been evident in social influence research. [3 + 3]

(c) Consider whether findings from studies of conformity can be applied beyond the research setting. [18]

AQA A style question

2

(a) Psychologists often refer to attitudes as containing three components. Identify **all three** of these components. [3]

(b) Using an example, explain what is meant by a *stereotype*. [3]

(c) A psychologist is interested in measuring attitudes towards genetically modified foods. He has decided to use a Likert Scale. Describe how he would do this. [4]

(d) The main purpose of measuring people's attitudes is to allow their future behaviour to be predicted. Discuss whether knowing a person's attitude allows for accurate prediction of their behaviour. Refer to relevant theory and evidence in your answer. [10]

AQA B specimen paper

3

A 'theory' counts as any set of interrelated facts which in some way account for the behaviour. When you describe a theory you can draw on material about its implications.

In this question the theory in parts (b) and (c) need not be the same one. Be sure to describe both a strength and a weakness.

(a) Define what is meant by the term obedience. [2]

(b) (i) Name **one** theory of obedience. [1]

(ii) Describe this theory of obedience. [4]

(c) Evaluate **one** theory of obedience in terms of one of its strengths and one of its weaknesses. [4]

Edexcel specimen paper

Chapter 7

Research

The following topics are covered in this chapter:

- *Quantitative and qualitative research methods*
- *Research design and implementation*
- *Data analysis*

7.1 Quantitative and qualitative research methods

After studying this topic you should be able to:

- *distinguish between quantitative and qualitative methods of research*
- *give examples of and evaluate quantitative methods of research*
- *give examples of and evaluate qualitative methods of research*
- *outline the ethical issues involved in these research methods*

Quantitative research methods

AQA A	U3
AQA B	U1
EDEXCEL	U3
OCR	U3

The term 'research' means the process of gaining knowledge either through the use of theories (to explain a behaviour) or empirical data collection. In this chapter we will look at the methods of **empirical data collection**. ('Empirical' means something which is based on observed facts, i.e. data that is collected through direct observation.)

In **quantitative** research, the information obtained from the participants is expressed in numerical form. It is concerned with how much there is of something – i.e. the quantity.

In **qualitative** research the emphasis is on the stated experiences of the participants and on the stated meanings they attach to the data. It is concerned with how things are expressed, what a behaviour feels like and what it means – i.e. the quality.

Experiments

In an experiment the relationship between two things is investigated by deliberately producing a change in the **independent variable (IV)** and recording what effect this has on the **dependent variable (DV)**. The main features of experiments are:

- **Causal relationships** between the independent and dependent variables can be demonstrated.
- **Greater control** – features of the experimental environment can be controlled by the researcher.
- **Replication** – the study can be repeated because all variables have been identified and operationalised.

The terms quantitative and qualitative actually refer to the data collected, not the research method. Quantitative data is concerned with 'how much' whereas qualitative data provides non-numerical information ('what something is like').

The laboratory experiment

Advantages

- This is the **ideal form** of the experiment because there is the possibility of good control of all variables, especially extraneous ones.
- **Replication** is good. The IV is the variable that is manipulated by the experiment and the DV is the one that is measured.

Disadvantages

- In reality, **total control is never possible**. The results may be affected by, for example: extraneous variables, experimenter bias, demand characteristics, volunteer bias, sample bias.
- The laboratory experiment is an **artificial situation**, therefore the results may not generalise to real life (it lacks **ecological/external validity**).

Ethical considerations

- **Informed consent** isn't always possible.
- Participants may not truly be able to exercise their **right to withdraw**.
- Participants should not be subjected to **stressful** or negative manipulations.

The field experiment

This is an experiment conducted in more natural surroundings, where the participants are unaware that they are participating in a psychology experiment. The independent variable (IV) is still manipulated.

Advantages

- Greater **ecological validity** (in general).
- The technique **avoids experimenter bias** and evaluation apprehension because the participants are unaware that they are part of an experiment.

Disadvantages

- Inevitably, extraneous variables are **harder to control**.
- Some **design problems** remain, such as sample bias.
- It is **more time-consuming** and expensive than laboratory experiments.

Ethical considerations

- It is not possible to gain **informed consent** or usually to give **debriefing**.
- Participants may be **distressed** by the experience (especially because they are not aware that it is 'make believe').

The natural experiment

If conditions vary naturally, the effects of an independent variable (IV) can be observed without any intervention by the experimenter. The research is still an experiment in the sense that a cause and effect are being identified, but it is not a 'true' experiment because:

- **the IV is not directly manipulated**; this means that one cannot be certain that the IV is the *cause* of any observed effect
- **participants are not randomly allocated to conditions**; therefore participants in different conditions may not be comparable.

Advantages

- It is the **only way to study cause and effect in certain situations** – for example, where there are practical and/or ethical objections to manipulating the variables (such as looking at the effects of deprivation).
- There is greater **ecological validity** (in general).
- If the participants are unaware of being studied, the technique **avoids experimenter bias**.

Disadvantages

- It cannot confidently establish **cause and effect** because so many other factors may influence the dependent variable (DV).
- A **lack of control** reduces internal validity. There may also be a lack of a suitable control group.
- It is not easy to **replicate** such studies, and may not even be possible.
- It can **only be used when conditions vary naturally**. Such conditions are not always possible to find.
- **Participants may be aware of being studied** and show improvements just because of this (the **Hawthorne effect** – see p.171).

Ethical considerations

- A natural experiment may involve **withholding treatment** from one group, as when a new educational programme is being tested and the research requires that one group of students do not have the new teaching method.

When comparing laboratory and field experiments you can see that each has advantages. Field experiments tend to have higher external validity whereas laboratory experiments have higher internal validity because of the greater control.

Natural experiments are sometimes called 'quasi-experiments' because they are not genuine experiments – which is what 'quasi' means (not quite the real thing).

- If participants are unaware they are taking part, there is the issue of **informed consent**.
- **Researchers need to be sensitive** to the problems of participants in unfavourable circumstances that may surround the behaviour being studied, as in the case of deprived children.

1 Name one difference between a laboratory and field experiment.
2 Name one difference between a laboratory and a natural experiment.

2 E.g. in a laboratory study the IV is directly manipulated by the experimenter.

1 E.g. field experiments involve more naturalistic surroundings, participants are not aware of being studied.

Investigations using correlational analysis

> What is the difference between an experiment and a correlational study? We study co-variables rather than an IV and DV, and cause and effect cannot be determined.

In this method a numerical value (coefficient) is calculated to represent the degree to which two sets of data are correlated. The terms IV and DV are not used because one does not depend on the other. The variables are called **co-variables**. Perfect positive correlation is +1.00, perfect negative correlation is –1.00.

Advantages

- Can be used where **experimental manipulation would be unethical** or impossible.
- Indicates **possible relationships** between co-variables, and might suggest future research ideas which would look at possible causal relationships.
- Can **rule out causal relationships** – if two variables are not correlated than one cannot cause the other.

Disadvantages

- Does not establish **cause and effect**.
- The relationship may be due to other **extraneous variables**. For example, in an experiment trying to establish a relationship between diet and IQ, the extraneous variable might be parent's IQ because intelligent parents might supply a better diet.

Ethical considerations

- Causal inferences shouldn't be made but often this **misinterpretation** of the data does happen.
- This is especially important with relation to **socially sensitive issues**, such as IQ, which tend to rely on correlational data.

Interviews and questionnaire surveys

> Interviews can produce qualitative data: in fact, **unstructured interviews** are *more* likely to produce qualitative data. So, it is difficult to categorise interviews and questionnaire surveys as being exclusively either quantitative or qualitative methods.

Interviews can be highly structured or little more than an informal 'chat'; they may be conducted face-to-face (interviews) or require written answers (questionnaires).

The structured interview

In these, all or most of the questions are decided beforehand. The questions may have a limited range of answers (e.g. 'Yes', 'No', 'Don't know').

Advantages

- Can collect information about people's **feelings and attitudes**, which cannot be obtained through observation or experiments.
- Requires **less skill** than unstructured interviews.
- Can be conducted on the **telephone**.

Disadvantages

- The interviewer's **expectations may influence** the interviewee's performance

The **halo effect** is the tendency to think that someone with one desirable characteristic also has other desirable characteristics, e.g. thinking that an attractive person is probably also nicer and more intelligent than someone who is less attractive.

Confirmatory bias refers to people's preference for things that confirm their existing stereotypes.

(halo effects, confirmatory bias, racial/sexual/ageist prejudices).

- People often don't actually know what they think and therefore their answers are **influenced by suggestion and response biases.**
- The method relies on self-report, which is open to problems such as **social desirability bias** (providing answers that make the interviewee 'look good').
- In comparison with unstructured interviews, the data collected will be **restricted** by a pre-determined set of questions.

Ethical considerations

- **Deception** may be necessary.
- Questions may concern **sensitive and personal issues.**
- **Confidentiality and privacy** must be respected.

The unstructured interview

The interviewer has a few questions, and lets the interviewee's answers guide subsequent questions. Clinical psychologists use this method with patients.

Advantages

- **Rich data** can be obtained.

Disadvantages

- It requires **well-trained interviewers,** which makes it more expensive to produce reliable interviews.
- Interviews may not be comparable because different interviewers ask different questions (**low inter-interviewer reliability**). Reliability may also be affected by the same interviewer behaving differently on different occasions.
- It is more affected by **interviewer bias.**

The questionnaire survey

Respondents record their own answers.

Advantages

- **Large amounts of data** can be collected at relatively little cost – both financial and in terms of time.

Disadvantages

- Answers may not be truthful (**social desirability bias**).
- Only **suitable for certain kinds of participants** – those who are literate and willing to spend time filling in a questionnaire, creating a biased sample.
- Designing questionnaires requires **considerable skill** (see p.169).

Progress check

1 What are the variables called in a study that uses correlational analysis?
2 What kind of interview is likely to produce the more qualitative kind of data?

2 Unstructured interview.
1 Co-variables.

Qualitative research methods

AQA A	U3
AQA B	U2
EDEXCEL	U3
OCR	U3

Observational studies

Naturalistic observation

Behaviour is observed in the natural environment. All variables are free to alter and interference is kept to a minimum. No IV is manipulated.

Advantages

- Study behaviour for the first time – observation is needed to **establish possible relationships**.
- It offers a way to study behaviour where there are **ethical objections** to manipulating variables.
- Gives a more **realistic picture** of spontaneous behaviour. It has high ecological validity.
- If the observer(s) remain undetected, the method **avoids most experimental effects**, such as experimenter bias, and evaluation apprehension.

Disadvantages

- It is not possible to infer **cause and effect**.
- It is **difficult to replicate** and therefore you cannot be certain that the result was not a 'one off'.
- It is not possible to **control** extraneous variables.
- **Observer bias**: the observer sees what he 'wants' to see.
- Where participants know they are being watched (disclosed observations) they may **behave unnaturally**. Even non-participant observers, by their mere presence, can alter a situation.

Ethical considerations

- Undisclosed observations preclude the right to **informed consent**.
- Disclosed observations may affect the individuals observed, creating **distress**.

Other kinds of observation

- **Experimental (controlled) observation**: Some observational studies are conducted in a controlled, laboratory environment. For example, Ainsworth's Strange Situation (p.62) and Milgram's 'experiment' (see p.150).
- **Participant and non-participant observation**: The observer may be a participant as well or may watch (non-participant).
- **Disclosed or undisclosed observation**: Participants may be observed through a one-way mirror (undisclosed) as in Bandura *et al.*'s study (see p.24).
- **Content analysis**: A detailed analysis of written or verbal material. Indirect observation of behaviour using, for example, books, diaries or TV programmes and counting the frequency of particular behaviours.

> Remember that observations may produce highly **quantitative** data. This is especially true for a content analysis.

Case studies

These are detailed accounts of a single individual, small group, institution or event. They might contain data about personal history, background, test results, and the text of interviews.

Advantages

- Only option when a behaviour is **rare**.
- Provide insights from an **unusual perspective** and rich data.
- Relate to real life (**high ecological validity**).

Disadvantages

- Usually involve recall of earlier history and therefore are **unreliable**.
- Close relationship between experimenter and participant introduces **bias**.
- **Cause and effect** are difficult to establish.
- Not a rigorous methodology: often unstructured and **unreplicable**.
- Limited samples, lack generalisability (**low in ecological validity**).
- **Time consuming** and expensive.

Ethical considerations

Confidentiality and **privacy** must be protected. Individuals should not be named.

7.2 Research design and implementation

After studying this topic you should be able to:

- describe and use different kinds of hypothesis formulated when planning research and describe different sampling procedures
- outline issues around the identification and control of variables in research
- discuss methods of experimental design
- identify the features of good research design

Planning research

AQA A — U3
AQA B — U3
EDEXCEL — U3
OCR — U3

When planning a research study there are various considerations to think about and these are described below.

Aims and hypotheses

> An example of a null hypothesis would be 'Any difference/relationship that is found is due to chance factors alone'.

> An example of an **alternative hypothesis** in an experiment could be 'Participants recall more words from list A than list B'. This is directional. (The DV would be recall, the IV would be differences between list A and list B.)

Research aims are the stated intentions of question(s) that are planned to be answered.

A **hypothesis** is a formal, unambiguous statement of what you believe to be true.

- The **null hypothesis** (H_0) is a statement of 'no difference' or 'no relationship' between the populations being studied.
- The **alternative hypothesis** (H_1) makes a prediction about the effect of the IV on the DV. In the case of a study using a correlational design, the alternative hypothesis makes a statement about the relationship between the co-variables.
- A **directional** (or **one-tailed**) hypothesis predicts the direction of the effect.
- A **non-directional** (or **two-tailed**) hypothesis anticipates a difference or correlation but not the direction.

Progress check

1 Is the following an example of a null or an alternative hypothesis: 'There is no relationship between variable A and variable B'?
2 Rewrite the following hypothesis so that it is non-directional: 'Younger participants do better on the test than older participants'.

2 'There is a difference in the performance of young and older participants in terms of their test performance.'

1 A null hypothesis.

Populations and sampling

The following list explains the terms used in relation to selecting samples for use in research.

- **Sample:** part of a population selected such that it is considered to be representative of the population as a whole.
- The **population** is the group of people from whom the sample is drawn. The population may be unrepresentative – e.g. selecting a sample from one school.
- **Sampling bias:** this occurs when some people have a greater or lesser chance of being selected than they should have, given their frequency in the population.

Sampling techniques (methods of drawing a sample)

- **Random sample:** Every member of the population has an equal chance of being selected, therefore it is an **unbiased sample**. This can be achieved using random number tables or numbers drawn from a hat. However, be aware that the population the sample is drawn from may be biased, e.g. if you take names from the phone book this only includes those people with telephones.

- **Systematic or quasi-random sample:** For example, using every 10th case or the name at the top of each page in the phone book. There is no bias in selection, however, every person does not stand an equal chance of being selected (therefore quasi-random).
- **Opportunity sample:** Selecting participants because they are available – for example, asking people in the street. This is sometimes mistakenly regarded as random whereas it is invariably biased.
- **Volunteer or self-selected sample:** Participants who become part of an experiment because they volunteer when asked. The results are likely to suffer from a volunteer bias because such participants are usually more highly motivated and perform better than randomly selected participants.
- **Stratified sample:** The population is divided in sections or strata in relation to factors considered relevant, for example, social class or age. The researcher then randomly selects a preset number of individuals from each strata.
- **Quota sample:** This also uses stratified methods but the sample is not randomly determined, because the researcher seeks any 5 individuals satisfying each criteria.

> Most research involves opportunity sampling. It is the easiest method in terms of both time and money.

Progress check

1 What method of sampling is unbiased?
2 What method of sampling is most commonly used?

2 Opportunity sampling.
1 Random sampling.

Research design

AQA A	U3
AQA B	U1
EDEXCEL	U3
OCR	U3

> In a study of the effects of stress on performance, some participants are given an impossible puzzle to solve, whereas others do an easy puzzle. Then all participants have to do further test (task B). In this case, the IV is the difficulty of the puzzle (task A) and the DV is the performance on the task.

Variables

Experimental variables

These are the ones that we are studying.

- The **independent variable (IV)** is the one which is specifically manipulated so that we can observe its effect on the **dependent variable (DV)**. The DV is usually the one we are measuring or assessing.
- **Operational definition** is necessary in order to make a variable measurable and unambiguous. The definition is based on a set of operations or objective components. For example, hunger might be defined in terms of the number of hours since a participant last ate or a rating scale of how hungry they feel.
- **Levels of measurement** – variables can be measured at different levels of detail. Each level expresses more information about the thing we are measuring:
  - **Nominal** – data is in discrete categories, such as grouping people according to which kind of foods they prefer (Italian, American, Indian, etc.).
  - **Ordinal** – data is ordered in some way, for example asking people to put various food products in order of liking: spaghetti could be 1st, followed by burgers, sausages and liver. The 'difference' between each item is not the same, i.e. the individual may like the 1st item a lot more than the 2nd one but there might only be a small difference between the items ranked as 2nd and 3rd.
  - **Interval** – data is measured using units of equal intervals. For example, when using a centigrade temperature scale or any 'public' unit of measurement. Many psychological studies use **plastic interval scales**

> The key issue in interval data is that the intervals are equal and not arbitrary. The intervals reflect a real difference.

(Wright, 1976) where the intervals are arbitrarily determined and therefore we can't actually know for certain that there are equal intervals between the numbers.

- **Ratio:** There is a true zero point, as in most measures of physical quantities.

Participant variables

This refers to features of the participants, such as their gender, age, social class, and education. These characteristics are important when assessing the extent to which a sample is representative, and are also used when matching participants in a matched participant design (see p.168).

Participant variables can be controlled using **random allocation** to conditions. Any bias in placing participants in experimental or control groups can be overcome by randomly determining the group they are placed in.

Situational variables

Features of the situation which may interfere with the effect of the IV on the DV and 'spoil' the research result.

- **Extraneous variable:** anything that may unintentionally affect the dependent variable. These need to be controlled (as described below).
- **Confounding variable:** an extraneous variable that has not been controlled. There are two kinds:
  - **Constant errors:** e.g. testing the effects of noise on memory, all of those tested in the noise condition are tested in the morning whereas those tested in no noise condition are tested in the afternoon. Time of day is a constant error. Better performance may be due to time of day rather than lack of noise.
  - **Random errors:** features of the experiment that occur with no pattern. They occur equally in both conditions and are assumed to cancel each other out. For example, if participants are randomly allocated to groups one would presume that any individual differences are randomly distributed and we would not find all the brightest or oldest individuals in one group.
- **Controlling extraneous variables**
  - **Standardised procedures** are used to ensure that conditions are equivalent for all participants, this includes the use of **standardised instructions.**
  - **Counterbalancing** to control **order effects**. Give half the participants condition A first, while the other half get condition B first. This prevents improvement due to e.g. practice, or poorer performance due to e.g. boredom.

Progress check

1 What is the difference between an extraneous and a confounding variable?
2 When is counterbalancing used?

2 When order effects may affect performance.
1 A confounding variable is one that confounds the findings because it acts as another IV, whereas an extraneous variable is one that was potentially confounding but has been controlled.

Experimental designs

Repeated measures design

In this design the same participant is tested before and after the experimental treatment. Therefore all participants are tested twice, for example doing a memory test with and without noise. Performance on the DV is compared to see if there was a difference before and after.

Advantages
- Good control for **participant variables**.
- Needs **fewer participants**.

Disadvantages
- **Order effects** (e.g. practice or boredom) can affect final performance.
- Participants may **guess the purpose** of the experiment after the first test.

Independent groups design

In this design comparison is made between two unrelated groups of participants. The participants are in groups. One group receives the experimental treatment, the other doesn't (control group) or receives a different experimental treatment. Performance on the DV is compared.

Advantages
- **Used where repeated measures are not possible** (because otherwise participants would realise the purpose of the experiment).
- **No order effects** and other problems of repeated measures.

Disadvantages
- **Lacks control** of participant variables.
- Needs **more participants**.

Matched participant design

In this design participant variables are controlled by matching pairs of participants on key attributes. One partner is exposed to the IV, and both are compared in terms of their performance on the DV.

Advantages
- **No order effects** or other problems of repeated measures design.
- **Participant variables** partly controlled.

Disadvantages
- Matching is **difficult**, time-consuming and may waste participants.
- Matching is **inevitably inexact**.

Design of naturalistic observations

Observational studies require methods of categorising behaviour to ensure consistency and to reduce time taken in situations where it is limited.

Methods of recording data
- **Rating system**: score each individual in terms of degree, such as amount of interest shown.
- **Coding system**: a system of symbols or abbreviations is developed as a shorthand. Tick occurrences of target behaviours. These categories may be derived from earlier research, for example **ethograms** (a record of the behavioural repertoire for a particular species).
- **Diaries**: participants and/or observers keep a diary of events, either at the time or at the end of the day.
- **Sketches or photographs**: showing who or what is where.
- **Tape or video recording**: keep record of all data for later analysis.

Sampling techniques
- **Event sampling**: a list of behaviours is drawn up and a record made every time they occur.
- **Time sampling**: observations are made at regular intervals, such as once a minute.
- **Point sampling**: observe one individual for a fixed period of time, such as five minutes, and then move on to the next individual.

Design of interviews and questionnaire surveys

Attitude scales

See p.131–132.

Structured interviews/questionnaires

- Develop research aims.
- Develop sub-topics to investigate. A 'top down' approach should be used in generating questions – start with broad questions and break each down into a number of different specific behaviours.
- Question style
  - **Avoid** complex, ambiguous, negative, emotive, and/or leading questions.
  - **Open versus closed**: Open questions can have an infinite variety of answers (e.g. 'How do you reduce stress?') and are best for obtaining maximum information. Closed questions (with a limited range of answers) are best for ease of scoring.
  - **Forced choice** questions (e.g. 'Do you smoke to reduce stress?' Yes/No) may bias the results because participants can't give their real answer. 'Don't know' categories may get overused.
  - **Filler questions**: it may help to include some irrelevant questions in order to mislead the respondent from the main purpose of the survey.
- **Sequence for the questions**: It is best to start with easy ones, saving difficult questions, or ones which raise emotional defences, until the respondent has relaxed. Also, respondents may resist answering 'yes' or 'no' too many times in a row (**response set**).
- **Write standardised instructions**, and debriefing notes.
- **Pilot run**: The questionnaire should now be tested on a small sample; use feedback to redraft the questionnaire.
- Decide on **sampling technique** (see p.165–166).

Progress check

1. Which method of experimental design avoids order effects?
2. Name one sampling technique used in observational studies.
3. What is meant by a 'closed question'?

3 One that only has a limited range of possible answers.

2 E.g. event, time, point sampling.

1 Independent measures.

Factors associated with good design

AQA A	U3
AQA B	U1
EDEXCEL	U3
OCR	U3

Pilot studies

These are smaller, preliminary studies which makes it possible to check out standardised procedures and general design before investing time and money in the major study. Any problems can be adjusted.

Reliability

Reliability is the extent to which something is consistent or stable.

Internal reliability

This is the extent to which a measure is consistent within itself. It can be checked using:

- **The split-half method:** test is randomly divided into two halves so that each half is equivalent. Internal reliability is demonstrated by participants' scores being similar on both halves.
- **Item analysis:** compare performance on each item with overall score. Good correlation suggests high internal reliability.

External reliability

This is the extent to which a measure varies from one use to another.
- **Test-retest:** the same person is tested twice over a period of time. Similar scores demonstrate high external reliability.
- **Inter-rater reliability:** the ratings from more than one person are correlated to check for agreement.
- **Replication:** any research study should produce similar findings if repeated.

Validity

Validity is the extent to which something is true.

Internal validity

This is the extent to which something measures what was intended to be measured.

- **Psychological tests:** Is the test 'true'? Does it measure what it says it measures? For example, in the case of a test of anxiety – does it actually measure anxiety? This can be assessed using, for example:
  - **Face validity:** the items look like they measure what the test says it measures, for example on a creativity test, do the items look like they are measuring creativity?
  - **Criterion validity:** do people who do well on the test do well on other things that you would expect to be associated. For example, does someone who does well on an intelligence test also do well at school?
- **Research studies:** Internal or **experimental validity** is the extent to which the experimental procedure is believable (see p.149). It is the extent to which all extraneous variables have been controlled and that we can be certain that any changes in the DV were due to manipulation of the IV. In order to maximise this validity, one should attend to experimenter bias, demand characteristics, order effects (in repeated measures designs), participant variables (in independent measures), and any other confounding variables.

> The more control an experiment has (high internal validity), the less ecological validity it may have.

External validity

This is the extent to which the experimental findings can be generalised to real life and other situations (see p.150).

Progress check

1 Why are pilot studies useful?
2 Name one method of assessing reliability.
3 What is the difference between internal and external validity?

3 Internal validity concerns what is happening inside the experiment (e.g. demand characteristics) and external validity concerns what is external.

2 E.g. split-half technique, item analysis, test-retest.

1 To test that your procedures work.

Relationship between researchers and participants

Examples of the influence of researchers on participants

Note that the **experimenter effect** is different from the **experimental effect**, which is the effect of the experimental treatment.

- **Experimenter (investigator) effect or bias:** an experimenter has expectations about the outcome of an experiment and may indirectly and unconsciously communicate these to the participant (human or animal). This affects the participants' behaviour. Rosenthal and Jacobsen (1968) provided empirical support for this self-fulfilling prophecy in their study of the effects of teacher expectations on IQ performance.
- **The Hawthorne effect:** a person's performance may improve, not because of the experimental treatment, but because they are receiving unaccustomed attention. Such attention increases self-esteem and leads to improved performance. The effect is named after the Hawthorne electrical factory where it was first observed.
- **The Greenspoon effect:** participants are subtly reinforced by the experimenter's comments. Greenspoon (1955) was able to alter participants' responses by using subtle reinforcement of 'right' or 'wrong' answers. He said 'mm-hmm' whenever the participant said a plural word or 'huh-uh' after other responses. This led to increased or decreased production of plural words in random word-generation.
- **Demand characteristics:** those features of an experimental setting that 'invite' the participant to behave in particular ways. They bias a participant's behaviour. One example is the participant's attempts (not necessarily conscious) to guess what the experiment is about, and to do (or not do) what is expected of them. Orne (1962) tested this by telling participants they were participants in an experiment investigating sensory deprivation. In fact, they were not deprived at all, yet they displayed the classic symptoms of being so. In other words, they did what they were expected to do.

Reasons why participants are likely to be influenced

- **The experiment is a social situation:** participants prefer to behave in a socially acceptable manner. This is true even when performing anonymously or when answering questions on paper.
- **Active participants:** Orne (1962) argued that the picture of the participant as automaton is a foolish ideal. Participants actively search for clues about how to behave.
- **Evaluation apprehension:** a participant is aware of being 'tested' and wants to appear normal and to create a good impression. In order to overcome anxiety and uncertainty, the participant tries to guess what the experimenter really wants.

Ways of overcoming researcher and participant reactivity

- **Single blind technique:** participants are not informed of the aim of the experiment until after it is finished. This attempts to control participant bias.
- **Double blind technique:** neither the participant *nor* the experimenter are aware of the 'crucial' aspects of the experiment. This aims to avoid both participant and experimenter bias. (The experimenter is the person actually carrying out the research, whereas the investigator designs and directs the research.)
- **Placebos** are a control for the effects of expectations because participants think they are receiving the experimental treatment when they are not. They receive a 'treatment' which appears the same as the real thing but does not have its critical effects.
- **Undisclosed observation:** in a field experiment, and in some natural experiments, the participant has no expectations because they are unaware of being part of an experiment.
- **Standardised instructions:** these help to prevent experimenter bias by controlling what the experimenter says to the participants.

7.3 Data analysis

After studying this topic you should be able to:

- *outline methods of analysing qualitative data*
- *define and evaluate measures of central tendency and of dispersion*
- *describe a method of representing correlational data*
- *explain the appropriate use and interpretation of graphs and charts*

Analysis of qualitative data

AQA A	U3
AQA B	U1
EDEXCEL	U3
OCR	U3

A common criticism of this form of analysis is that it tends to be subjective. However, when the same data are analysed qualitatively by various people it becomes more objective.

Interviews

These may have open-ended questions and/or questions which are unstructured. Foster and Parker (1995) suggest the following possibilities for analysing the data produced by these:

- **'Giving voice'**: represent and/or summarise what the interviewee has said using selective quotations and describing the key details of the entire interview.
- **Grounded theory**: use the text to develop theoretical accounts of the interview data. What you write is 'grounded' in the text; it is 'theoretical' in the sense that it is an attempt to produce a coherent account of the facts. You might identify certain themes which recur, or categorise types of behaviour.
- **Thematic analysis**: organising the interview material in relation to certain research questions or themes that had been identified before the research started. This differs from 'grounded theory' in that the themes arise *prior* to the research. (Grounded theory comes out of the interview text.)
- **Discourse analysis**: aims to reveal how the text is organised by a number of competing themes or discourses (see p.130).

Observation

- **Quantitative analysis**: analyse data from time, event and point sampling using descriptive and inferential statistics.
- Produce **a detailed record** of observed behaviour ('giving voice').
- Produce **interpretations** (as above for interviews, e.g. thematic analysis, grounded theory), which may lead to further quantitative analysis.

Measures of central tendency and dispersion

AQA A	U3
AQA B	U1
EDEXCEL	U3
OCR	U3

Descriptive statistics are ways of *describing* the data so that the meaning of the data becomes more apparent, e.g. by reporting the mean or drawing a bar chart: you can see at a glance the meaning of the data.

Measures of central tendency

'Central tendency' refers to ways of giving the most typical or central value.

- **Mean**: Add up all the values and divide by N. *Advantage*: it is a sensitive measure. *Disadvantage*: it can be misleading with extreme values.
- **Median**: The middle or central value in an ordered list (see box below). *Advantage*: it is not affected by extreme scores. *Disadvantage*: it is not as sensitive because not all scores are used in calculation.
- **Mode**: The modal group is the most commonly used group. Bi-modal means two modes. *Advantage*: it is the only measure appropriate for nominal data. *Disadvantage*: it is not useful in data with more than one mode.

Measures of dispersion

'Dispersion' refers to the spread of the data.

- **Range**: the distance between lowest and highest value. *Advantage*: it is quick to calculate. *Disadvantage*: it is affected by extreme values.
- **Standard deviation**: The difference between each value and the mean is calculated, and then the mean of these differences is worked out. *Advantage*: it is the most accurate measure because it takes the distance between all values into account. *Disadvantage*: it requires extensive calculation and it is also not immediately obvious (whereas the range is).

Progress check

1 Which measure of central tendency would be suitable for nominal data?
2 Which measure of central tendency uses most of the data?
3 Which measure of dispersion is easiest to calculate?

1 The mode. 2 The mean. 3 The range.

Correlational data

AQA A	U3
AQA B	U1
EDEXCEL	U3
OCR	U3

Scattergrams are used to plot correlational data. Each pair of values is plotted against each other to show if a consistent trend is present. The correlation may be positive (trend from bottom left to top right), negative (trend from top left to bottom right) or none (even spread).

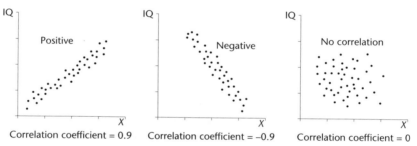

Correlation coefficient = 0.9   Correlation coefficient = –0.9   Correlation coefficient = 0

Graphs and charts

AQA A	U3
AQA B	U1
EDEXCEL	U3
OCR	U3

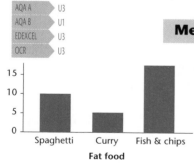

Methods which can be used with any level of measurement

- **Tables**: numerical data is arranged in columns and rows.
- **Bar charts**: a visual display of frequency, with the highest bar being the mode (see opposite). The data on the *x*-axis can be categories (nominal), i.e. not continuous. The *y*-axis represents frequency.

Methods suitable for ordinal and interval data only

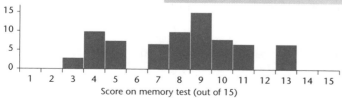

- **Histogram**: this differs from a bar chart in that the area of the bars must be proportional to the frequencies represented, and the *x*-axis must contain continuous data (see opposite).

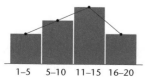

- **Frequency polygon**: the midpoint of each bar is joined to show continuous change; it is not suitable for data that is not continuous (see opposite).
- **Curved lines**: a sketch of an approximate line may be the best way to represent the data rather than using a jagged line graph.

173

Sample questions and student answers

(Comment on research methods and techniques)

A group of psychology students design a memory experiment to investigate the effects of organisation on recall. Previous research has shown that organisation improves recall. The researchers gave one group of participants a list of words that was unorganised. A second group of participants are given the same words but the words were organised into categories.

After the list of words had been studied for 30 seconds, the word lists were collected back in and the participants were asked to write down as many words as they could remember. Afterwards they were debriefed and thanked for taking part. The findings from the study are displayed in Table 1.

Group 1: Unorganised list	Group 2: Organised list
10	15
11	16
11	16
13	17
14	18
14	19
16	19
18	20
18	21
27	23
	25
	25

Table 1: Number of words recalled after 30 seconds

(a) (i) Give an appropriate experimental/alternative hypothesis for this study. [2]
 (ii) State whether your hypothesis is directional or non-directional and justify why you choose this form of hypothesis. [3]

(b) (i) Name the experimental design used in this study. [1]
 (ii) Give **one** advantage and **one** disadvantage of this kind of design in the context of this study. [2 + 2]

(c) Suggest a suitable sampling method for this study and explain **one** strength of this method of sampling. [3]

(d) After the experiment the participants were debriefed. Describe **two** things that might have been included in this debriefing. [2 + 2]

(e) Name **one** possible extraneous variable in this study and explain why this might affect the findings. [1 + 2]

(f) What measure of central tendency is most suitable to describe the data in Table 1? Explain your choice of measure of central tendency. [3]

(g) Explain what is meant by a pilot study and give **one** reason why it might be appropriate to use a pilot study as part of this investigation. [1 + 2]

(h) Give **two** conclusions that can be drawn from the data in Table 1. [2 + 2]

(a) (i) Participants will recall more words in the organised list condition than in the unorganised list condition. [3]

 (ii) This is a directional hypothesis. I used a directional hypothesis because past research suggests that organising word lists leads to better recall. [1]

(b) (i) Independent groups design. [1]

 (ii) One advantage is that there wouldn't be a practice effect, in a repeated measures design you would have to use different lists of words for both conditions and this could bring in an extraneous variable. One disadvantage is that you need to have a lot more participants. [2 + 1]

Only the first answer has been contextualised.

(c)   An opportunity sample could be used. This is easy to conduct
      because you just take whoever is available.   [3]

(d)   The experimenter would have told the participants the true purpose of the
      study (to study the effects of organisation on recall) and could also
      have assured them that their data would remain confidential.   [2 + 2]

(e)   The participants in one condition might have been tested at a different
      time of day. People might have better memories earlier in the day and that
      would explain why they had better recall rather than the actual memory
      condition.   [1 + 2]

(f)   The median would be best because it is not affected by extreme values
      (there is one in Group 1) which would affect the mean.   [3]

(g)   A pilot study is a small-scale practice run of a study to check for any
      problems in methodology that might need adjusting. It would have been
      useful in this study to see whether, for example, the standardised
      instructions were clear and if 30 seconds is a long enough delay. [1 + 2]

> Both answers are correct but require some further detail for full marks.

(h)   One conclusion is that organisation does enhance memory. The second
      conclusion is that there are individual differences.   [1 + 2]

TOTAL: 27 out of 30 marks

Practice examination questions

A psychology lecturer notices that he can clearly see one of the tables in a college coffee bar from an upstairs window. The lecturer decides to carry out an observation study to discover if males differ from females in the number of *friendly acts* displayed in their interaction with other people. *Friendly acts* are defined as smiling and touching. For interaction that was observed the lecturer recorded the number of smiles and incidents of touching displayed by each *participant*.

To qualify as a participant in the study, the person had to be at the table in the coffee bar and in full view of the lecturer. The participant had to be with only one other person (companion).

The lecturer conducted the observations over a two-week period for a total of 12 separate hours. The same number of male and female participants were observed. The following data were obtained.

		Gender of participant	
		Male	Female
Gender of companion	Male	102	140
	Female	184	225

Table 1 Number of friendly acts displayed by male and female participants when interacting with either a male or female companion.

(a)   What type of observational study did the lecturer conduct?   [2]

(b)   Describe the data depicted in *Table 1*. What may be said about the patterns
      of friendly acts displayed by males and females when interacting?   [3]

(c)   There may be a danger that *observer bias* could be present in this study.
      i) What is meant by the term *observer bias*?   [3]
      ii) Explain **one** way in which the lecturer might overcome this problem?   [2]

(d)   Name **two** variables (other than observer bias) the lecturer might have controlled
      for in his study. Why might it have been important to control for these?   [4]

(e)   Explain why the lecturer should be cautious about generalising his results
      to all males and females.   [3]

(f)   Discuss **one** ethical issue raised by this study.   [3]

AQA B specimen paper Unit 1 Introducing psychology question 3

Index

abnormality 111-3, 114-19
accommodation 53
activation synthesis 92
adoption 86, 87
affectionless pyschopathy 72
age prejudice 139
aggression 24
alpha and beta tests 88
amnesia 32
anaclitic depression 71
androgyny 108
animal experiments 66, 89, 99-100
anorexia nervosa 120-3
arousal-cost-reward model 133
assimilation 53
attachments 60-8, 69-76
attitudes 131-5
authoritarian personality 138, 152
authority 148-53
autonomy 122, 153
autonomic nervous system 80, 93
aversion therapy 117

bar charts 173
behaviour 17, 19, 21, 24, 28, 80, 85-8, 101, 112, 118, 123, 125, 132, 150
behaviourist approach 21-4, 28
bias 163
biochemical abnormalities 114, 121, 124
biofeedback 101
biological abnormality 114, 115, 121, 124, 125-6
bodily rhythms 89
bond disruption 70, 77
Bowlby's Theory 61, 66-8, 70-2
brain damage 29, 32, 84
brain scan 29, 82
British Psychological Society 156
bulimia nervosa 120, 124, 125-6
bystander effect 133

cardiovascular disorder 95
caregiving sensitivity 62-3
case studies 164
central executive 35
central tendency 172
cerebral cortex 80
childminding 75
classical conditioning 21, 65, 117, 123, 125, 136
cognitive approach 28-9, 123, 125
cognitive development 50, 53-9, 73, 75-6
cognitive dissonance 134
cognitive model 118-9
cognitive restructuring therapy 119
conditioning theory 21
confidentiality 156
conformity 141, 142-5
cohort effect 52
compliance 141
concrete operational stage 54
conservation 55, 57
control 24, 99, 103, 124
correlational analysis 162-3
cortical function 81
cost-benefit analysis 157
counter-attitudinal behaviour 134
critical period 67
cross-sectional studies 52

cultural relativism 110, 113
cultural variation 63-4, 100, 106-7, 109, 110, 123, 125, 148
data analysis 17, 19, 172
data recording 165-6, 168-9
day care 75-7
debriefing 154, 156
deception 154-5, 156, 163
declarative memory 31
deindividuation 148
delinquency 71-2
demand characteristics 51, 130, 144, 145, 149, 171
deprivation 69, 70, 71-2
deprivation dwarfism 72
developmental approach 50-2
deviation 111
diathesis-stress model 116
discourse analysis 130
discrimination 136-40
dispersion 172-3
displacement 38
dissonance 134-5
dreams 19, 20, 91, 92, 116
drug therapy 101, 115
dysfunction 112

eating disorders 120-8
ecological validity 145, 150, 160, 161, 164
education 58
ego 17, 18, 116, 131
egocentrism 55, 58
Electra Complex 18
electroconvulsive therapy 114-5
electro-encephalogram 82
emotion 45, 76-7, 91
encoding 31, 39
environment 86
episodic memory 31
equilibrium 53
Erikson 19
ethics 19, 22, 110, 118, 145, 150, 154-7, 161, 162, 164
ethnocentrism 139-40
ethogenics 25
ethology 66
evolutionary theory 90-1
experimental approach 51
experimental design 167-8
experimental validity 149
experiments 23, 24, 28, 29, 32, 34, 57, 109, 147, 160
external validity 150
extinction 22
evaluation apprehension 130
eyewitness testimony 43, 45-6

face recognition 46-7
failure to function adequately 111
familial studies 85-7, 122
feature recognition 46-7
field experiments 148-9, 161
flashbulb memory 41-2, 45
flooding 118
forced compliance 134
forgetting 38-42
formal operational stage 54, 55
free recall 30
frequency polygon 173
Freud 17, 20-1, 40, 65, 91, 116

gender 24, 100, 108, 136, 138-9, 148
gender prejudice 138
gender schema theory 108
generalisation 22, 106

General Adaptation Syndrome 94
genetics 85-8, 114, 121, 124
genotype 87
Greenspoon effect 171

hardiness 103
Hawthorne effect 171
hippocampus 29
histogram 173
homosexuality 111
homeostasis 102
horizontal décalage 53
hormones 81, 108, 121
hospitalisation 71
humanistic approach 25
hypotheses 165

id 18
identification 141
identity 108
idiographic approach 106
imitation 24
immune system 96
implosion therapy 118
imprinting 66
independence 141
individual differences 106-28, 145, 148, 153
informational social influence 141, 145
informed consent 154-5, 156, 161-2
influence 135
inheritance 50
initial perception 44
insecure attachments 61, 62-3
institutionalisation 73, 74
intelligence 19, 58, 73, 76, 85, 88
interference 30, 39
internal validity 149
internal working model 67
internalisation 141, 169
interviews 19, 162, 172
investigator bias 18, 19, 56, 161, 163, 164, 171
introspectionism 21

Jung 18, 19

language 44, 53, 55, 56, 58, 81
learning theory 65, 118
lesioning 82
levels of processing model 36-7
Likert scale 131
long-term memory 31, 33, 34-6, 39, 40-1
longitudinal studies 51-2

majority influence 146
material deprivation 70, 74
maternal deprivation 70-1
mean 172
median 172
memory 29, 30-46, 150
mental health 112
mental illness 112, 113, 114, 116, 125
minority influence 141, 146-7
mode 172
monotropy 61, 67, 68
multi-store model 35

nature 50, 108
neo-behaviourism 23
neo-Freudians 19
nervous system 80
neuroanatomy 114, 121
neurons 81

neurosurgery 83
new paradigm research 25
NICHD 77
nomothetic approach 106
nonsense syllables 30
normative social influence 142, 145
neurons 81
nurseries 75
nurture 50, 108

obedience 148-54
object permanence 54
observation 51, 163-4, 168, 171
obsession 20
Oedipus Complex 18, 21
operant conditioning 21-2, 65, 101, 118, 123
operational stage 53

paired associate learning 30, 39
participant reactivity 130
participant variables 167
personality 17, 18, 19, 100, 134
persuasion 135
phenotype 87
phobia 20
phonological loop 35
physical illness 94-6, 115
physiological abnormality 114
physiological approach 80-4, 101
physiology 80-105
Piaget's Theory 53-7, 59
pilot studies 169
placebos 171
plastic interval scales 166
pleasure principle 18
population validity 150
populations 165-6
positivism 21
post-decisional dissonance 134
pre-operational stage 54, 55
prejudice 136-40
privation 69, 72-4
procedural memory 31
projective techniques 132
protest-despair-detachment model 69
psychoanalysis 17, 66, 117
psychodynamics 17-21, 65-6, 116, 122-3, 125, 131
psychometric testing 19, 107
psychosexuality 18, 20-1, 65, 117
psychosurgery 115
punishment 22

qualitative research methods 163-4
questionnaires 138, 155, 162, 163, 169

racial prejudice 134, 138
rational-emotional therapy 119
range 173
rapid eye movement 89
reactance 135
reactive attachment disorder 73
realistic conflict theory 137
reality principle 18
reasoned action 134
rebellion 153
recall 33, 39, 40, 43, 45
recognition 30, 46
reconstructive memory 43, 44
reinforcement 22, 123
reliability 169-70
repressed memories 40-1, 45

repressors 29
research 149, 154-7, 160-75
resistance to obedience 152-3
restoration theory 90
Reunion behaviour 62
reverse learning 91
role play 149, 155
Rorschach test 132

Samaritanism 133
sampling 165-6, 168, 169
scans 29
scattergrams 173
schema 43, 53, 136
schizophrenia 83-4
secure attachments 61, 62-3
self determination 25
self-perception theory 135
semantic differential technique 131
semantic memory 31, 36
sensorimotor stage 53, 54
sensory memory 31
separation 69
separation anxiety 60, 62
separation protest 60, 69
serial position effect 32
shaping 22
short-term memory 31, 32-6, 45
situational variables 167
skin-to-skin contact 66
sleep deprivation 90
sleep-wake cycle 89
sociability 77
social approach 129-30
social desirability bias 130, 163
social effects 76
social identity theory 136-7
social influence 141
social learning theory 23, 65, 123, 125
social norms 111, 145
social support 148
socio economic status 86-7
somatic nervous system 80
split brains 83-4
standard deviation 173
statistical norm 111
stereotype 108, 110, 123, 136
Strange Situation 62-3, 64, 77
stranger anxiety 60, 62
stress 93-6, 97-100, 101-5
stress inoculation 102-3, 119
stressor 93, 98-9
superego 18
surveys 130
systematic desensitisation 118

tables 173
temperamental hypothesis 61
Thematic Apperception test 132
therapy 17
trace decay 38, 39
transference 116
twin studies 52, 72, 85, 87, 121-2, 124, 125-6

unconscious 17, 116

validity 170
variables 166
variant cognitive structures 53
vision 82, 85
visuo-spacial sketchpad 36
Vygotsky's Theory 58-9

working memory 35
workplace stress 98-100